Churchill's Atlantic Convoys

Churchill's Atlantic Convoys

Tenacity and Sacrifice

William Smith

Pen & Sword
MARITIME

First published in Great Britain in 2023 by
Pen & Sword Maritime
An imprint of
Pen & Sword Books Ltd
Yorkshire – Philadelphia

ISBN 978 1 39905 097 5

A CIP catalogue record for this book is
available from the British Library.

Typeset by Mac Style
Printed in the UK by CPI Group (UK) Ltd, Croydon, CR0 4YY.

Pen & Sword Books Limited incorporates the imprints of Atlas,
Archaeology, Aviation, Discovery, Family History, Fiction, History,
Maritime, Military, Military Classics, Politics, Select, Transport, True
Crime, Air World, Frontline Publishing, Leo Cooper, Remember
When, Seaforth Publishing, The Praetorian Press, Wharncliffe Local
History, Wharncliffe Transport, Wharncliffe True Crime, White Owl
and After the Battle.

For a complete list of Pen & Sword titles please contact

PEN & SWORD BOOKS LIMITED
47 Church Street, Barnsley, South Yorkshire, S70 2AS, England
E-mail: enquiries@pen-and-sword.co.uk
Website: www.pen-and-sword.co.uk

Or

PEN AND SWORD BOOKS
1950 Lawrence Rd, Havertown, PA 19083, USA
E-mail: Uspen-and-sword@casematepublishers.com
Website: www.penandswordbooks.com

In memory of my father

Chief Officer William Neville Dougall Smith MBE

Merchant Navy

Master Mariner

Who served in

Atlantic, Arctic and Mediterranean Convoys
1939 to 1945

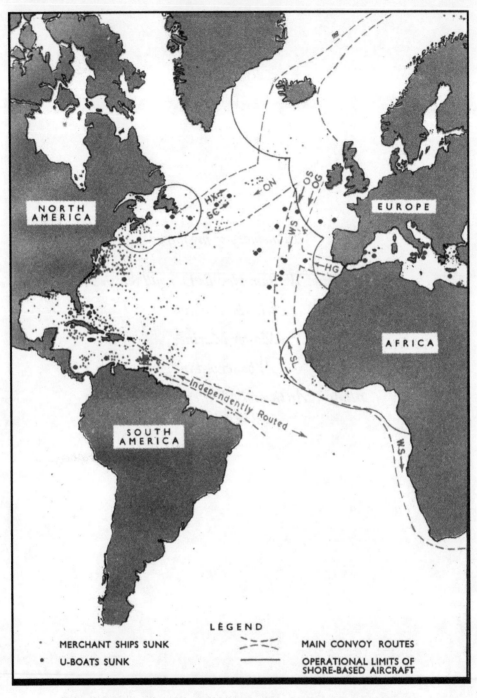

LEGEND

· MERCHANT SHIPS SUNK   – – –<   MAIN CONVOY ROUTES

• U-BOATS SUNK   ———   OPERATIONAL LIMITS OF
SHORE-BASED AIRCRAFT

THE BATTLE OF THE ATLANTIC (IV), JANUARY–JULY 1942

Note (i) Extension of patrols over S.W. approaches and off W.
Africa.

   (ii) Aircraft now operating from Newfoundland and Nova
Scotia up to 250 miles from shore.

Contents

Introduction

In 1939 Britain, an island and maritime nation, unlike Germany, a continental European nation, was highly dependent on imports, being only self-sustainable for two months of the year and importing about fifty million tons of food, fuel, and materials annually – over one million tons per week. The country's continuing survival and ability to fight would be entirely dependent on the re-supply by sea of essential foodstuffs, raw materials, arms, ammunition, fuel and other necessities, especially those imported from North America and the countries of the British Empire. Much of this would be transported across the North Atlantic – a vast sea area of some 16 million square miles – in thousands of merchant ships vulnerable to attack by enemy U-boats, warships (particularly surface raiders) and aircraft.

It was this vulnerability that Hitler and the Kriegsmarine (German Navy) sought to exploit from the very first day of hostilities. 'Directive No. 1 for the Conduct of the War' signed by Adolf Hitler in Berlin on 31 August 1939 included at Paragraph 4 the order:

> If Britain and France open hostilities against Germany … the Navy will carry on warfare against merchant shipping, directed mainly at England.

It continued:

> In conducting the war against England, preparations are to be made for the use of the Luftwaffe in disrupting British supplies by sea.

As Admiral Karl Dönitz later acknowledged:

> When the war came in September 1939, the following, therefore, obtained for the navy: England was in every respect dependent on sea-borne supply for food and import of raw materials, as well as for development of every type of military power. The single task of the Kriegsmarine was, therefore, to interrupt or cut these sea communications. It was clear that this object could never be obtained by building a fleet to fight the English fleet and in this way win the sea communications. The only remaining method was to attack sea communications quickly. For this purpose only the U-boat could be considered, as only this weapon could penetrate the main areas

of English sea communications in spite of English sea supremacy on the surface.

No one knew better than Churchill the importance of the Atlantic convoys to the sustainment of the British war effort by means of imported raw materials, munitions, oil and food. As he later recorded in his memoirs, it was

the dominating factor all through the war. Never for one moment could we forget that everything happening elsewhere, on land, at sea, or in the air, depended ultimately on its outcome, and amid all other cares we viewed its changing fortunes day by day with hope or apprehension.[1]

He also claimed that 'The only thing that ever really frightened me during the war was the U-boat peril.'[2]

Some sources have suggested that despite these recollections Churchill took considerably less interest in the day-to-day management of the anti-U-boat war than these quotations might suggest and only became directly involved when shipping losses began to approach crisis levels. The detailed evidence to be found in close scrutiny of the Minutes of War Cabinet Meetings and papers including the War Cabinet Weekly Resumés, Hansard records of Parliamentary debates and Churchill's public speeches suggests that this represents a less than generous perception of his personal involvement and commitment between 1939 and 1945, considering the climate of uncertainty, the conflicting operational priorities and the resources to be managed on a day-to-day basis.

The Admiralty had assumed control of all British merchant shipping on the evening of 26 August 1939. This control was chiefly exercised through the Director of the Trade Division and his Naval Control Service staffs stationed in ports used by British shipping all over the world. The procurement of merchant shipping tonnage by purchase, charter or other means remained the responsibility of the Ministry of Shipping (later amalgamated with the Ministry of Transport to become the Ministry of War Transport), as did the manning of the merchant navy.[3] The Admiralty's responsibility began shortly before a ship sailed on an outward voyage and ended with her safe arrival after completing the journey. The organization of convoy escorts and the conduct of convoys at sea, the routes used by all shipping and the instruction of masters in the execution of the Admiralty's policy and orders all rested with the Trade Division. On 4 September 1939 the Admiralty ordered the introduction of the convoy system for merchant ships.

The principal sea lines of communication across the North Atlantic stretched from the north-east coast of Canada to the Western Approaches to the British Isles, a distance from Halifax, Nova Scotia to Londonderry, Northern Ireland, or Liverpool, of approximately 2,500 nautical miles. Once arrangements were in place, merchant ships crossing the Atlantic eastbound assembled in convoy at either Halifax for fast convoys (designated 'HX') or Sydney, Cape Breton for slow convoys (designated 'SC'). Ships travelling from the Pacific via the Panama Canal and from the Caribbean would assemble at Bermuda prior to joining the HX convoys at sea. Those merchant ships sailing westbound in either fast ('ON') or slow ('ONS') convoys assembled close to one of the principal UK west coast ports, with merchant ships joining in UK coastal waters before heading out into the Atlantic. It would take, subject to weather conditions and enemy activity, a 'slow' convoy roughly seventeen days and a 'fast' convoy about eight days to cross the North Atlantic. These convoys would represent Britain's vital life support system throughout the war. The first outward-bound ocean convoy (ON.1) sailed for Halifax on Thursday, 7 September 1939. The first return convoy from Halifax (HX.1) sailed on Saturday, 13 September.[4] These convoys were subsequently reorganized as the 'Outbound to North America' (ON) series, subdivided into fast (ON) and slow (ONS) convoys. Details of the convoy sailing programme are in the Appendix.

Although the Atlantic convoy programme ran between September 1939 and May 1945, there were periods of time, sometimes months, when the merchant ships crossed the ocean unchallenged by the enemy. The narrative which follows is therefore structured through a series of time-related phases to better define and describe the ebb and flow of Atlantic convoy operations and the military and political factors which shaped these, and to deliver a definitive and authoritative assessment of the outcome and provide a valuable reference. Interwoven with the narrative are some descriptions of key encounters with German forces, especially the U-boat fleet.

Chapter 1

Phase One: August 1939 to March 1940

As the storm clouds gathered over Europe, Admiral Karl Dönitz, Commander of the German U-boat fleet, despite all his efforts at pre-war preparation, found himself on 29 August with just fifty-six U-boats, nine large, seventeen medium and thirty small, of which forty-nine were ready for operational duties. The Atlantic boats took up their positions in the second half of August 1939; the large and medium U-boats were to attack merchant shipping west of Ireland and in the Bay of Biscay. Two days later, Dönitz received Supreme HQ Instruction No.1, which defined the main task of the Kriegsmarine as 'the waging of war on shipping, with Britain as the principal enemy'.

It would now be only a matter of hours rather than days before that instruction took effect.

On Friday, 1 September 1939 the passenger liner *Athenia* sailed from Glasgow via Belfast to Liverpool, from where at 13.00 on 2 September she was, despite clear indications war would break out any day, allowed to leave Liverpool bound for Montreal. Less than twenty-four hours later, at 11.15 on 3 September, Prime Minister Neville Chamberlain announced in a radio broadcast that Britain and France had declared war on Germany. Shortly before 13.00, an encoded message sent to all German naval units informed them hostilities with Britain were effective immediately. This was followed one hour later by a further message from Dönitz ordering the 'prize' regulations to be adhered to, under which unarmed merchant ships had to be boarded and searched, and only sunk if carrying cargo relating to the war effort and then only after their crews had been evacuated into lifeboats. Passenger ships were not to be boarded or sunk at all. Both of these messages were received and logged by *U-30*.

To avoid confusion with the order given on 31 August, a further radio message sent at 15.50 to U-boats read: 'Open hostilities against England immediately; do not wait to be attacked first.'

An earlier message at 14.00 from the Naval War Staff had ordered:

U-boats to make war on merchant shipping in accordance with operations order. This should exclude any misunderstanding, as the operations order expressly orders war against merchant shipping in accordance with prize law.

Around 16.30, *U-30* sighted the passenger liner *Athenia* 60 nautical miles south of Rockall and 200 nautical miles north-west of Inishtrahull,[1] Ireland sailing on a course away from Britain and observed that she seemed to be blacked out and taking an evasive zigzagging course. *U-30's* commander, Fritz-Julius Lemp, decided *Athenia* was an armed merchant cruiser and fair game within the prize rules. At 19.40 Lemp gave the order to fire two torpedoes at the *Athenia*, but when the radio operator on board *U-30* picked up the distress call of a passenger liner, Lemp realized he had made a terrible mistake. Of the 1,418 people on board, a total of ninety-eight passengers and nineteen crew members died in the sinking and two subsequent accidents during the rescue operation, or died later of injuries. Fifty-four were Canadian, twenty-eight were US citizens and four were German. The *Athenia* remained afloat for more than fourteen hours, and finally sank stern-first at 10.40 the following morning.

This was the opening shot in what Churchill, who arrived at his desk as the newly appointed First Lord of the Admiralty at 18.00, and his contemporaries would refer to for the next eighteen months as 'the war at sea'.

After learning of the sinking Dönitz, under orders from Berlin, swore the crew of *U-30* to secrecy and falsified the U-boat's logs. The full truth would not emerge until Dönitz admitted to Lemp's error and the alteration of the logs at the Nuremberg Trials in 1945/46. Goebbels, the German Minister of Propaganda, claimed in a radio broadcast on 22 October that Churchill had ordered the *Athenia* sunk as a means of drawing America into the war. The same day, the German newspaper *Völkischer Beobachter*, a mouthpiece of the Nazi regime, carried the headline 'Churchill Sank the Athenia'.

On 4 September, in one of his first Minutes as First Sea Lord, Churchill wrote to the Parliamentary and Financial Secretary to the Admiralty and to all departments:

> To avoid confusion, German submarines are always to be described officially as U-boats in all official papers and communiqués.

In his first speech as First Lord of the Admiralty in the House of Commons on Monday, 4 September[2] Churchill informed the House about the sinking of the passenger liner *Athenia* by a U-boat in the first attack on civilian shipping of the war:

> A signal was received in the Admiralty at about 11 p.m. last night giving the information that the steamship *'Athenia'* had been torpedoed in a position about 200 miles north-west of Ireland at 8.59 p.m.

After describing the event he added:

Since the 26th of August all British merchant ships in the Atlantic have been diverted from their normal routes. Orders were given for the institution of convoy on one route as soon as war was declared. Of course it will take a little time to institute a general system of convoy, but that is being pressed to the utmost.

Asked then whether he could tell the House if it was certain in the minds of the Board of Admiralty that the convoy system could be quickly and efficiently expanded to cover all reasonable precautions on these routes within a very short time, Churchill replied:

We have every belief that the convoy system will be brought into complete operation at a comparatively early date. In the meanwhile, all that is possible is being done.

The sinking of the *Athenia* led the Admiralty to believe unrestricted submarine warfare had been launched, and full convoy plans were put into operation; but just before midnight, the German Naval War Staff radioed all U-boats: 'By the Führer's orders no hostile action is to be taken for the present against passenger ships, even if in convoy.'

Churchill held his first Admiralty conference on the night of 4 September. The record of the conference dated 5 September[3] read in part:

The convoy system is being set up. By convoy system is meant only anti-submarine convoys. All question of dealing with raiding cruisers or heavy ships is excluded from this particular paper. The First Sea Lord is considering movement to the western approaches of Great Britain of whatever destroyers and escort vessels can be scraped from the Eastern and Mediterranean theatres, with the object of adding, if possible, twelve to the escorts for convoys.

Churchill in his memoirs noted that the organization of outward-bound convoys was brought into force almost at once. By 8 September three main convoy routes were operating – from Liverpool and from the Thames to the Atlantic, and along the east coast between the Thames and the Forth. Staff for the control of convoys at these ports and many others at home and abroad were included in the war plan and had already been dispatched. Meanwhile, all ships outward bound in the Channel and Irish Sea and not in convoy were ordered to Plymouth and Milford Haven, and all independent outward sailings were cancelled. Overseas, arrangements for forming homeward-bound convoys were pressed forward. The first two of these sailed from Freetown, Sierra Leone on 14 September and from Halifax, Nova Scotia, two days later. Three days later, the first Atlantic convoy (designated OA.1) sailed for Halifax. The first eastbound (HX.1) departed Halifax on 16 September. The convoy system would remain in place until May 1945.

On 7 September there were only eighteen U-boats available for Atlantic operations against merchant shipping, although the BdU[4] hoped that by October there would be twenty-six.

The sinking of the *Athenia* was discussed at the 7 September Führer Conference on Naval Affairs, at which Hitler decided no attempt should be made to solve the *Athenia* affair until *U-30* returned home, and ordered U-boats in the Atlantic not to attack passenger and French ships.

U-boat attacks on merchant shipping up to now received little publicity, but on 13 September the press reported the losses of merchant shipping and introduction of the convoy system. A typical article read:

U-BOAT ATTACKS CONTINUE

Convoys Assembling

LONDON, Tuesday
Introduction of the convoy system should reduce the losses of British merchantmen of which more have been sunk by enemy submarines. It is believed that the number torpedoed is comparatively small but no official confirmation of losses appears to be forthcoming.

Generally successful torpedo attacks are not quickly made known to the public unless survivors are picked up by foreign ships or are landed in Great Britain.

Two foreign vessels picked up members of the crews of British freighters sunk in the Atlantic. An American ship (*American Shipper*) picked up the crew of the *Blairlogie* (Clydesdale Navigation Co 4,425 tons gross) and a Swedish ship (*Castor*) picked up survivors from the *Gartavon* (Gart Line 1,777 tons gross). Both were sunk in the Atlantic.

The Ministry of Information announced that the convoy system had been put into force but was not yet operating completely.

When war was forced on us, British merchantmen were scattered over trade routes throughout the world. It takes time to collect convoys and it is obviously undesirable to give details as this would afford invaluable assistance to the enemy, said the announcement.

Both the ships referred to had been unescorted when sunk. It was not long before the first U-boat attack on a convoy was attempted; OB.4 was attacked by *U-31* on 16 September, when the steam merchantman *Aviemore* was sunk

220 miles south-west of Cape Clear.[5] Although OB.4 is frequently claimed to have been the first Atlantic convoy attacked by a U-boat, the *Aviemore* was not in that convoy but unfortunately in the wrong place at the wrong time, sailing on a course crossing ahead of OB.4. Thus although the *Aviemore* was the first merchant ship sunk by a U-boat during an attack on an Atlantic convoy in the Second World War, she was technically not the first to be sunk from a convoy.

The following day, Churchill presented his first report to the War Cabinet[6] on the 'Progress of the War at Sea' including the introduction of the convoy system. This read:

1. In less than a week from now practically all ships will arrive in convoy. These convoys will be protected in the approaches against anti-submarine attack, though for some time the anti-submarine escorts will be weaker than desired. None the less considerable relief may be expected in this sphere; first from the institution of the convoy system; secondly from the gradual growth of our anti U-boat forces in the theatre; and thirdly by the mounting of guns on all our vessels. Meanwhile, the ASDIC method is yielding good results and a serious toll has been exacted from the German U-boats engaged. All our measures will progressively increase in power.

2. The institution of convoys presents targets which may be found more tempting to the German armed merchant cruisers. We are endeavouring to work up protection against surface attack for our convoys as fast as possible.

5. We must expect serious recrudescence of the U-boat warfare during the summer and autumn of 1940.

There were in fact still very few U-boats at sea in the early weeks of September. On 20 September Hitler was informed[7] that twenty-one were in the Atlantic when war broke out but only four to five would be operating at any one time; at the beginning of October, however, there would be about ten to twelve.

Prime Minister Chamberlain remained confident the U-boat threat to British merchant shipping was being safely contained. On 20 September, addressing the House of Commons on 'the War Situation,'[8] he claimed:

We are now carrying out an offensive against the U-boats and they are continually and relentlessly attacked whenever they disclose themselves ... I am confident that I am understating the case when I say that already six or seven German submarines have paid the full penalty for their attacks on British shipping.[9] In some cases their crews have been captured.

I am quite confident that with the full operation of the convoy system, and the rapid increase in the numbers, power, and efficiency of our hunting craft this submarine menace will dwindle with corresponding speed ... It is, however, already clear that the Navy and the Merchant Service by their unceasing efforts will be able to maintain essential supplies of raw materials and food for our population and our industries.

He may have spoken a little too soon, as the following afternoon, in the first successful U-boat attack on a convoy (OA.7) south-west of the Scillies, *U-35* damaged the tanker *Teakwood*. The first actual sinking of a merchant ship from an Atlantic convoy by a U-boat was still months away.

On 23 September Admiral Raeder advised Hitler in what seems, given earlier BdU reports, an exaggeration of U-boat numbers:

The first phase of the submarine war in the Atlantic and the Channel is over. When war broke out, numerous submarines were at sea; a great stream of ships was returning home to England and France; as yet there were no armed merchantmen; defences were not fully organized. It is true the submarines have sunk 232,000 tons of shipping so far, but they are hampered by political restrictions, e.g., no attacks on passenger vessels and no action against French naval and merchant shipping.

The expression 'submarine warfare' is to be replaced by the expression 'war against merchant shipping'.

Three days later, Churchill briefed the House of Commons on the emergent U-boat threat:[10]

The war at sea opened with some intensity. Our ships going about the world were set upon by lurking U-boats, carefully posted beforehand. We immediately replied in three ways. First, we set in motion the convoy system. This could be very quickly done for all outgoing ships but took a fortnight to organise convoys of homeward-bound ships. Meanwhile, however, large numbers of ships who started independently, under the ordinary conditions of peace, had day after day to run the gauntlet of the waiting U-boats without being either armed or escorted; consequently a serious, though, I am glad to say, diminishing, toll was exacted. The convoy system is a good and well-tried defence against U-boat attack, but no one can pretend that it is a complete defence. Some degree of risk and a steady proportion of losses must be expected. There are also other forms of attack besides U-boats, attacks from surface craft and from the air, against which we must be on our guard. I can assure the House that every preparation is being made to cope with such attacks, but I must again warn the House that we cannot guarantee immunity and that we must expect further losses.

During September over 900 ships sailed in convoy without the loss of a single vessel. The lack of knowledge of the existence of ASDIC probably accounted for early U-boat tactics, as they preferred to attack targets during the day, generally by torpedo from periscope depth, but they also sank unarmed merchant ships with gunfire. The majority of sinkings of unescorted ships took place in the waters around the British Isles, the North-West and South-West Approaches and the Bay of Biscay; there were no sinkings in the North Atlantic, the sea area being beyond the range of the few U-boats operational at the time.

There was then a lull in U-boat activity during the first ten days of October, during which, although U-boats were at sea, only a handful of ships were attacked. This seems to have reflected the political situation at the time, coinciding as it did with Hitler's offer of peace terms on 6 October. The British Government rejected the offer on 12 October, and U-boat activity flared up again the same day. By the end of the month twenty-three independent merchant ships had been sunk by U-boats, but no Atlantic convoys were attacked.

Churchill certainly seemed optimistic. In a radio broadcast from London on 1 October he offered reassurance that the U-boat attacks were so far unsuccessful:

> Here I speak as First Lord of the Admiralty and with special caution. It would seem that the U-boat attack upon the life of the British Isles has not so far proved successful.
>
> It is true that when they sprang out upon us and we were going about our ordinary business, with 2,000 ships in constant movement every day upon the seas, they managed to do some serious damage.
>
> But the Royal Navy has immediately attacked the U-boats and is hunting them night and day.
>
> A week has passed since a British ship, alone or in convoy, has been sunk or even molested by a U-boat on the high seas.
>
> We must of course expect that the U-boat attack upon the sea-borne commerce of the world will be renewed presently on a greater scale. We hope, however, that by the end of October we shall have three times as many hunting craft at work as we had at the beginning of the war; and by the measures we have taken we hope that our means of putting down this pest will grow continually. We are taking great care about that.

Two weeks later, on 17 October in his 'Statement on the Progress of U-boat Warfare'[11] Churchill informed the House of Commons:

> Towards the end of last week the U-boat warfare, which had for a fortnight been mainly directed upon neutrals, became again intensified. Four ships, including two French ships, were sunk upon the Western Approaches

during Saturday and Sunday, and three others were attacked but made their escape. The British ships sunk aggregated 13,000 tons.

On the other hand, it should not be supposed that all the losses are upon one side. The Admiralty have hitherto refrained from giving the figures of the slaughter of U-boats which has been proceeding and is still proceeding with increasing severity. On Friday last, for instance, four U-boats were certainly destroyed, including two of the largest and latest ocean-going U-boats in the German Navy. Nothing like this rate of destruction was attained at any moment in the last war. During the last week for which I can give figures, that is to say to the end of the sixth week of the war, seven U-boats were sunk. If we look back over the whole period of six weeks since the war began we may estimate that thirteen U-boats have been sunk, that five have been seriously damaged, and possibly sunk, and several others damaged. These figures are probably an understatement. Besides this, two-thirds of the U-boats which have been out raiding have suffered attack from depth-charges. The French Navy, which is powerful and in the highest state of efficiency, has also been active, and has certainly taken its toll, but it is not for me to give figures upon this subject.

We believe, therefore, that out of about sixty U-boats ready for action at the beginning of the war about one-third have already been sunk or seriously damaged; and of the largest and latest ocean-going U-boats the proportion is at least one-fifth. We actually hold survivors from the crews of three vessels of this highest class.

We may thus take stock of the general position reached in the first six weeks of the U-boat war against British commerce. Something from a third to a quarter of the total U-boat fleet of Germany has been destroyed, and the gaps made in the skilled officers and crews cannot be speedily replaced.

I cannot close my examination of the first phase of this severe sea-struggle without inviting the House to realize the intensity of the effort and devotion which has been required from all the ever-increasing hunting-craft and from those engaged upon convoy, not only in narrow waters but amid the storms of the oceans; and the constancy of the merchant officers and seamen who face all the hazards with buoyant and confident determination. I feel we may commend this part of our war business with some confidence to the House.

Again Churchill was prone to exaggeration, possibly for dramatic effect. The actual total of U-boats destroyed was six, including two sunk by the minefields off Dover. A typical international press report of the time on the U-boat war published on 27 October read:

U-BOAT WAR

German U-boats have intensified their indiscriminate sinkings of merchant vessels during the past week. From October 18 to October 25, no fewer than seventeen ships have been sunk.[12]

Such a state of affairs takes us back to September 26, when the First Lord of the Admiralty, Mr Winston Churchill, addressed the House of Commons. Among other things, Mr Churchill said ... 'such is the U-boat war – hard, widespread and bitter – a war of groping and drowning – a war of ambuscade and stratagem – a war of science and seamanship.' A better description could not have been given. In the first week of the war, British shipping losses by U-boat sinkings amounted to 65,000 tons, in the second week they were 46,000 tons, and in the third 21,000 tons. A further lull was noted in the six days prior to Mr Churchill's statement, our losses amounting to only 9,000 tons. It was then that 'we were advised' not to dwell upon such reassuring figures too much, for war is full of unpleasant, surprises. It certainly is. Of the seventeen vessels sunk during the past week, nine, of 43,947 tons, have been British. This brings the British total since the *Athenia* outrage to forty-seven vessels, totalling 216,984 tons, a situation demanding a much more vigorous reply by the Admiralty. The convoy system has been in full operation both ways in the Atlantic for five weeks now, and there has been no report of successful U-boat attacks. This suggests that only those vessels which have sailed independently have been sunk in the past few weeks. Elimination, or at least curtailment of these sailings would make war at sea less profitable for the enemy.

During October three Atlantic convoys were attacked and five ships sunk – two in convoy, two stragglers and one dispersed.

Hitler was advised on 1 November that U-boat attacks on enemy shipping had been intensified as much as possible. Even passenger steamers proceeding without lights and in convoy could now be torpedoed without warning. All that was lacking was the declaration of a state of siege against England, which would allow neutral ships to be torpedoed without previous warning once the neutral states had been notified. The Commander-in-Chief of the Luftwaffe was to give orders for action to be taken by warplanes without warning against merchant ships sailing in convoy, this being judged entirely in accordance with international law. The moment for the declaration of a state of siege would depend on political developments in the near future and on the time and nature of Army operations. Should these violate the neutrality of neutral states, then the appropriate moment for the most drastic measures on the part of the Navy would also have come.

Churchill returned to the progress of 'the War at Sea' on 8 November,[13] when he assured the House of Commons, 'We are gaining a definite mastery over the U-boat attack.'

After giving an account of losses during the previous eight weeks, the defensive arming of merchant ships and delays in the passage times for merchant ships imposed by convoys, he continued:

Now I turn to the offensive against the U-boats. It is very difficult to give assured figures ... But I think it would be a fairly sound conservative estimate that the losses of U-boats lie between two and four in every week according to the activity which prevails. Of course, when many are out there are more losses to commerce and more U-boats are killed. On the other side, however, there is a factor which has to be considered. I have not hitherto mentioned to the House the German building. We must assume that perhaps two new U-boats are added every week to the hostile strength, and in ten weeks of war this would be twenty. At any rate our expectation is that we must face a hundred U-boats available in January, less whatever sinkings have occurred in the interval. It will be seen, therefore, that, although we are making headway, a long and unrelenting struggle lies before us. For this our preparations are moving forward on the largest scale. Three times as many hunting craft are now at work as at the outbreak of the war, and very large reinforcements of vessels, specially adapted to this task, will flow in increasingly from the spring of 1940 onwards. Therefore, it would seem that, judged upon the material basis alone, we may face the future with confidence.

I must warn the House again that continual losses must be expected. No immunity can be guaranteed at any time. There will not be in this war any period when the seas will be completely safe; but neither will there be, I believe and I trust, any period when the full necessary traffic of the Allies cannot be carried on. We shall suffer and we shall suffer continually, but by perseverance, and by taking measures on the largest scale, I feel no doubt that in the end we shall break their hearts.

In addition to the U-boat menace we have to face the attack of the surface raider. It is certain that one and possibly two of the so-called pocket battleships has been out upon the Atlantic trade routes during the last six weeks. But what is remarkable is that although these powerful vessels have been lying athwart the stream of convoys and the individual vessels crossing the Atlantic, they have not been able, or have not dared, so far – and I speak under the greatest reserve – to make any captures worth considering. Thus up to the present not only has the U-boat campaign been controlled, but also the attack by surface raiders both by warships or by armed merchantmen has not developed in any serious way.

The U-boat operation reports produced by the BdU during November offer a rather more objective account:

> Seven U-boats lost through enemy action. The number available still too small for the force to be split up to attack the enemy in different parts of the world, with or without the co-operation of auxiliary cruisers. For the moment, they are to work as a compact unit. The element of surprise is needed to make operations successful, and therefore new tactics must be devised. They are to operate only where likely to achieve success. The policy of sending out several U-boats to make a concerted attack on a convoy has not achieved the success expected, because of the enemy's use of direction-finding by bearings, and owing to the fact only a maximum of nine Atlantic U-boats could be sent out on concerted attacks.

No merchant ships were lost from Atlantic convoys during November.

Churchill was given, as we have already seen, to providing the House of Commons with regular updates on the progress of the war at sea. On Wednesday, 6 December[14] he reported:

> The main attack of the enemy had been concentrated on the Royal Navy and the sea-borne commerce upon which the British Islands and British Empire depend. We have considerably more than 2,000 ships at sea. This immense traffic has to be maintained in the teeth of a constant U-boat attack.

He continued:

> I must again repeat the warning which I gave to the House in September … a steady flow of losses must be expected … occasional disasters will occur … any failure upon our part to act up to the level of circumstances would immediately be attended by grave dangers. [This was a theme to which Churchill would regularly return.] The convoy system is now in full operation. Very few ships have been attacked in convoy; less than one in 750 has been sunk. Nevertheless we must remember that convoy involves a certain definite loss of carrying power, since the ships have to wait during the assembly of the convoy, and the convoy must travel at the speed of the slowest ship. This loss is being steadily reduced by the institution of slow and fast convoys, and by other appropriate measures; but a certain delay must always remain, a certain diminution, that is to say, in the actual fertility of our convoys.

With few U-boats on patrol in the North Atlantic, the threat to the convoys was minimal. However, two Atlantic convoys were attacked. On 5 December the Royal Mail Lines steamer *Navasota*, sailing in OB.46 from Liverpool for Buenos Aires, was sunk by *U-47* (Günther Prien) 150 miles west of Bishop Rock in the South-Western Approaches; and four days later, the motor tanker *San Alberto* in convoy OB.48 was torpedoed by *U-48* in the same area. Two days earlier, the *Brandon*, a straggler from OB.48, had been sunk south of Fastnet by the same U-boat. These were the only losses from Atlantic convoys during the month.

The return of *U-48* to the North Sea on 19 December left no U-boats in the Atlantic, although a concentration of about fifteen was expected to arrive in January and February. This lack of activity was partly due to the small number of U–boats ready for sea in December and January, when it had been necessary to change engine installations in the old 500-ton boats, make extensive repairs to all U-boats and to withdraw many of the small boats to support U-boat training. U-boat losses during the first few months of the war had also not been replaced by new construction.

Many of the merchant ships attacked by U-boats during January were neutrals sailing independently, a fact referred to by Churchill in a radio broadcast on 20 January 1940:

> Everyone wonders what is happening about the war.
>
> Neutral ships are sunk without law or mercy – not only by the blind and wanton mine, but by the coldly considered, deliberately aimed torpedo. The Dutch, the Belgians, the Danes, the Swedes, and, above all, the Norwegians, have their ships destroyed whenever they can be caught upon the high seas. It is only in the British and French convoys that safety is to be found. There, in those convoys, it is five-hundred-to-one against being sunk. There, controlling forces are at work which are steadily keeping the seas open, steadily keeping the traffic going, and establishing order and freedom of movement amid the waves of anarchy and sea-murder.
>
> It seems pretty certain that half the U-boats with which Germany began the war have been sunk,[15] and that their new building has fallen far behind what we expected. Our faithful ASDIC detector smells them out in the depths of the sea, and, with the potent aid of the Royal Air Force, I do not doubt that we shall break their strength and break their purpose.
>
> Here we are, after nearly five months of all they can do against us on the sea, with the first U-boat campaign for the first time being utterly broken, with our shipping virtually undiminished, and with all the oceans of the world free from surface raiders.

The end of January brought the first surfaced U-boat attack on a convoy, when *U-55* conducted two attacks on OA.80G in the Celtic Sea south-west of the Isles of Scilly, sinking one merchant ship in each attack – the only ships lost from an escorted convoy during the month. The U-boat was then counter attacked and sunk, an event referred in a speech by Prime Minster Neville Chamberlain to the National Defence and Public Interest Committee the following day, and widely reported in the press. A typical account of the action read:

U-BOAT SUNK

Pays For Loss of Tanker

RESCUED GERMANS IN LONDON

LONDON, 1 February
A German submarine was destroyed on Tuesday after it had attacked and sunk the British tanker *Vaclite* (5,026 tons), which was under convoy. Survivors from the U-boat were picked up. They arrived in London last night strongly guarded, on their way to an internment camp. Most of them appeared to be in their teens. They were practically all bearded.

The Prime Minister, in referring during a luncheon speech yesterday to the sinking of the U-boat, said, 'Contrary to the German practice, we saved the lives of the majority of the crew.' It was the first submarine attack on a British convoy for some time. The escorting naval vessels immediately dropped depth charges in an effort to destroy the U-boat. Contact with the submarine was lost, but soon afterwards a Coastal Command flying-boat, which had been escorting the convoy, saw the U-boat proceeding on the surface, apparently too damaged to submerge.

The plane dropped a bomb, to which the submarine replied with anti-aircraft fire. The flying-boat then brought its machine-guns into action. Clouds were now touching the sea and the flying-boat lost sight of the submarine. It informed warships of the submarine's position, and when they arrived they found the U-boat had sunk. Some survivors were rescued from a rubber dinghy, and later others were picked up from the sea. There were no casualties aboard the *Vaclite*, whose crew were rescued by an Italian ship.

The absence of attacks on convoys during the month was further explained by the BdU War Log for 23 January, which noted:

At present it is not possible to make the desired mass attacks on merchant shipping, as there are not enough boats available.

On 2 February, in what would prove a remarkable outburst in the light of later developments and his own personal admissions, Dönitz denied that the success of U-boat attacks on convoys had been impaired by the enemy's use of direction-finding, or that huge packs of U-boats were needed for concerted attacks on convoys. He referred to the recent success of a concerted attack on a convoy by only three U-boats, and insisted best use was being made of the U-boats available. With the current shortage of boats, the long-distance operations proposed for U-boats would weaken the chances of effective 'kills' in nearer waters. In January thirty-seven enemy steamers had been sunk by torpedo.[16] There were in fact, as the BdU War Log for 23 February confirmed, 'only about six submarines continuously operating in the Atlantic. The recent losses of *U-15*, *U-55*, and *U-33* bring the total to date to twelve – an average of two per month.'

February saw a further increase in U-boat operations, Allied and neutral ships being attacked without prior warning. There were also sporadic attacks on Atlantic convoys during the month, with one merchant ship sunk on 5 February in the attack on OA.84 and two stragglers from HX.18 torpedoed and sunk in separate incidents on 14 February, followed on 22 February by the sinking of a straggler from HX.19. Most of the sinkings took place in the North-Western and South-Western Approaches – usually single ships or stragglers from convoys, when there was little risk of the U-boat being detected and attacked by escorts.

Up to March 1940 the U-boats preferred to attack single ships or stragglers, the usual method being to approach on the surface and use the deck gun to stop the vessel; then if the ship was British or a neutral carrying contraband, to sink it by torpedo. Only seven of 169 merchant ships sunk by U-boats during the first six months of the war were in convoy when sunk. The U-boat campaign against neutral merchant shipping was exposed in press reports which appeared on 1 March:

Nazi Admission of War on Neutral Shipping
WARNING IN BROADCAST ANNOUNCEMENT

An admission by Germany of the Nazi campaign against neutral shipping was contained in a broadcast from Berlin. The radio complained that British statements of shipping losses did not include those of neutrals, thus striving to detract from the success of the Nazis naval warfare. The announcer said that Germany would put out of action all merchant shipping going to the enemy. 'This has been done, and is being done, regardless of nationality,' said the announcer.

The broadcast has been accepted in London as an admission of the campaign against neutral shipping. It has also been pointed out in London that Germany's attention has not wholly been given to neutral ships trading with the Allies.

During March only one merchant ship from dispersed Atlantic convoy OA.152 was sunk, on the 4th. There would be no further attacks during the remainder of March whilst most U-boats were withdrawn from the Atlantic and other operational areas to support the invasion of Norway – Operation *Weserübung*. Only one U-boat was operating west of Ireland and two off the English south and west coasts. None would be detected in the Atlantic after about 12 March. The German Naval Staff Operations Division War Log for 4 March commenting on plans for Operation *Weserübung* noted: 'The war against merchant shipping must be relegated to second place.'

On 6 March it was announced the restrictions on air attacks on neutral shipping had been lifted. Newspaper reports of the announcement appeared two days later:

NAZIS ORDER AIR ATTACKS
ON NEUTRAL SHIPPING

Australian Associated Press

LONDON, 7 March

A fresh move against neutral shipping was announced from Berlin yesterday. An official statement declared that neutral ships which were escorted by Allied warships, either in a voluntary convoy or forcibly, to a contraband control base were liable to be treated as enemy ships and attacked from the air. The statement denied the accusations that Germany was sinking neutral ships indiscriminately.

'It is impossible for German pilots to distinguish whether a ship is being escorted voluntarily or forcibly,' added the statement. 'Such convoys can legitimately be attacked. Our pilots have strict orders not to attack unconvoyed neutral ships, and they have never machine-gunned the crews of ships.'

The Oslo newspaper *Aftenposten* declares that it is impossible for neutral countries to trade with a country which is simultaneously sinking her ships, killing her sailors and forbidding her to trade with other countries. 'It is high time,' it adds, 'that Germany clearly specified her claims to Norwegian ships and trade.' The Oslo newspaper *Tidens Tegn* states that

German ships are using Norwegian waters to carry arms to Russia, and
Norwegian pilots are not allowed to go aboard.

As the BdU War Log later noted,[17] from mid-March 1940 the Atlantic U-boats
kept watch on the western and northern Norwegian harbours, as far north
as Narvik, and on the English bases in the north. This interrupted Atlantic
operations for two months, and restricted operations in the North Sea to a few
boats. During the invasion of Norway, all U-boats were withdrawn to carry
supplies, and for escort duties and attacks on English bases. As a result, there
was a pause in U-boat attacks on Atlantic convoys until May 1940. Dönitz later
wrote of these months:

> The declaration of an operational area around England and freedom of
> attack on all British merchant ships followed after England had publicly
> declared that all English merchant ships had been armed. Very soon after
> the beginning of the war, the convoy system was instituted by England to
> an ever-increasing degree. By this, merchant ships lost the protection of
> all international rules, as under the protection of their own warships they
> had put themselves outside the prize law. The U-boats were then given
> freedom of attack on all merchant ships escorted by enemy warships.
>
> With the very small number of U-boats available, it was clear U-boat
> command could only inflict pinpricks on England's trade and conduct of
> the war at sea. The number of U-boats at sea in operational areas during
> the winter 1939–40 never exceeded ten and at times fell as low as two. It
> was clear U-boat command could achieve results only if they took the bull
> by the horns and attacked, as far as possible, the concentration point of
> traffic in or near harbours.

Chapter 2

Phase Two: April to June 1940

May 1940 was dominated by a series of major events with significant implications for the war at sea in the Atlantic. The first was the British occupation of Iceland, which would play a key role in defence of both the Atlantic and Arctic convoys. Following the German invasion of Norway and Denmark on 9 April 1940, the British Government, increasingly concerned Germany would establish a military presence in Iceland and so threaten British control of the North Atlantic sea lanes, offered Iceland assistance in maintaining her independence. The Admiralty led by Churchill was also eager to establish bases in Iceland to strengthen the Northern Patrol.[1] The strategic location of Iceland, together with the islands of Newfoundland and Greenland, meant that if Germany took them, their forces based there could have exercised control over the whole sea route across the North Atlantic. As Churchill later said, 'Whoever possesses Iceland holds a pistol firmly pointed at Britain, America and Canada.'[2]

It was the recognition of this threat, Churchill later postulated, that prompted Britain, when Denmark was invaded by Germany, to occupy Iceland. Although Churchill rather disingenuously claimed this occupation of Iceland was 'with the concurrence of its people', in reality the Icelanders were offered little real choice.

On 6 May Churchill advised the War Cabinet[3] that Britain should occupy Iceland immediately to secure it as a base for flying boats and for refuelling facilities for the Northern Patrol,[4] and obtained approval for the immediate occupation of Iceland by military forces, with a view to the establishment there of naval and air facilities. After a two-day debate in the House of Commons on the failures of the British campaign in Norway, Prime Minister Neville Chamberlain resigned on 8 May – the day the landings in Iceland (Operation Fork) took place. Churchill now assumed the role of Prime Minister and responsibility for inter-service co-ordination, with the title of Minister of Defence. As subsequent events confirm, the decision to base Allied naval and air forces in Iceland would prove vital to the successful outcome of North Atlantic and Arctic convoy operations. The early weeks of May were also dominated by the German invasion of Holland, Belgium, Luxembourg, and France on the 10th, followed by the Allied retreat to, and beginning of evacuation from, Dunkirk.

During the second half of May, as the BdU War Log explained, it was at last possible to return U-boats gradually to the Atlantic, where they were to operate with great success. Five U-boats sailed for the Atlantic between 18 and 22 May, but only eight merchant ships were sunk between 22 and 31 May. No Atlantic convoys were attacked.

From May to October 1940 outward bound convoys would only be escorted as far as 12° west, and later as far as 19° west. At approximately the same longitude the homeward-bound convoys were then picked up by the escort. Canadian destroyers escorted convoys from Halifax for some 400 miles east into the Atlantic. For the rest of the crossing they were escorted by a single Royal Navy Armed Merchant Cruiser (AMC).

Operation Dynamo, the evacuation of Allied forces from Dunkirk, began on 26 May. Three days later, the Germans announced U-boat warfare was about to recommence and warned neutral shipping not to sail under the protection of British convoys. The promised resumption of U-boat activity was presaged in press reports which appeared on 31 May:

INTENSIFICATION OF U-BOAT CAMPAIGN THREATENED

LONDON, Thursday
The German news agency threatens an intensification of the submarine warfare. It says, 'the training of additional crews has been completed and the submarine fleet will how concentrate its activities on British sea routes, especially as ports in Eastern England are already blocked.'

In the early morning of 4 June the departure of the destroyer *Shikari* from Dunkirk brought Operation Dynamo to a close.

Until June the numbers of merchant ships attacked both by U-boats and German surface raiders in the Atlantic remained relatively low, given the U-boats' restricted operating range from their bases in Germany and competing operational priorities in Norway. After Dunkirk the perceived threat of an invasion of the east and south coasts of Britain resulted in the diversion to anti-invasion patrols of naval escorts from convoys and aircraft from anti-submarine patrols in the Western Approaches. Churchill was now prompted to appeal to President Roosevelt for assistance. In the first of an extended series of exchanges on the subject he cabled Roosevelt on 11 June:

I have already cabled you about aeroplanes including flying boats which are so needful to us in the impending struggle for the life of Great Britain. But even more pressing is the need for destroyers.

The Italian outrage[5] makes it necessary for us to cope with much larger number of submarines which may come out into the Atlantic and perhaps be based on Spanish ports. To this the only counter is destroyers. Nothing is so important as for us to have 30 or 40 old destroyers you have already had reconditioned. We can fit them very rapidly with our ASDICS and they will bridge over the gap of 6 months before our wartime new construction comes into play. We will return them or their equivalents to you without fail at 6 months' notice if at any time you need them. The next 6 months are vital.

In fact, the destroyers were transferred in batches, the first on 9 September 1940 and the last on 5 December 1940. The last of the December batch arrived in Plymouth on 9 March 1941. A number required subsequent refit and/or repair.

The BdU War Log for 12 June noted that seventy-four U-boats had been commissioned or were already in service between September 1939 and the end of May 1940. Of these, sixty-six had operated against the enemy. Twenty-four (36.4 per cent) had been lost. Dönitz promised these losses would fall as soon as a counter-measure to ASDIC was found.

June 1940 also saw the experimental introduction of the wolfpack tactic to replace attacks by individual U-boats. This involved two small groups of U-boats codenamed *Rosing* and *Prien* (after Günther Prien) formed on 12 June. *Prien*, of six U-boats with *U-47* in tactical command, attacked HX.47 on 14/15 June 60 miles west of the Scilly Isles and sank three merchant ships. *Prien* was also tasked to attack HX.48 on 16 June but failed to make contact, and on the afternoon of 17 June the operation was terminated. Wolfpack *Rosing* of five U-boats formed to operate against SL convoys and independents in the Bay of Biscay sank two unescorted merchant ships and two from SL.34 between 12 and 14 June, but had no further success and was dissolved on 23 June. Both groups were relatively unsuccessful; the attempt to operate as an integrated wolfpack to intercept and destroy a convoy failed as a result of the difficulties in exercising effective command and control at sea. As a result, Dönitz would in future exercise tactical control from his headquarters, at Lorient and later in Paris.

On 16 June fourteen U-boats were operational in the Atlantic. Two days later, Rear-Admiral Fricke, of the Operations Division, Naval Staff, pointed out the advantages which would accrue to the U-boat arm if the Wehrmacht reached the west coast of France. There would then be new bases on the French coast for U-boats, and airfields in France would provide reconnaissance in the eastern Atlantic to scout for targets. The Wehrmacht captured the port of Lorient on 21 June, and Dönitz arrived there two days later and chose it as the first of his five French bases (to be followed by Brest, Saint-Nazaire, La Pallice, and Bordeaux). Lorient had escaped large-scale sabotage damage by the French military. As Dönitz later wrote:

> Conditions were made particularly favourable for the U-boat war against shipping in the Atlantic, which was resumed at the conclusion of the Norwegian expedition. The possession of the Biscay ports eliminated the long journeys to and fro which had taken up almost the whole radius of action of the U-boats. The sea routes were now, so to speak, at the front door.

On 22 June the French signed an armistice, surrendering to the Germans. British forces had been evacuated from Brest and Saint-Nazaire by 19 June and from La Rochelle/La Pallice and Bordeaux on 20 June; by 25 June the evacuation of Allied forces from French Atlantic ports was complete. Britain now stood alone in the war against Germany, her ability to sustain the war effort dependent on keeping the sea lanes open. The number of U-boats fortunately remained no greater than in September 1939, with never more than fifteen on patrol out of the twenty-five operational.

The acquisition of the French Atlantic ports enabled Dönitz to fully implement his wolfpack tactic. He now had control of powerful land-based radio transmitters on the coast of France capable of sending messages to U-boats across the Atlantic and sufficient U-boats to deploy wolfpacks from July 1940 onwards.

Prior to July 1940, U-boats had to sail 450 miles through the North Sea and round the north of the British Isles to reach the Atlantic. Operating from the French bases now relieved U-boats of this hazardous journey. Passage time was reduced by seven days, with a corresponding saving in fuel and a doubling of the numbers available in the operational areas, which now extended further west into the Atlantic. Although fewer U-boats were available, the number actually operating rose to eight or nine, and they could now sail directly into the Atlantic convoy routes with, in the early months at least, less risk of detection.

Chapter 3

Phase Three: July to September 1940

The threat to Atlantic convoys following the German occupation of France was not confined to U-boats. The dangers to merchant ships setting off across the Atlantic sometimes lay closer to home. Convoy OA.178 of thirty-five merchant ships departed Southend on 3 July with a single escort for the English Channel, prior to the merchantmen dispersing to their transatlantic destinations. In the afternoon of 4 July the convoy was attacked in the English Channel, some 20 miles to the south of Portland Bill, by two groups of Ju.87 dive-bombers. A number of ships sought refuge in Weymouth Bay, where again they came under air attack. At dusk those merchant ships which had remained at sea, now 13 miles to the south of Portland, were attacked by aircraft and E-boats. In the course of both attacks five merchantmen were sunk and twelve were damaged and unable to continue. The following day, the escort was joined by the destroyer *Broke*, which remained with the convoy until 6 July, when it was dispersed in the South-Western Approaches. The severity of OA.178's losses led to the decision to route all subsequent OA convoys from Methil in Fife around the north coast of Scotland, to avoid the English Channel and the threat of air and E-boat attack from northern France. The first Atlantic U-boat base in France was established at Lorient on 6 July, and the following day, *U-30* became the first U-boat to make Lorient its home port.

Churchill sought in a radio broadcast on 14 July to provide reassurance and give an upbeat assessment of the impact of the war at sea on food reserves and merchant shipping tonnage; but he also called for increased effort and vigilance in meeting the challenge which lay ahead:

> Around all lies the power of the Royal Navy. With over a thousand armed ships under the White Ensign patrolling the seas, the Navy, which is capable of transferring its force very readily to the protection of any part of the British Empire which may be threatened, is capable also of keeping open communication with the New World, from whom, as the struggle deepens, increasing aid will come. Is it not remarkable that after ten months of unlimited U-boat and air attack upon our commerce, our food reserves are higher than they have ever been, and we have a substantially larger tonnage under our own flag, apart from great numbers of foreign ships

in our control, than we had at the beginning of the war? Why do I dwell on all this? Not, surely, to induce any slackening of effort or vigilance. On the contrary. These must be redoubled, and we must prepare not only for the summer, but for the winter; not only for 1941, but for 1942; when the war will, I trust, take a different form from the defensive, in which it has hitherto been bound. I dwell on these elements in our strength, on these resources which we have mobilized and control – I dwell on them because it is right to show that the good cause can command the means of survival; and that while we toil through the dark valley we can see the sunlight on the uplands beyond.

Until the middle of July, U-boats were most active off the South-Western Approaches to the British Isles. As shipping losses mounted, the Atlantic convoys were re-routed to approach the Irish Sea through the North-Western Approaches. The North Channel and the sea-lanes leading to it now became the focal point for all merchant shipping leaving or arriving in British waters. The first convoy to be re-routed was HX.55, the main body of which arrived at Liverpool on 18 July.[1] Even this new route did not guarantee safety. On 16 and 17 July three merchant ships were sunk, two off the Bloody Foreland and one off Cape Wrath.

By 17 July the BdU had confirmed from radio intelligence and Luftwaffe reports the change of convoy route, and numerous convoys had been observed sailing north of Scotland to east coast ports. The North Channel, Minch and Moray Firth areas would now become the focus of operation by the next wave of U-boats.

Until June 1940 U-boats had tended to conduct submerged attacks on convoys and surface attacks on unescorted merchant ships. July brought a change in tactics. Following the realization that submerged U-boats were vulnerable to detection by ASDIC and counter-attack by escorts, they now began to attack on the surface at night, becoming less visible, more difficult to detect and able to operate at higher speed with greater manoeuvrability to evade counter-attack. They would shadow a convoy until dark, approach 'trimmed down' on the surface for the attack, then retire at high speed. During daylight they continued to attack ships sailing independently or stragglers from convoys.

There were sporadic attacks on eight Atlantic convoys during July, with ten merchant ships sunk. In the most serious, on the afternoon 26 July, convoy OB.188 was attacked 350 miles west of Ireland by U-34 and a passenger liner and a merchant ship sunk. A merchant ship and a tanker were sunk by the same U-boat in the early hours of the following day.

In the first strike of August, convoy HX.60 was attacked on the 4th about 300 miles west-north-west of Bloody Foreland; three merchant ships were sunk. Two stragglers from HX.62 would be sunk on 13 and 15 August in the North-West Approaches.

Churchill had appealed to Roosevelt on 11 June for assistance in the form of additional destroyers. Roosevelt's reply on 13 August confirmed that 'it might be possible to furnish to the British Government as immediate assistance at least 50 destroyers'. But Roosevelt set two preconditions: firstly seeking assurance from Churchill that in the event that the waters of Great Britain became untenable for British ships of war, the destroyers would not be turned over to the Germans or sunk, but sent to other parts of the Empire for continued defence; and secondly, an agreement that the British Government would authorize the use of Newfoundland, Bermuda, the Bahamas, Jamaica, St Lucia, Trinidad and British Guiana as naval and air bases by the United States … with the understanding the land necessary for the above could be acquired by the United States through purchase or a 99-year lease.

Two days later, Churchill replied in the affirmative to Roosevelt's proposals. Clearly anxious to obtain the destroyers at almost any cost, he said:

> We can meet both the points you consider necessary to help you with Congress and with others concerned, but I am sure you will not misunderstand me if I say that our willingness to do so must be conditioned on our being assured that there will be no delay in letting us have the ships.

OB.197 was attacked by two U-boats on 16 August with two merchant ships sunk and one damaged. In August long-range FW200 bombers began patrols off the coast of Ireland, operating from the airbase at Merignac, near Bordeaux. As well as vectoring U-boats onto convoys, they would attack and sink many ships and remain a major threat for the following two years.

Slow convoys, designated 'SC', to include ships making between seven and a half and nine knots, were organized in August to assemble at Sydney, Nova Scotia. SC.1 sailed on 15 August 1940. The convoy was attacked by U-boats several times between 24 and 28 August, when one escort and three merchant ships were sunk. This measure reduced the HX convoys to a reasonable size of about forty-five ships. The HX convoys sailed on a four-day cycle, and the SC convoys on an eight-day cycle.

Winston Churchill addressed the House of Commons on 20 August on the War Situation:[2]

> It is our intention to maintain and enforce a strict blockade not only of Germany but of Italy, France and all the other countries that have fallen into the German power. I read in the papers that Herr Hitler has also proclaimed a strict blockade of the British Islands. No one can complain of that.

Our Navy is far stronger than it was at the beginning of the war. The seas and oceans are open. The U-boats are contained. Our stocks of food of all kinds are far more abundant than in the days of peace and a large and growing programme of food production is on foot.

There is, however, one direction in which we can see a little more clearly ahead. We have to think not only for ourselves but for the lasting security of the cause and principles for which we are fighting and of the long future of the British Commonwealth of Nations. Some months ago we came to the conclusion that the interests of the United States and of the British Empire both required that the United States should have facilities for the naval and air defence of the Western hemisphere against the attack of a Nazi power which might have acquired temporary but lengthy control of a large part of Western Europe and its formidable resources. We had therefore decided spontaneously, and without being asked or offered any inducement, to inform the Government of the United States that we would be glad to place such defence facilities at their disposal by leasing suitable sites in our transatlantic possessions for their greater security against the unmeasured dangers of the future ...

His Majesty's Government are entirely willing to accord defence facilities to the United States on a 99 years' leasehold basis, and we feel sure that our interests no less than theirs, and the interests of the Colonies themselves and of Canada and Newfoundland will be served thereby.

He ended by saying:

For my own part, looking out upon the future, I do not view the process with any misgivings. I could not stop it if I wished; no one can stop it. Like the Mississippi, it just keeps rolling along. Let it roll. Let it roll on full flood, inexorable, irresistible, benignant, to broader lands and better days.

The same day, a report of the German announcement threatening a resumption of unrestricted submarine warfare appeared in the newspapers. This read:

Except for its threat of an intensification of unrestricted submarine warfare, Germany's announcement yesterday of a 'total blockade' of the British Isles does not foreshadow any sort of action which Germany has not done her utmost to carry out for months past. The trumpet-blast with which the Nazi announcement was issued through the German news agency, heralding that Germany would do what she was already attempting to do, can only be interpreted as an over-elaborate piece of propaganda and bluff, possibly designed to improve the unimpressive effect upon neutrals of the air blitzkrieg, or the growing uneasiness in Germany at the tremendous

German losses and the stern and magnificent counter-action by the Royal Air Force – despite the claims that all British aerodromes have been destroyed and that the R.A.F. is demoralised.

The spokesman described the blockade area as being smaller than the war zone designated by President Roosevelt, but it would comprise Eire and all the coast around England.

The German radio last night warned all neutral shipmasters that the blockade includes an area eastward of a line drawn from the Breton coast 600 miles into the Atlantic, then north and back to the Norwegian coast, but missing Iceland and the Faroe Islands.

British Naval Comment

A typical British naval comment on the German announcement is: 'Germany threatens to overlap our minefields? That's fine. We alone are able to use surface ships. We can sweep the passages for our convoyed and unconvoyed ships. Germany is now able to use bombers with a wider range, in addition to submarines, against shipping. We are carrying on. Let's see what happens.'

On 22 August the War Cabinet[3] discussed the response to be made to President Roosevelt's proposal for supply of destroyers and proposed grant of base facilities in certain British territories and agreed in principle an affirmative answer should be sent to the President's proposals; the Foreign Secretary was invited to draft the text of an interim reply to be dispatched by the Prime Minister that evening. This interim reply indicated the British government was in favour of the scheme but had to consult the Governments of Canada and Newfoundland before finally signifying acceptance.

One of the early re-routed convoys, HX.65, was attacked on 24 August as it neared the North-Western Approaches and ran into a group of five U-boats lying in wait across its path. One straggler was sunk in the afternoon of 24 August. In the evening, the main transatlantic crossing completed, the convoy split in two sections, HX.65A and HX.65B. HX.65A set off eastwards towards Cape Wrath and the Pentland Firth, to then sail on around the north coast of Scotland en route to the convoy anchorage at Methil Roads, from where the ships would sail on to various ports down the east coast. HX.65B headed off down the west coast of Scotland towards Liverpool.[4] The U-boat threat had not passed; on 25 August, in a position 90 miles east by north of the Flannan Isles,[5] HX.65A was attacked by *U-48*, which sank two merchant ships. Throughout the 25th six tankers unable to keep up, trailing less than a mile behind the main body of the convoy and presenting tempting targets were attacked by a

U-boat; one tanker was sunk. HX.65A was sighted by U-boats the same day. Fortunately, the timely arrival of a Sunderland flying boat probably deterred the U-boats from attacking. Then just before midnight, the convoy was attacked again 23 miles north of the Butt of Lewis in the Outer Hebrides; two merchant ships were sunk and a third badly damaged. Following this latest attack, two destroyers were dispatched from Scapa Flow early on 26 August to reinforce the convoy's anti-submarine escort, and later that day the convoy came within range of UK-based air cover. At dusk, 15 miles north-east of Kinnaird Head (12 miles north-east of Peterhead), HX.65A was attacked by eight Ju.88 bombers and four He.115 torpedo-bombers, which spotted the straggling convoy spread out below them. Two merchant ships were sunk and two damaged. One of those sunk was the victim of an He.115 torpedo-bomber in what was reportedly the Luftwaffe's first confirmed successful torpedo attack on a convoy.[6]

As HX.65B sailed down the west coast, the twenty-eight surviving merchant ships dispersed to the Clyde, Belfast, Liverpool, Dublin and Avonmouth, arriving between 26 and 28 August. Of the fifty-one merchant ships which sailed in HX.65, eight were sunk and one wrecked. Five of the original twenty-two of the Bermuda section were lost, and a further two were badly bomb-damaged. A total of 162 merchant seamen lost their lives, a figure greater than the casualties incurred in the ill-fated and much publicized convoy PQ.17, in which although twenty-four merchant ships were sunk, 153 seamen lost their lives.

By 28 August the protracted negotiations on the destroyers for naval bases agreement were approaching a conclusion, with a draft agreement forwarded from Washington to London. Churchill replied to Roosevelt the following day:

> We are prepared in friendship and good will to meet your representatives forthwith, in order to consider the lease for ninety-nine years of areas for the establishment of naval and air bases in the following places: Newfoundland, Bermuda, Bahamas, Jamaica, Antigua, St Lucia, Trinidad, British Guiana. Subject to later settlements on points of detail.

In the final attack of the month on an Atlantic convoy, OB.295 lost four ships sunk and two damaged between 30 August and 1 September. One of those damaged was the Dutch passenger liner *Volendam* assigned to the child evacuation programme and carrying 273 crew members, 320 children with their leaders and 286 other passengers, all of whom abandoned ship and were rescued by three other vessels from the convoy. Only one crew member was lost.

At the end of the month the BdU review of the first year of U-boat operations noted new construction had not covered U-boat losses. As a large number of vessels (up to twenty at times) had been required for training purposes, only about eighteen had been available for operations in the Atlantic, and eight to twelve small U-boats for operations elsewhere. The operational U-boats had been sent out very frequently, with harbour time restricted to essential repairs. U-boats had conducted 288 operations against the enemy.

The proportion of sea time – an average of 45.5 per cent – meant each U-boat spent six months at sea in one year. Of sixty-one operational U-boats, twenty-eight (46 per cent) had been lost. Seventy-nine officers, 273 petty officers and 412 men had been killed, and 33 officers, 114 petty officers and 280 men taken prisoner.

In the opinion of the German Naval Staff, the difficulty facing the U-boat offensive was not so much the enemy's escort forces which, though numerically small, were fitted with good locating devices, but rather enemy air cover, which had been surprisingly evident and which might become dangerous. It was hoped the longer, darker nights would ease this problem, and there would be a more rapid increase in the number of U-boats. They declared the next U-boat offensive would take place in the North Atlantic, for which there would be a welcome reinforcement in the next few months of some forty Italian U-boats; together with an increase of some six U-boats per month, this should result in some decisive successes in the battle to halt English imports.

Notwithstanding the small numbers available, U-boats were now carrying out attacks as far as 27° west, as their area of operations extended out into mid-Atlantic, accompanied by a marked increase in the frequency and scale of attacks on Atlantic convoys. As a result, eight OB convoys and five HX convoys were attacked during the month, losing eleven and four ships respectively.

In September 1939 Dönitz had fifty-seven U-boats; on 1 September 1940 there were still only fifty-seven, since although twenty-eight had been commissioned, another twenty-eight had been lost. Of the fifty-seven, only thirty-nine were operational. Only twelve were engaged in operations at any one time, a large number being employed on training and exercises.

During June, July, and August 1940 the numbers of merchant ships sunk by U-boats showed a steady increase over the previous three months.

On 3 September President Roosevelt notified Congress that he had completed an arrangement by which the United States would transfer to Great Britain fifty over-age destroyers in return for 99-year leases of sea and air bases at eight strategic continental and island points in the Western Hemisphere. The defence line thus established would run, he said, 4,500 miles from Newfoundland to British Guiana, and include other bases on the islands of Bermuda, the Bahamas, Jamaica, St Lucia, Trinidad and Antigua. It was intended, through the use of these bases, to make difficult, if not impossible, naval and air attacks on the United States and much of the Western Hemisphere. He referred to the naval and air bases as 'generously given and gladly received' and said:

The Anglo-American agreement is not inconsistent in any sense with our status of peace. Still less is it a threat against any nation. It is an epochal and far-reaching act of preparation for continental defence in face of grave danger, the most important action for the reinforcement of our national defence taken since the Louisiana purchase from France in 1803 … These outposts of security are essential to the protection of the Panama Canal, Central America, the Antilles, Canada, Mexico, and our own eastern and Gulf seaboards.

The night attacks on convoys now led, in September 1940, to the fitting of radar to the aircraft of Coastal Command and the Fleet Air Arm. September also saw the first organized U-boat wolfpack attacks on the Atlantic convoys, personally directed by Admiral Dönitz. Luftwaffe FW200 Condor long-range bombers, now also operating from Norway as well as France, continued to attack shipping off Ireland.

The target of one of the first planned wolfpack attacks on an Atlantic convoy was SC.2, an eastbound convoy of fifty-four merchant ships which sailed from Sydney, Cape Breton, Nova Scotia on 25 August 1940 bound for Liverpool, escorted by the sloop *Scarborough*. B-Dienst, the German signals intelligence branch, had broken the Admiralty cipher codes and informed U-boat Command (BdU) of SC.2's departure. Only five U-boats were on station in the Atlantic at the time, and BdU ordered one of these, *U-47*, to intercept and shadow the convoy while the other boats homed in. En route, *U-47* encountered and attacked convoy OA.207 on 3 September, about 80 miles south-west of Rockall, and in the early hours of 4 September sank one merchant ship. Of the five U-boats tasked to attack, *U-124* was unavailable, being on weather-reporting duty, and *U-28* was short of fuel and unable to proceed further west. It was thus left to *U-65* and *U-101* to move west to join the search. On 4 September the three U-boats formed a patrol line at longitude 20° west, on the fringe of the Western Approaches.

Two days later, *U-65* sighted the convoy and notified BdU and the other U-boats, but was unable to attack in heavy seas. *U-101* then fell out of the pursuit with engine trouble, leaving *U-47* to carry out the attack. This came in the early hours of the following morning, when in a series of attacks *U-47* sank three merchant ships. *U-47* continued to shadow the convoy but was unable to mount a further attack until the early hours of 9 September, when two more merchant ships were torpedoed and sunk. With this the assault on SC.2 ended; the U-boats had sunk five ships at no cost to themselves. This was one of the first occasions on which U-boats made a joint attack on a convoy, although its success was largely down to a single experienced U-boat commander, Günther

Prien of *U-47*, who accounted for four of the five ships sunk. The escort failed to inflict any damage on the attackers, but forty-nine ships reached Liverpool without further loss on 10 September.

The Führer Conference of 6 September discussed the extensive operational possibilities provided by the strategic position of bases at Trondheim, Lorient and Bordeaux. The main operational area – the western part of the North Channel and the waters west of Scotland – was recognized as very productive. Operations were being directed from Lorient and from home bases, and the results at present were considerable. A further gradual increase in successes might be expected with the declaration of an operational area around the British Isles and permission to open fire without previous warning on all targets, eliminating all previous restrictions. At the moment, anti-submarine defence was provided not so much by naval escort vessels, of which there were few, but by strong air cover. Since the outbreak of war twenty-eight out of sixty-one operational submarines, or 46 per cent, had been lost. Hitler was asked to acknowledge the contribution of the submarines in his next speech and promised to do so. Submarine warfare in the Atlantic was to be supported by Italian submarines, and Bordeaux expanded into a base. The first submarine had arrived at Bordeaux. At the moment there were three boats in the Atlantic and six en route. Thirty-six boats were to be sent into the Atlantic before the end of October.

A similar operation to that mounted against SC.21 took place two weeks later, the target the forty merchant ships of HX.72. At this time convoys were still unescorted or accompanied by a single armed merchant cruiser (AMC) as protection against surface raiders until reaching the Western Approaches. HX.72's ocean escort (to 20 September) was the AMC *Jervis Bay*. HX.72, not due to meet its Western Approaches escort until the afternoon of 21 September, was unescorted when sighted by *U-47*. At this time only a small number of U-boats were deployed in the North Atlantic, operating at the edge of the Western Approaches to intercept convoys before their escort joined. *U-47* on weather duty, her armament depleted after the earlier attack on SC.2, was only able to report the contact and began to shadow the convoy. Over the next few hours, BdU began to assemble a group of six U-boats. In the ensuing attack on the convoy seven merchant ships were sunk and one damaged. A further four were sunk and another damaged the following day, the U-boats' success only limited by the lack of torpedoes to carry out further attacks.

The U-boats involved included those commanded by the aces Kretschmer, Preen and Schepke. Seven of the eleven ships were sunk and two damaged by Schepke's *U-100* in one night. The German B-Dienst was instrumental in directing U-boats to the convoys, where they held the advantage as they manoeuvred on the surface between the merchantmen and their escorts. At the same time, the lack of radar deprived the escorts of the ability to detect the U-boats, force them to dive and deny them their speed advantage, before hunting them with ASDIC. The Convoy Commodore insisted at least two U-boats had worked together to attack the convoy, but apparently his comments were dismissed at the time.

Between 25 and 30 September four successive Atlantic convoys – OB.217, OB.218, OB.219 and OB.220 – were attacked by six U-boats, losing a total of thirteen ships sunk and one damaged, bringing the total sunk during the month to forty-seven. The early period of the war at sea between July and October 1940, when significant numbers of merchant ships were sunk, was referred to by U-boat crews as 'the Happy Time' (*die Glückliche Zeit*), and later as 'the First Happy Time'.

Chapter 4

Phase Four: October to December 1940

The inadequacy of the arrangements for protection of merchant ships in convoy was reviewed by the War Cabinet on 4 October 1940,[1] when they considered a Memorandum by the Ministers of Shipping and Food, and the First Lord of the Admiralty. The Memorandum dated 3 October 1940 argued that the principal cause of the losses by U-boat attack was the lack of escorting vessels. Additional reasons given for the increased losses included the employment of new tactics by the U-boats, their new French bases enabling them to operate much further westward than formerly and the size of the convoys. New enemy tactics seemed to indicate U-boats were now working as surface torpedo-boats, shadowing a convoy until after dark or locating it in the dark, and then attacking by 'browning'[2] from long range and escaping at high speed on the surface. This made the task of the meagre escorting forces with large convoys much more difficult. They were separated from each other by long distances, sometimes so far away that the escort was unaware an attack had taken place. Every possible step was being taken to develop new methods to counter these new tactics. As to the size of the convoys, a reduction, which would be most welcome to the Admiralty, could only be achieved at the expense of the import programme or by increasing the number of convoys. The latter was clearly impossible without an increase in the number of escorts.

Churchill noted the matter had been discussed on the previous evening at a meeting of the Defence Committee. The conclusion reached, in view of the fact that suitable weather for an invasion was unlikely to prevail during the winter months and taking into account the very heavy losses being sustained, was that it would be right to divert a number of destroyers and anti-submarine trawlers from anti-invasion duties to reinforce the convoy escorts in the North-West Approaches. Some of these could be recalled at short notice to assist in repelling any invasion attempt. In addition to these vessels, it was hoped to have ten further destroyers and six corvettes available for service in the next four weeks, including vessels received from the USA.

During October U-boat attacks on Atlantic convoys resumed with increasing intensity. There was still no air cover in the mid-Atlantic for merchant ships once they left American coastal waters, a deficiency which would not be remedied until early 1943. Convoys were now being attacked on a daily basis, usually losing only one or two ships, until on 16 October SC.7 sailed into the path of a group of U-boats operating in the North-Western Approaches and over a period of three nights was attacked by seven U-boats, which sank twenty merchantmen. One of those attacked in the dying minutes of 18 October was the British steamship *Fiscus*, torpedoed and sunk east of Rockall by *U-99* with the loss of her master, thirty-six crew and one gunner. Remarkably, the sole survivor, Edward Sidney King, was found later standing on some debris by the crew of a lifeboat from the steamship *Sneffeld*. In his Survivor's Report – sworn at Cardiff on 19 November 1940 – Edward described the circumstances of the sinking and his extraordinary survival:

This vessel had reached a point about 350 miles west of Eire. Position in Convoy, third ship in column three from port. Other columns having from three to six ships in each. Deponent [the legal term for Edward King] was lying dozing in his bunk when a violent explosion occurred, and ship took a heavy list to starboard. One packing case was lying alongside No. 2 hatch. It was not lashed to the deck. Deponent got on to the packing case, when the sea washed him into No. 2 hold, the hatches of which had been blown off by the explosion. Evidently, the torpedo had struck No. 2 hold, starboard side, blowing off beams and hatch covers. The hold was full of water. Deponent sank and rose to the surface when he grabbed the rope lashing around the packing case. The case floated away, the fore deck of the ship being by this time under water. The packing case swept clear of the ship and when deponent looked around the ship had disappeared, and the sea was a mass of wreckage. In deponent's opinion vessel sank within a minute of the explosion. After about two hours on the packing case deponent sighted three Indian firemen clinging to the ice box about 20 yards away. He called to them and helped them on to the packing case. They died from exposure the next morning. Deponent did not see any other members of the crew. He remained on the packing case until picked up on 21/10/40 by a lifeboat full of survivors from Norwegian ship *Thalia*.[3] This vessel had been in deponent's convoy and had been sunk about an hour and a half after the *Fiscus*. The lifeboat was sighted by a flying boat on 24/10/40 and the occupants picked up on the same day by one of H.M.S. [this was HMS *Clematis*]. The boats of the *Fiscus* were swung out ready for launching. One raft was in the starboard fore rigging and two others aft in main rigging, one on each side. Master had given strict orders on 17/10/40 that every man was to wear his life-saving waistcoat continuously and deponent knows that all deck personnel wore them accordingly.

Ninety minutes later, *U-101* sank the *Assyrian*, the ship of the convoy's Commodore. The master of the *Assyrian*, Reginald Sanderson Kearon, was later awarded both the OBE and the Lloyd's War Medal for Bravery at Sea. The Citation[4] for the award of the OBE describes the sinking and the heroism of Captain Kearon:

> The ship was torpedoed, and the damage was such that it was clear she would not last long. One boat was smashed but the other was put in the water and rafts were got over the side. Wreckage knocked men off the rafts into the water and holed the boat. Those left on board pulled all the men they could out of the water and then lowered the rest of the rafts. They then set to work to make a new raft and launched it when the ship began to sink. All but four were got on to it. The Master floated off the ship and was sucked down but came up by a large spar to which the Chief Officer, an elderly man, was clinging. The Master lashed him to it and they were later joined by two others. After two hours they were picked up, but two, including the Chief Officer, were dead from exposure.

When the corvette *Scarborough* passed through the scene of the action the following day she found only wreckage and no signs of any more survivors. During a six-hour period, seven U-boats sank a total of sixteen merchant ships. Twenty of the thirty-five which set out from Canada were lost, seven falling victim to *U-99* alone, with a further six badly damaged. From the German perspective, the attack on SC.7, the most successful of all U-boat attacks on Atlantic convoys, was a vindication of the wolfpack tactic.

The U-boats only broke off their attack on SC.7 to focus attention on HX.79, now entering their patrol area. HX.79 had departed Halifax at 13.30 on 8 October 1940 bound for Liverpool. On 19 October, just four days before making landfall, HX.79 entered the Western Approaches, caught up with SC.7 and was spotted by *U-47*, which sent a sighting report then began to shadow its progress. On receipt of the sighting report, four U-boats which had attacked SC.7 and were still able to fight (three had to depart to re-arm having expended all their torpedoes) were directed by Dönitz onto the scene. Meanwhile the Admiralty, concerned about the fate of SC.7 and anticipating an attack on HX.79, quickly despatched reinforcements to arrive on 19 October. Undeterred, however, by the presence of the escort, five U-boats attacked the convoy on the surface under cover of darkness, sinking twelve merchant ships and badly damaging two more. *U-47* (Prien) and *U-46* (Schepke) sank seven and damaged two between them – a loss rate of 25 per cent – and eighty-four merchant seamen lost their lives. Not one U-boat was damaged.

The sinking of thirty-two merchant ships (twenty-eight in a short forty-eight-hour period) from SC.7 and HX.79 made 18 and 19 October the two worst days for merchant shipping losses in the war at sea in the Atlantic. If not quickly stemmed, this continued rate of loss of men, ships and precious cargoes could soon have brought Britain to her knees, given the country's dependency on more than one million tons of imports per week to enable her to survive and fight.

Dönitz later claimed that 'over three days eight U-boats sank thirty-eight ships from three convoys for no losses' in what he later described as 'the opening phase of the battle of the Atlantic'. He had carefully co-ordinated these attacks from his HQ at Kerneval, and the wolfpack concept now become a deadly reality. It is notable that the sinkings occurred during and immediately after the full moon, when potential targets were clearly visible to U-boats operating on the surface at night.

The convoy escorts were subsequently shown to have been ineffective in protecting SC.7 and HX.79 from attack. But at this early stage in the war, convoy defence tactics remained rudimentary and the escorts' responses uncoordinated; their commanding officers were unaware that U-boats were attacking on the surface between the merchant ships inside the convoy formation. Additionally, they were unable to mount any serious counter-attacks, being unaccustomed to working together to a common battle-plan. Overall command of the escort lay in the hands of the most senior naval officer present at any one given time and could change as each new warship arrived. Apart from all this, much of the escorts' time was devoted to rescuing survivors. They could find themselves torn between staying with the convoy and abandoning survivors in the water as DEMS regulations demanded, or stopping to pick them up, thus leaving the convoy unprotected whilst running an increased risk of being torpedoed themselves. Yet there was a positive outcome, for the experience gained in these two convoys contributed significantly to the improvements in convoy defence developed through the subsequent operational analyses carried out by the Western Approaches Tactical Unit in Liverpool.

During the month a total of eight Atlantic convoys had been attacked, losing a total of fifty-two merchant ships. In reviewing the outcome of U-boat operations between April and October 1940 Dönitz later commented:

Conditions were made particularly favourable for the U-boat war against shipping in the Atlantic, which was resumed at the conclusion of the Norwegian expedition. The possession of the Biscay ports eliminated the long journeys to and fro which had taken up almost the whole radius of action of the U-boats. The sea routes were now, so to speak, at the front door. The U-boat command took energetic steps to insure that U-boats in the Atlantic were able, when their fighting resources were exhausted, to return to the Biscay ports for repairs and refitting as early as July 1940. The advantage of avoiding the long journey home was seen immediately in the doubling of the number of U-boats available in the actual operational area.

From October 1940 the picture west of England began to change for the U-boat arm. For England the danger of invasion was over. The English defence vessels were apparently once more available for A/S defence. The Royal Air Force was being used on an increasing scale for guarding shipping routes and for A/S defence. The convoy system was apparently being most extensively used. In any case it was becoming more difficult for U-boats to operate close in to shore and convoys were located less frequently. The U-boats were often at sea for lengthy periods without meeting any traffic, and the great successes of the summer came to an end. The U-boat command decided, therefore, in October 1940, on the controlled operation of U-boats at sea against convoys located by systematic search. These so-called pack tactics were developed in the clear knowledge that location would be the main problem in the U-boat war. Because of the concentration of shipping in convoys, the empty area of the ocean would be greatly increased. On the other hand, what mattered was to direct as many U-boats as possible to a convoy once found and thus set a concentration of U-boats against a concentration of shipping.

These tactics correspond to the principle held for thousands of years by every military command: that of being as strong as possible in the right place at the right time. Organization and control of U-boats was carried out by radio on long and short wave from the command post in Paris, and after November 1940 from Lorient.

The first convoy attacks at the end of October 1940 had very good results. In these engagements the U-boats quickly exhausted their torpedoes. This resulted in very short but successful operations. After the convoy battles there were no U-boats in the operational area. Because of the ever-present shortage of boats there were no replacements ready for sea.

There was now a lull in U-boat attacks on the convoys during the first weeks of November. The Atlantic was for the time empty of U-boats since, having expended all their torpedoes, they now returned to base earlier than planned to replenish weapons and stores. Meanwhile, the battle-cruisers *Scharnhorst*, *Gneisenau* and *Bismarck*, and heavy cruisers *Deutschland* (later renamed *Lutzow*), *Admiral Graf Spee*, *Admiral Hipper*, *Admiral Scheer* and *Prinz Eugen* now presented the principal threat to convoys in the western waters of the North Atlantic, between the Canadian coast and Greenland.

There would now follow one of the first and perhaps the most famous surface battles of the war at sea in the Atlantic, when convoy HX.84 was attacked on

5 November by the *Admiral Scheer*. Five merchant ships were sunk in short order, but the sacrifice of the armed merchant cruiser *Jervis Bay* and armed merchant ship *Beaverford* in attacking the *Scheer* allowed the rest of the convoy to escape in the failing daylight. As a result of the action, the captain of the *Jervis Bay*, Edward Fegen, was awarded a posthumous Victoria Cross. The citation[5] for the award read:

> For valour in challenging hopeless odds and giving his life to save the many ships it was his duty to protect. On the 5th of November 1940, in heavy seas, Captain Fegen, in His Majesty's Armed Merchant Cruiser Jervis Bay, was escorting thirty-eight Merchantmen. Sighting a powerful German warship he at once drew clear of the Convoy, made straight for the Enemy, and brought his ship between the Raider and her prey, so that they might scatter and escape. Crippled, in flames, unable to reply, for nearly an hour the Jervis Bay held the German's fire. So she went down: but of the Merchantmen all but four or five were saved.

Following the attack on HX.84, the North Atlantic convoys were temporarily suspended, and the Home Fleet put to sea in an attempt to intercept the *Admiral Scheer*. HX.85, which sailed from Halifax on 1 November, was diverted to Sydney, Cape Breton (arrived 9 November), and sailed again as HX.85/1 on 11 November. The attempt to intercept was unsuccessful, and the *Admiral Scheer* disappeared into the South Atlantic. A sixth merchant ship from HX.84 was bombed and set on fire west of Co. Donegal by an FW200, then torpedoed and sunk the next day by the Italian submarine *Guglielmo Marconi*.

Churchill addressed the Commons on the War Situation on 5 November:[6]

> More serious than the air raids has been the recent recrudescence of U-boat sinkings in the Atlantic approaches to our islands.
>
> However, this period of stringency is perhaps passing. The fifty American destroyers are rapidly coming into service just when they are most needed, and the main flow of new construction started at the outbreak of war is now coming on. In spite of serious losses, we have still very nearly as much shipping tonnage as we had at the outbreak of the war, and a great deal of neutral tonnage which used to trade freely with us is now under our control. Moreover, our U-boat hunting is still having its successes.
>
> I, personally, cannot doubt that they will be able to cope with them and will be able to bring in all the vital supplies of food and munitions which we shall require.
>
> We must expect that next year a still heavier U-boat attack will be made upon us, and we are making immense preparations to meet it.
>
> We have to look a long way ahead in this sphere of the war. We have to think of the years 1943 and 1944 and of the tonnage programmes which

we shall be able to move and which we shall have to move across the oceans then. Every endeavour must be made to use the time available to produce the greatest volume of food of which this fertile island is capable and so liberate our Navy and our merchant shipping for the movement of the considerable armies which will certainly be required in those years if the enemy do not surrender or collapse in the meanwhile. Having dwelt upon this sea communications aspect rather openly and bluntly this morning, I should not like to leave it without assuring the House that I, personally, have no doubt whatever that we shall make our way through all right.

Raeder advised Hitler on 14 November that the great U-boat success at the end of October was now waning, due in part to the need for U-boats to be overhauled and relieved. But this would be offset by the operations of Italian submarines in the North Atlantic. He noted that there had recently been appreciable losses in supplies reaching Britain as a result of the successful warfare waged against merchant shipping by submarines and the Luftwaffe. Reports from Britain confirmed the seriousness of the situation and the anxiety felt regarding the supply situation. In his last speech Churchill had said the submarine danger was more serious than the continual air attacks, and that large-scale preparations would be necessary in order to meet the very serious dangers from submarines in the coming year. It was therefore imperative to concentrate all the forces of the Kriegsmarine and the Luftwaffe to interrupt all supply shipments to Britain. This had to be the chief operational objective in the war against Britain. The weakness of British defence and escort forces so far was of great advantage to the U-boats. In view of the support given to Britain by the USA, and as the result of new ships being built, a considerable increase in the number of destroyers and anti-submarine vessels must be expected. An increase in anti-submarine activity was already perceptible. Raeder called for priority to be given to the submarine programme, still handicapped by the fact that too many projects had been awarded special priority. Already the state of affairs was such that at the end of 1940 thirty-seven submarines fewer would have been completed than planned.

The number of merchant ship sinkings increased after 21 November as U-boats returned to the Atlantic. Between 21 and 23 November two convoys, westbound OB.244[7] and eastbound SC.11,[8] were attacked by two groups of U-boats west of the North Channel.[9] Twelve merchant ships were sunk and one damaged beyond repair, including seven sunk from SC.11 by *U-100* (Schepke) on the night of 22/23 November. During the month fourteen Atlantic convoys were attacked by U-boats and twenty-five ships were sunk, mostly stragglers or attacked after convoys dispersed in the North-West Approaches and sea areas south of Iceland.

The attacks continued into December. An early victim was the eastbound HX.90, whose sole escort was the armed merchant cruiser *Laconia*. The Western Approaches escort, the destroyer *Viscount* (1 December), sloop *Folkestone* and corvette *Gentian* (both 2 December), were not to meet HX.90 until south of Iceland, reckoned to be the limit of any patrolling U-boat's range at the time. Several other convoys were at sea. SC.13 to the north of HX.90 was also heading east, while heading towards them was westbound OB.251. To the south, returning from Gibraltar, was HG.47. Ranged against them in the Atlantic was a pack of seven U-boats, reinforced by three Italian submarines deployed in a patrol line at the fringe of the Western Approaches, hoping to intercept eastbound convoys before they met their escorts.

The passage of HX.90 was uneventful until, on 1 December, some 500 nautical miles south of Iceland, it was sighted and reported by *U-101*, which was then ordered to shadow. During the day, the first of the Western Approaches escort, the destroyer *Viscount*, arrived from OB.251. Over a period of three days the merchant ships of HX.90 were attacked by a group of eight German and three Italian U-boats, and ten merchant ships were sunk and two damaged. The AMC *Forfar*, as she left HX.90 to join OB.251, was sunk by *U-99* (Otto Kretschmer) with the loss of 172 of her crew, leaving only 21 survivors. An eleventh merchant ship was bombed and sunk on 3 December by an FW200 about 200 miles west of Ireland with the loss of five crew; thirty survived. None of the attacking U-boats had been sunk or damaged. However, thirty ships of HX.90 arrived safely, as did forty-one ships of SC.13, thirty ships of HG.47 and thirty-one ships of OB.251. Nevertheless, the attack on HX.90 represented a setback and another serious Atlantic convoy loss.

Early in December a westerly movement of the U-boats became noticeable, with most of them stationed as far out as 20° west. The cycles of convoys were also opened out (to increase the time between sailings), with the object of reducing the strain on escorting forces.

The BdU War Log for 3 December complained at length about the urgent need for air support in the operational area. Raeder had made this point to Hitler at a meeting on 3 December, when he demanded that aircraft used for this reconnaissance should be under the direction of the Kriegsmarine with their crews drawn from trained seagoing officers, noting that the Do.217 aircraft was suitable for the task and could carry aerial torpedoes. The BdU War Log two days later noted the wolfpack had been an experiment based on multiple U-boat attacks, and the results had proved the validity of the concept and tactics. The hours of darkness had presented the best opportunity to attack, allowing the U-boats to manoeuvre within firing range more quickly and more frequently, with less risk of detection than in daylight. This was now to become the preferred option for concentrated attacks, and daytime attacks were to be undertaken only in favourable conditions.

The damage caused to British merchant shipping by the U-boat campaign was the subject of lengthy discussion at the 27 December Führer Conference, which re-emphasised the significance of greatly intensified submarine warfare. The German High Command was firmly convinced submarines were the decisive weapon against Britain, but the number newly constructed or nearing completion was totally inadequate. The maximum monthly output amounted to eighteen boats at most, possibly only twelve. If such a situation continued, all hope for the decisive effect of this most important weapon would have to be relinquished. The monthly output of submarines must be increased from twenty to thirty boats. The Führer wished for the greatest possible progress in submarine construction; twelve to eighteen submarines were too few.

During the twelve months of 1940 only twenty-four U-boats were lost.[10] Dönitz in his later review of U-boat operations between October and December 1940 recalled:

The first convoy attacks at the end of October 1940 succeeded with very good results. In these engagements the U-boats quickly exhausted their torpedoes. This resulted in very short but successful operations. After the convoy battles there were no U-boats in the operational area. Because of the ever-present shortage of boats there were no replacements ready for sea.

Thus the operational area in November 1940 was empty and it was filled only at the beginning of December. This led immediately to another successful convoy battle. Tactically it was proved already with these first experiments that pack tactics had been developed correctly. It was necessary to keep strict control of the boats, having regard to their disposition for contacting the convoy, their keeping contact with a view to directing other boats to the scene and the issuing of the order to attack. In the attack itself, however, the boats must have complete freedom. It was, therefore, a control in a tactical sense but did not hamper the actual attack by the individual U-boat.

It was further proved that night was by far the most opportune time for attack, because the U-boats could get within firing range much quicker and more often. Therefore, the night was used basically for concentrated attacks by U-boats, and day attacks were undertaken only in favourable conditions. The comparatively small and manoeuvrable Type VIIC proved itself excellent for night attacks.

During December eleven Atlantic convoys were attacked, and twenty-four merchant ships were sunk.

Chapter 5

Phase Five: January to March 1941

By 1 January 1941 Dönitz had 379 U-boats. Of these, forty-eight were on operations, forty-eight were engaged in training, fifty-two were with U-boat Acceptance Command (U.A.K.) and 231 were still under construction. There was, however, little evidence of U-boat attacks on convoys except when on 6 January, when one straggler from OB.269 was sunk 100 miles north-north-east of Rockall.

Raeder received some limited air support when the BdU announced on 7 January that Hitler had ordered No. 1 Combat Group/40 (an FW200 group) to be made operationally subordinate to the BdU with immediate effect. Dönitz therefore expected the conduct of U-boat warfare to take a decisive step forward, although tangible results would be some way off, with few aircraft available and a number of technical problems to be solved. Nevertheless, he had great hopes this co-operation would eventually lead to substantial success.

The Atlantic convoy routes fell quiet between 19 December 1940 and 28 January 1941, with no attacks on escorted convoys until 29 January, when SC.19 was attacked south of Rockall. Five merchant ships were sunk by three U-boats, and a straggler was sunk the following day. A seventh merchant ship, also a straggler, was bombed by an FW200 and sank about 400 miles west of Malin Head on 28 January.

With the increasing numbers of U-boats now about to enter service, and in a portent of things to come, Hitler in a speech at Berlin Sports Palace on 30 January declaimed:

> In the spring our U-boat war will begin at sea, and they will notice that we have not been sleeping.

The speech was widely reported in the international press the following day:

LONDON, Thursday
Apart from a further warning to America to withhold aid to Britain, Hitler in his speech on the occasion of the eighth anniversary of his accession to power, did not break any new ground. He made his usual attack on the democracies and England in particular.

After declaring that the U-boat war would begin in the spring he added: 'When the hour comes we will launch a decisive last stroke that will stand out in this historic year.'

In his warning to America, he said, 'Whoever believes that the Americans are able to help the English must know that every ship with or without convoy that comes to their help will be torpedoed.'

By the end of January 1941 shipping losses to U-boats had fallen to twenty-one ships of 127,000 gross tons, the lowest monthly figure since the Germans announced their intensified U-boat campaign in May 1940. At the same time, the average number of U-boats at sea in the Atlantic had increased to around twelve. Eight merchant ships were lost from three Atlantic convoys during January – two stragglers/independents and six from SC.19.

Thirteen German U-boats and seven Italian submarines operated in the North Atlantic in February, most deployed against the 156 merchant ships in four convoys bound for North America – OB.287, OB.288, OB.289 and OB.290. The month would also see the heavy surface ships *Scharnhorst* and *Gneisenau* carry out attacks on the eastbound convoys from Halifax. Between 1 and 6 February OB.289 lost two stragglers, OB.280 one merchant ship and one escort, and SC.20 three stragglers in the North-Western and South-Western Approaches, and SC.21 one straggler.

The 4 February Führer Conference noted that the meagre submarine successes were due to few boats being deployed on operations and the hampering effect of the weather, although an increase in submarine operations might be expected shortly. Twenty-one more submarines would become available for operations in a few weeks, since ice conditions in the Baltic had made it necessary to temporarily discontinue submarine training. Submarine warfare alone was for the time being not in a position to cut off British imports effectively because of the small number of submarines available and the current weather conditions.

The battle-cruisers *Scharnhorst* and *Gneisenau* had broken out into the open Atlantic on 3 February in an attempt to intercept convoys between Canada and Britain. Now, five days later, they established contact with HX.106 some 900 miles west of Slyne Head, Ireland. Fortunately, on approaching the convoy the *Scharnhorst* sighted the battleship *Ramillies*, and as his Operation Orders prohibited the captain of the *Gneisenau* from engaging Allied capital ships, the attack was called off. *Scharnhorst*, however, closed to 25,000 yards in an attempt to lure the *Ramillies* away from the convoy so the *Gneisenau* could attack; but the manoeuvre was discontinued by the *Gneisenau*, and the two battleships steamed off to the north-west to search for other victims.

Dönitz's War Log entry for 12 February declared the results achieved by U-boats during previous few weeks to be unsatisfactory. He concluded that bad weather, poor visibility and long hours of darkness could not be the only causes and suspected convoys had been diverted onto a more northerly route. An attempt to counter this by transferring the U-boat patrol line north had, however, not proved entirely satisfactory, so he decided to transfer the boats' attack areas another 50 miles to the north to cover the whole area between Iceland and the northern approach to the Minch. This meant the approach routes from the west to the North Channel would be temporarily unoccupied. This change of tactics proved more successful when, on 13 February, two stragglers from HX.106 were sunk by *U-96*, and the following day a straggler from SC.21 was torpedoed and sunk 300 miles west of Ireland, followed by four stragglers from HX.107 sunk between 17 and 19 February. A number of Atlantic convoys were also attacked by the Luftwaffe during the last two weeks of the month. On 19 February an FW200 en route for Stavanger sighted westbound convoy OB.287 80 miles north-west of Cape Wrath. All the U-boats, then in a group south of Iceland, were directed to proceed south-east at maximum speed to form a patrol line ahead of the reported convoy course. On 20 February the convoy was picked up by two aircraft, whose sighting reports were so inaccurate that searching on that day achieved no result. Further patrol lines by the boats on the next day also failed to find the convoy, and the operation was abandoned on the evening of 21 February. The Luftwaffe had rather more success, the convoy being bombed on three consecutive days by a single aircraft. Two ships were bombed and sunk on 19 February, and two stragglers bombed and damaged the following day, after OB.287 dispersed, returned to port. On 21 February another straggler from convoy OB.287, damaged by bombs from an FW200, was abandoned, to be sunk the following day by *U-96*.

The *Scharnhorst* and *Gneisenau* now reappeared. Two weeks after the abortive attack on HX.106, on 22 February they located and attacked dispersed merchant ships of OB.285 and OB.286 some 600 miles east of Newfoundland. *Gneisenau* sank four and *Scharnhorst* a fifth. They then left the area when surviving members of the dispersed convoy sent distress signals, and sailed south for the Cape Town–Gibraltar convoy route.

The same day, a Luftwaffe aircraft returning from Stavanger sighted westbound convoy OB.288 40 miles south-east of the Lousy Bank.[1] Approaching the position given by the aircraft, *U-73* was able to make temporary contact a few hours later. The aircraft which took off on the following morning had insufficient range to find the convoy, but the U-boat report of the previous day was sufficiently accurate for the U-boats to find it again east of their patrol line. In an FW200 attack at 07.00 three ships were bombed – two of which returned to port. The following day, U-boats sank two merchant ships and a naval auxiliary. Six merchant ships were sunk on 24 February after the convoy dispersed. In all, 246 merchant seamen lost their lives. OB.289 was then attacked south-west of the Faroe Islands by *U-97*, which sank three merchant ships and damaged a fourth.

Adolf Hitler's lengthy speech on the 21st anniversary of the founding of the National Socialist Party on 24 February 1941 in Munich contained a new threat in one of the two statements later referred to by Churchill in his Battle of the Atlantic Directive. Hitler declared:

> As I told you the other day, our warfare at sea is just beginning. The reason for this is that we first wanted to train new crews for the new submarines which will now make their appearance on the scene. Let no one doubt that they are about to appear.
>
> Just two hours ago I received a communiqué from the Commander-in-Chief of the Kriegsmarine stating that the reports of the last two days from our ships and submarines on the high seas reveal that another 215,000 tons have been sunk, that of this total 190,000 tons were sunk by submarines alone, and that this figure includes a single convoy of 125,000 tons which was destroyed yesterday.
>
> From March and April on, those gentlemen will have to be prepared for something very different. They will see whether we have been asleep during the winter, or whether we have made good use of our time. During the long months when we had so few submarines to fight our battles, Italy kept large forces engaged. It does not matter to us whether our Stukas attack British ships in the North Sea or in the Mediterranean; the result is always the same. One thing is certain: wherever Britain touches the continent she will immediately have to reckon with us, and wherever British ships appear, our submarines will attack them until the hour of decision comes.

The following day, *U-47* chanced upon convoy OB.290 just after noon, sent a sighting report and prepared to attack during the early hours of the next morning. When intercepted German radio signals confirmed the convoy was being shadowed, various evasive changes of course were ordered in an attempt to throw the U-boat of the scent, but *U-47* doggedly remained in close contact. Between midnight and 02.00 on 26 February, 190 miles north-west of Ireland, *U-47* attacked from the rear of the convoy, sank three merchant ships and damaged a fourth. The escort counter-attacked *U-47* with depth charges, and the U-boat then called for assistance, which arrived later in the form of FW200 long-range maritime bombers of I. Gruppe KG 40 based in Bordeaux. At around 10.00 the Senior Officer of the Escort (SOE) reported three merchant ships hit and two sunk. A second attack developed shortly after 18.30, and at 18:37 the Convoy Commodore reported, 'Five merchant ships sunk and three damaged'. After the air attacks the convoy was dispersed. These air attacks by I/KG 40 represented the highest ever number of successes in a single day for the FW200. But the danger was not yet over. The following day, 27 February, the Italian submarine *Michele Bianchi* sank the British freighter *Baltistan*.

In summary, of the forty merchant ships which set out four days previously, seven returned to port – two with battle damage, one with survivors. Eleven were sunk – three by U-boats and one by the Italian submarine. FW200s sank five more ships and badly damaged seven, two of whom sank during the following two days. Only twenty – half the number which had sailed – reached their intended destinations. There were in total 102 deaths. Lost cargoes included aircraft, military stores and vehicles.

Details of the attack on OB.290 were reported to the War Cabinet[2] on 27 February, when Churchill announced:

> We have sustained heavy losses in an attack on an outward-bound convoy by submarines and aircraft, between 240 and 300 miles off Bloody Foreland. Four vessels, totalling 10,000 tons, have been sunk for certain. Nine other vessels, totalling 61,000 tons, have been either sunk or damaged to a greater or less degree. The highest possible priority must be given to the measures necessary to deal with the double menace to our shipping constituted by submarines and Focke-Wulf aircraft, acting in combination. Our effort against this renewed danger must, for the moment, be our supreme exertion. [He then gave details of the action in hand to counter enemy attacks on shipping and to increase imports.]

A report on 'U-boat Successes' signed by Dönitz on 27 February claimed:

> In December 1940 fourteen U-boats operating in the Atlantic sank fifty ships (345,125 G.R.T.). In December 1940, the full number of sixteen U-boats operated together. An average of 1,135 G.R.T. of enemy shipping was sunk by each U-boat for every day at sea. One hundred and twenty-six torpedoes were fired in action during the month, seventeen were failures, seventy-five were hits, and there were thirty-three misses.

Hitler's speech of 24 February was later widely reported in the press, a typical article of 28 February reading:

U-BOAT CAMPAIGN

According to a Berlin spokesman, Hitler's threatened U-boat offensive has begun. The U-boats will hunt in packs, and the system was first tried in attacks on shipping west and north-west of Britain on February 23.[3]

The only other attack on a merchant ship from a convoy occurred on 28 February, when one straggler from HX.109 was sunk. During the month eleven Atlantic convoys were attacked and thirty-five ships sunk, again most in the Atlantic south of Iceland out to 25° west. With four of these attacked during the last week of February[4] and nineteen merchant ships sunk, it became evident the expected spring offensive had begun.

In March the main focus of U-boat operations shifted to the sea area south of Iceland which BdU now believed was being used as a more northerly route by convoys. Three unescorted ships from HX.109 were sunk on 1 and 2 March in the North-Western Approaches. The lack of effective naval control over Luftwaffe operations led Raeder to write to Hitler on 4 March:

> I am definitely of the opinion that the war against England can be won only at sea. The Navy has to wage war not only against a considerably stronger enemy, but against an enemy who has full use of the necessary naval air forces.

The average number of U-boats at sea in the Atlantic rose to sixteen in March.

The first official reference to the 'Battle of the Atlantic' appeared on 4 March, when during a War Cabinet discussion[5] Churchill described the measures being taken to improve the merchant shipping situation. This was, he said

> the Battle of the Atlantic, which must be fought out in the shipyards and the docks and on the seas. Special steps [are] being taken to reduce the volume of merchant shipping awaiting repair. Above all, the offensive spirit must be retained in meeting the enemy's attacks on our merchant shipping. If resolutely tackled over the next four months, the position should show great improvement.

The following day in the House of Commons debate on the Navy Estimates 1941,[6] the First Lord of the Admiralty, A. V. Alexander, reported:

> The enemy is now able with long-range aircraft to attack ships far out in the Atlantic. I can give the House this assurance, that counter-measures to this new form of attack are being developed.
>
> The enemy raider, whether warship or converted merchantman, is, of course, another major problem which the Navy must deal with. We are exercising all our ingenuity within the limits of our resources to frustrate this form of attack.
>
> The enemy has undoubtedly gained great advantages from his acquisition of French submarine bases. The Admiralty never relaxes its efforts to maintain constant attack on the U-boats. With the expansion of the reconnaissance forces available to the Coastal Command, which

I hope will take place progressively throughout the year, the watch from above will become more difficult for the enemy to avoid. No doubt, too, the Royal Air Force, for whose assistance the Navy is most grateful, will continue to dislocate the organization of the U-boat patrols by attacking them in their bases. At sea an increased number of escorts will enable us to provide greater protection for the convoys themselves. To these advantages will be added all the improvements in antisubmarine tactics and devices which experience and experiment can suggest to us.

Let me say, also, that although it is not our policy to make regular statements as to U-boat sinkings, we continue to inflict loss upon the enemy submarine flotillas. The very success of our earlier anti-submarine methods has given rise to a new wariness on the part of the U-boats themselves. To give the German Naval Staff their due, they have changed their U-boat tactics frequently and whenever they have become too costly; and new tactics demand changes in our own measures, which sometimes take time to perfect. Moreover, the results of the war against the U-boats are, by its very nature, uncertain.

After meeting Admiral Pound in the Prime Minister's office in the House of Commons, Churchill decided to proclaim the 'Battle of the Atlantic' as 'a signal to concentrate all minds and all departments concerned about the U-boat war'. And so on 6 March Churchill, faced with the emergent threat of an increased German U-boat and aircraft offensive in the Atlantic and mounting losses of merchant shipping, issued his now famous 'Battle of the Atlantic Directive', the opening paragraphs of which read:

In view of various German statements, we must assume that the Battle of the Atlantic has begun.

The next four months should enable us to defeat the attempt to strangle our food supplies and our connection with the United States. For this purpose we must take the offensive against the U-boat and the Focke-Wulf wherever we can and whenever we can. The U-boat at sea must be hunted, the U-boat in the building yard or in dock must be bombed. The Focke-Wulf and other bombers employed against our shipping must be attacked in the air and in their nests.

He went on to call for, inter alia, Catapult Armed Merchantmen (CAM)[7] to be fitted out, merchant ships to be equipped with AA weapons as a first priority, and more Coastal Command squadrons to be formed and fitted with radar. Port and dockyard congestion was to be dealt with, and the defence of seaports greatly improved as a matter of the very highest national priority; the survival of

Britain depended upon them. Overall direction was to be exercised by a Battle of the Atlantic Committee[8] chaired by the Prime Minister himself.

As a result of the Directive a number of long-awaited ship types and weapons would come into service over the following months and contribute significantly to the eventual defeat of the U-boats. The first CAM ships equipped with a single 'one-way' Hurricane would be ready in April, followed in June by the introduction of the first escort carrier. New scientific developments would also begin to play their part. In May, the first High-Definition Radar (Type 271) would be installed in a corvette. Later still, high frequency, direction-finding radar (HF/DF or 'Huff-Duff') would be deployed on escorts to supplement the work of the shore stations. Inter-service co-ordination would be further improved when RAF Coastal Command was placed under the operational control of the Admiralty.

Meanwhile, the assault on the Atlantic convoys continued with a failed attempt to attack OB.292. An account of the operation appeared in the BdU War Log for 7 March:

An extensive but unsuccessful operation began on 2 March, when an aircraft proceeding to Stavanger sighted OB.292 just west of the North Channel. All available boats were assembled in patrol line by 3 March, while three FW200s searched in vain for the convoy. The three aircraft reconnoitred the area south-west of North Channel more fully than the north-western sector, so it was assumed that the convoy had been diverted to the north, and the boats were ordered to proceed slowly northwards. On the third day of the operation an aircraft returning from Stavanger found a convoy of the same composition 150 miles north of the position reported on the first day. Presumably the weather had forced it to heave to. The boats were drawn up in a new patrol line. At dawn on 5 March they proceeded eastwards to meet the convoy but were unsuccessful. It had passed out of the range of our aircraft, and as there was no way of finding out which direction it had taken, the operation was abandoned that evening.

After this unsuccessful operation, F.O. [Flag Officer] U-boats decided that for the time being no more U-boats should be sent against convoys reported by aircraft. The aircraft had hardly sufficient range to direct the U-boats to outward-bound convoys. They were able to maintain contact for one or two hours (as far as 10° west) on the day of sighting, but on the second and most important day the westbound convoys would be beyond their range. In the case of convoys on north-westerly and south-westerly courses, air contact could be made only if the ships happened to be on the direct route of the aircraft, and even then there was not enough fuel for searching, shadowing or sending homing signals. The aircraft could not even remain long enough over a convoy to deduce its mean line of advance. No air reconnaissance could be provided for attacks on homeward-bound convoys as the aircraft could not reach the northern area. Aircraft reports on convoy positions were often badly in error. A comparison of convoy positions reported by aircraft, U-boats and the Radio Intercept Service showed that the aircraft reports were sometimes as much as 70 miles out. This was the reason for the failure of the actions against OB.287 and OB.292.

OB.292 was dispersed on 6 March. One unescorted straggler was sunk by a U-boat the following day. The outcome of the operation demonstrated that whilst U-boats could successfully vector aircraft onto convoys, the Luftwaffe lacked aircraft with sufficient range and capabilities to successfully and accurately vector U-boats onto them. The attacks continued; the following convoy, OB.293, was attacked on 7 March, with three merchant ships sunk. The same day, *U-47* (commanded by U-boat ace Günther Prien, who sank the battleship *Royal Oak* in Scapa Flow) was reportedly sunk by the destroyer *Wolverine* with the loss of all forty-five crew while pursuing OB.293. Although this report is disputed, it is confirmed that *U-47* sent its last radio message at 04.54 on 7 March and was later listed as missing after repeatedly failing to report its position; there is no other verified explanation of its loss. Prien had sunk thirty merchant ships and one warship, and damaged eight merchant ships.

President Roosevelt signed the Lend-Lease bill into law on 11 March 1941 which permitted him to 'sell, transfer title to, exchange, lease, lend, or otherwise dispose of, to any such government [whose defence the President deems vital to the defence of the United States] any defence article'. Britain and her allies were now able to receive American arms and supplies without immediate payment.

The second week of March saw the return of the *Scharnhorst* and *Gneisenau* to the North Atlantic. After being sighted by the battleship *Malaya*, on 8 March they moved back into the mid-Atlantic to join up with their supply ships. On the evening of 12 March all four spread out in line abreast so as to cover a patrol line 120 miles wide and commenced sailing in a north-westerly direction towards the HX convoy routes. In the morning of 15 March they encountered merchant ships of dispersed convoy OB.294 in mid-Atlantic. *Scharnhorst* sank two. *Gneisenau* sank five and captured three tankers, two of which were later scuttled by their prize crews. The following day, *Scharnhorst* sank a further four merchant ships and *Gneisenau* three, including an independent (the *Chilean Reefer*) and one merchant ship dispersed from OB.292.

One week after the loss of *U-47*, on 15 March, U-boats commanded by two of the most celebrated commanders and heroes of propaganda, *U-99* under Otto Kretschmer and *U-100* commanded by Joachim Schepke, were sunk during attacks on convoy HX.112 of forty-one merchant ships which had sailed from Halifax, Nova Scotia on 1 March escorted by the 5th Escort Group including the destroyers *Walker* and *Vanoc*. Five merchant ships straggled on the night of 10/11 March leaving thirty-six in the convoy, when on 15 March it was sighted and reported by *U-110*, which then commenced shadowing, to be joined during the day by four other U-boats. After shadowing the convoy on the surface during the day, the U-boats attacked at nightfall on 15 March. In the early hours of 16 March, *U-110* torpedoed and damaged a tanker. *U-99* then managed to penetrate the convoy from the north, on its port side, and within seventy-five minutes sank three tankers and two freighters, and damaged another tanker, before leaving the scene.

Meanwhile, in the evening of 16 March the battleship *Rodney*, escorting HX.114, sighted the *Gneisenau*, which made off at high speed. *Rodney* attempted to follow, but the speed differential was too great, and in poor visibility she gave up the chase and returned to pick up survivors from the *Chilean Reefer*. The *Scharnhorst* and *Gneisenau* were ordered back to Brest. They met air and sea escorts on 21 March and docked the next day. In total, they had sailed nearly 18,000 miles in sixty days and destroyed or captured twenty-two merchant ships.

In the early hours of 17 March the escorts of HX.112, searching for U-boats outside the convoy perimeter, detected *U-100* approaching on the surface. *U-100* dived and was attacked with a depth charge pattern set at close range. The U-boat evaded further damage but then surfaced, to be sighted and rammed by *Vanoc* just after 03.00. The U-boat commander and ace, Joachim Schepke, was killed when the *Vanoc* smashed into his periscope structure, and *U-100* sank. *U-100* attained the dubious honour of becoming the first U-boat in the Second World War to be detected by radar, mounted aboard *Vanoc*, during an overcast night that should otherwise have shielded a U-boat from lookouts. Thirty-eight of her crew were killed; there were only six survivors. Schepke had been responsible for sinking twenty-six merchant ships and damaging four more.

As this was taking place, *U-99* making her escape almost collided with a destroyer in the dark and dived. Picked up on ASDIC by *Walker*, *U-99* was depth-charged and severely damaged. To avoid his U-boat being crushed as it sank deeper and deeper, Kretschmer brought it to the surface, where it was fired on by the destroyers, then scuttled. Kretschmer and all but three of his crew were rescued and taken prisoner. Kretschmer had sunk thirty-six merchant ships and three warships and damaged five merchant ships. There were no further attacks on HX.112, and the convoy arrived in Liverpool on 20 March.

Also on 17 March the War Cabinet[9] received the following briefing on recent attacks against merchant shipping:

> The known losses during the last four days amounted to 27,000 tons. In addition, however, 7 ships of a total tonnage of some 35,000 tons had been attacked by enemy raiders on the previous day, although it was not yet known if all 7 had been sunk..
>
> The Destroyer escort of a homeward-bound convoy had sunk 2 U-boats, one by ramming (the crew of which had been saved) and the other by depth charges. The crew of a third submarine had been on board one of these U-boats. The Admiralty were asked to consider whether the usual rule should not be waived, and this information made public.
>
> One of our capital ships had sighted one of the enemy battle cruisers, together with a ship believed to have been a tanker, some 400–500 miles south-east of Newfoundland, but had lost them in the gathering darkness.

Churchill was greatly troubled by the extent of losses from the Atlantic convoys:

> The position resulting from the present shipping losses presents a most formidable problem, and one which must be tackled by every means in our power. We [are] at the moment completely on the defensive at sea, and the Admiralty has had to disperse many important units from the Home Fleet for convoy duties and to hunt the raiders on the Atlantic routes … A very heavy toll has been taken of our merchant shipping, and … at the present time our Naval resources are at a fuller stretch than they have been at any time in the last war. One method of relieving our difficulties would be if the United States would convoy ships west of the 30th meridian. Another way would, be if the United States would allow some of their warships to cruise in the Atlantic and to pass on to us information obtained by them as to the whereabouts of German raiders. Such an act would be less un-neutral than the convoying of ships.
>
> [Churchill advised he had consulted Mr Harriman who said the United. States might be prepared to escort their own ships outside the prohibited area. He was working out a scheme whereby United States ships would take over the long hauls, leaving us with the short hauls. They were also planning a very big merchant shipbuilding programme, which would mature in 1942.]

He continued:

Our shipping difficulties are the blackest cloud which we have to face. But we must remember that we have dealt with, and overcome, equal perils in the past.

The following day, Churchill gave a speech at the Pilgrims Club in London to welcome the new US Ambassador Charles Winant, the details of which were reported in the newspapers the following day under the banner headline:

BATTLE OF ATLANTIC

Confident That We Shall Overcome Dangers

'We welcome you here, Mr Winant,' said Mr Churchill, 'at the moment when a great battle in which your Government and nation are deeply interested, is developing its full scope and severity. The Battle of the Atlantic must be won in a decisive manner. It must be won beyond all doubt if the declared policies of the government and people of the United States are not to be forcibly frustrated.

'Not only German U-boats, but German battle cruisers have crossed to the American side of the Atlantic and have already sunk some of our independently routed ships not sailing in convoy. They have sunk the ships as far west as the 42nd meridian of longitude.

'Over here upon the approaches of our island an intense unrelenting struggle is being waged to bring in the endless stream of munitions and food without which our war efforts here and in the Middle East, for that shall not be relaxed, cannot be maintained.

'Our losses have risen for the time being, and we are applying our fullest strength and resource and all the skill and science we can command in order to meet the potentially mortal challenge. Not only does our shipping suffer by the attacks, but also the fertility of its importing power is reduced by many of the precautions and measures which we must take to master and dominate the attacks which are made upon us. But our strength is growing every week.

'American destroyers which reached us in the autumn and winter are increasingly coming into action. Our own flotillas are growing in number. Our air power over the island and over the seas is growing fast. We are striking back with increasing effect. Only yesterday I received news of the certain destruction of three German U-boats.[10] Not since October 13, 1939, have I been cheered by such delectable tidings of a triple event.

'It is my rule not to conceal the gravity of the danger from our people and therefore I have the right to be believed when I also proclaim our confidence that we shall overcome them. But anyone can see how bitter is the need of Hitler and his gang to cut the sea roads between Great Britain and the United States, and, having divided these mighty powers to destroy them one by one.

'We must regard the Battle of the Atlantic as one of the most momentous ever fought in all the annals of war. Therefore, Mr Winant, you come to us at a grand turning point in the world's history.'

The same day, the Service Chiefs submitted Notes to Churchill[11] reporting the action being taken in response to his Directive to meet the new German attack on shipping. The content covered a broad spectrum of actions being taken within a short timescale, illustrating the way in which the art of the possible was being stimulated by Churchill's encouragement. One might wonder why it took Churchill's direct intervention for some of these to be put in hand.

The toll taken of U-boats during the month continued to increase. On 23 March a fifth, *U-551*, was sunk by the armed trawler *Visenda*. All five U-boats were sunk to the south of Iceland, notably the first U-boat casualties since *U-104* in November 1940, four months earlier.

Despite all his evident concerns, Churchill remained, in public at least, in a buoyant mood, as press reports of his address to the Conservative Party meeting on 27 March published the following day illustrate:

'I cannot doubt that before many months we shall be able to declare that the Battle of the Atlantic has been won,' said Mr. Churchill in his address to the Conservative Party meeting yesterday.

'The Battle of the Atlantic must be won so that food, supplies, munitions and every form of American aid can come with ever-growing volume,' he said.

'The battle is being fought against surface raiders, against aircraft stealing out daily from the French and Norwegian coasts, and against U-boats. It is being fought by the Royal Navy and the Merchant Marine; by men working in the docks, ports and harbours; by women standing at their side in equal dangers.'

Referring to the war situation generally, he said:

We already take the rough with the smooth. We must have spirits so constant that we can derive added strength from misfortune.

If we are cheered with victory we must also be inspired to greater efforts by a rebuff.

I cannot tell how long the road will be. I only know it will be a stony, painful, uphill road and that we will march along it to the end.

The absence of shipping activity in the area south of Iceland now led Dönitz to withdraw his U-boats from the area and concentrate them farther to the south-west. The only subsequent attack during the month took place on 29 March against HX.115, the thirty-two merchant ships of which left Halifax on 17 March for Liverpool. Two tankers returned (later sunk in SC.26). As the *Scharnhorst* and *Gneisenau* were still thought to be at sea in the North Atlantic, the ocean escort, AMC *California*, was reinforced on 20 March by the battleship *King George V* and submarine *Thunderbolt*. On 28 March one merchant ship bound for Iceland left the convoy, followed by the AMC *California*, *Thunderbolt* and eventually the battleship, leaving the remaining twenty-nine ships unescorted. Early the following morning, *U-48* sighted the unescorted convoy south of Iceland in moderate weather. The U-boat immediately attacked to utilize the few remaining hours of the moonless night, firing six single torpedoes at six different targets and sinking three merchant ships with one torpedo each. Fortunately for HX.115, no other U-boats were in the vicinity.

During March eighteen merchant ships were sunk and four damaged from seven Atlantic convoys. In the space of a few days the U-boats also suffered their first major defeat at the hands of the escorts, losing five U-boats including those of three U-boat aces. All three had operated independently of other U-boats in attacking and sinking merchant ships and single-handedly spearheaded the most successful attacks. After the three U-boat commanders were captured or killed, the pattern of conflict in the North Atlantic shifted to actions between wolfpacks and convoy escorts.

Chapter 6

Phase Six: April to December 1941

I n April 1941 bases for use by escort groups and aircraft were established in Iceland, extending the range of surface escorts to 35° west. This still left a gap in air protection further to the west.

As a result of the successes achieved by the convoy escorts in the North-Western Approaches during March, in April the U-boats abandoned their tactic of close attack on the surface when anti-submarine escorts were present. They now extended their operations away from the Western Approaches further into the eastern Atlantic, where they could attack convoys before the anti-submarine escorts joined.

There now followed one of the most serious attacks to date on an Atlantic convoy. SC.26 of twenty-four merchant ships with a rescue ship had departed Halifax on 20 March bound for Liverpool, escorted by the AMC *Worcestershire*. One merchant ship returned and two diverted to Iceland, leaving twenty-one to continue. SC.26 was sighted and reported by *U-76* on 1 April, and the following day, a patrol line of eight U-boats formed to intercept. The convoy was located by *U-74*, which vectored *U-46*, *U-69* and *U-73* onto the position and commenced shadowing. In a series of attacks between 2 and 4 April ten merchant ships were sunk, one damaged and the AMC *Worcestershire* torpedoed and damaged – a casualty rate of almost 50 per cent. Almost a hundred sailors lost their lives. *U-76*, attempting to attack the convoy at daylight on 5 April, was attacked and sunk by the escort, although all but one of her crew survived.

Churchill later commented (somewhat erroneously):

> In early 1941 the focus of U-boat activity shifted from the Western Approaches farther west beyond the reach of flotilla escorts and air protection. Cover could only be provided over about a quarter of the route to Halifax.[1] Between 2 and 4 April, convoy SC.26 from Halifax (escorted only by the AMC *Worcestershire*) was attacked by a pack of eight U-boats in 28 degrees west before the escort had joined. Twenty ships out of the twenty-two in the convoy were sunk.[2]

The lack of escorts to bridge the gap in convoy escort cover led Churchill on 4 April to appeal again to President Roosevelt for assistance in reinforcing naval and air cover in the North Atlantic.[3] His telegram read:

1. I am most grateful for your message just received from the Ambassador about the shipping.
2. During the last few weeks we have been able to strengthen our escorts in Home North Western Approaches and in consequence have hit the U-boats hard (Stop) They have now moved further west and this morning sunk four ships on the 29th Meridian one day before our escort could meet them (Stop) Beating the U-boats is simply a question of destroyers and escorts but we are so strained that to fill one gap is to open another (Stop) If we could get your ten cutters taken over and manned we would base them on Iceland where their good radius would give protection to convoys right up to where they meet our British based escorts (Stop) Another important factor in North Western Approaches is long distance aircraft (Stop) These are now coming in (Stop) Meanwhile though our losses are increasingly serious I hope we shall lessen the Air menace when in a month or six weeks' time we have a good number of Hurricane fighters flying off merchant ships patrolling or escorting in the danger zone (Ends)

The War Cabinet heard on 5 April[4] that 'A large homeward-bound convoy from America is being attacked by U-boats. So far, two ships had been sunk.'

Churchill, clearly concerned by the extent of the shipping losses, addressed the House of Commons on 9 April:[5]

Everything turns upon the Battle of the Atlantic, which is proceeding with growing intensity on both sides. Our losses in ships and tonnage are very heavy, and vast as are the shipping resources which we control, these losses could not continue indefinitely without seriously affecting our war effort and our means of subsistence. It is no answer to say that we have inflicted upon the Germans and Italians a far higher proportion of loss compared with the size of their merchant fleets and the fleeting opportunities they offer us, than they have upon us, with our world-wide traffic continually maintained. We have, in fact, sunk, captured, or seen scuttled over 2,300,000 tons of German and Italian shipping. But we have ourselves lost since the beginning of the war nearly 4,000,000 tons of British tonnage. As against that, we have gained under the British flag over 3,000,000 of foreign or newly-constructed tonnage, not counting the considerable foreign tonnage which has also come under our control. Therefore, at the moment our enormous fleets sail the seas without any serious or obvious diminution, as far as the number of ships is concerned.

But what is to happen in the future if these losses continue at the present rate? Where are we to find another three or four million tons to fill the gap which is being created and carry us on through 1942? We are building merchant ships upon a very considerable scale and to the utmost of our ability, having regard to other calls upon our labour. We are also making a most strenuous effort to make ready for sea the large number of vessels which have been damaged by the enemy and the still larger number which have been damaged by the winter gales. We are doing our utmost to accelerate the turn-round of our ships, remembering – this is a striking figure – that even ten days' saving on turn-round on our immense fleets is equal to a reinforcement of 5,000,000 tons of imports in a single year. I can assure the House that all the energy and contrivance of which we are capable have been and will continue to be devoted to these purposes, and we are already conscious of substantial results. But, when all is said and done, the only way in which we can get through the year 1942 without a very sensible contraction of our war effort is by another gigantic building of merchant ships in the United States similar to that prodigy of output accomplished by the Americans in 1918. All this has been in train in the United States for many months past. There has now been a very large extension of the programmes, and we have the assurance that several millions of tons of American new-built shipping will be available for the common struggle during the course of the next year. Here, then, is the assurance upon which we may count for the staying power without which it will not be possible to save the world from the criminals who assail its future.

The Battle of the Atlantic must, however, be won, not only in the factories and shipyards, but upon the blue water. I am confident that we shall succeed in coping with the air attacks which are made upon the shipping in the Western and North-Western Approaches. I hope that eventually the inhabitants of the sister Island may realize that it is as much in their interest as in ours that their ports and air fields should be available for the naval and air forces which must operate ever further into the Atlantic. But, while I am hopeful that we shall gain mastery over the air attack upon our shipping, the U-boats, and the surface raiders, ranging ever farther to the Westward, ever nearer to the shores of the United States, constitute a menace which must be overcome if the life of Britain is not to be endangered and if the purposes to which the Government and people of the United States have devoted themselves are not to be frustrated. We shall, of course, make every effort in our power. The defeat of the U-boats and of the surface raiders has been proved to be entirely a question of adequate escorts for our convoys. It would be indeed disastrous if the great masses of weapons, munitions, and instruments of war of all kinds, made with the toil and skill of American hands, at the cost of the United

States, and loaned to us under the Aid to Britain Act, were to sink into the depths of the ocean and never reach the hard-pressed fighting line. That would be a result lamentable to us over here, and I cannot believe that it would be found acceptable to the proud and resolute people of the United States. Indeed, I am now authorised to state that 10 United States Revenue cutters, fast vessels of about 2,000 tons displacement, with a fine armament and a very wide range of endurance, have already been placed at our disposal by the United States Government and will soon be in action. These vessels, originally designed to enforce prohibition, will now serve an even higher purpose.[6]

Two days later, Roosevelt informed Churchill that the US government proposed to extend their so-called security zone and patrol areas to a line covering all North Atlantic waters west of about 26°, using ships and aircraft operating from Greenland, Newfoundland, Nova Scotia, the US, Bermuda and the West Indies. This line of demarcation, which would be formally declared on 18 April, then became in effect the virtual sea frontier of the United States; the US nevertheless remained non-belligerent and unable to provide direct protection for the convoys, which remained a British responsibility over the whole route.

In the face of mounting merchant shipping losses Churchill now directed the Minister of Information on 14 April to discontinue with immediate effect the weekly publication of details of sinkings, to be replaced by monthly statements. He would answer any questions on the subject himself in the House of Commons.

The Führer Conference held on 20 April confirmed that the main objective of submarine warfare remained the attack on imports to the British Isles – 'the waging of war on shipping, with Britain as the principal enemy'. The concentration of supply ships into convoys demanded a similar concentration of attacking forces. Sufficient reconnaissance was lacking, since air reconnaissance could not operate as far out as the submarine operational area. Only thirty operational boats were available, including those being overhauled. About half of this number were at sea, counting submarines either outward or homeward bound; therefore only one third, or ten, were in the operational area. This small number was sufficient to locate and attack an occasional convoy in the two main operational areas west of Britain and west of Africa. Any division of forces necessarily reduced the chances for intercepting and destroying convoys

Churchill cabled Roosevelt again on 24 April:

In the Battle of the Atlantic we have two main problems to deal with ... the U-boats and the raiders.

As regards the U-boats, we have had considerable success in dealing with these pests when they were working somewhere in the longitude of 22 degrees west in the North-Western Approaches. Whether it was because of our success or some other reason, they are now working in about 30 degrees west.

We have however been able gradually to strengthen our escorting forces, thanks to the United States destroyers which were sent us, and by the use of Iceland as a refuelling base for escorts

It may be expected that the enemy's reaction to this will be to send his U-boats still farther west, and as most of them are based in Lorient or Bordeaux they can do this without operating farther from their bases than at the present time.

It is quite likely therefore that the areas to the westward of 35 degrees west and to the southward of Greenland will be the next danger area and it is one which it is difficult for us to deal with. Aerial reconnaissance which could be carried out from Greenland to cover this area would therefore be of greatest value, as if a U-boat were located we should be able to re-route our convoys by signal so as to pass clear of the danger.

Later in the same message, Churchill referred to the danger presented by the *Scharnhorst* and *Gneisenau* and expressed the view that 'Any additional long-range reconnaissance which could be carried out from Newfoundland or Nova Scotia would be of the greatest assistance.'

Three days later, Churchill, in a radio broadcast on 27 April entitled 'THE ATLANTIC LIFE-LINE', made clear the most important theatre of the war for Britain lay in the Atlantic:

But how about our life-line across the Atlantic? What is to happen if so many of our merchant ships are sunk that we cannot bring in the food we need to nourish our brave people? What if the supplies of war materials and war weapons which the United States are seeking to send us in such enormous quantities should in large part be sunk on the way? What is to happen then? In February, as you may remember, that bad man in one of his raving outbursts threatened us with a terrifying increase in the numbers and activities of his U-boats and in his air-attack – not only on our Island but, thanks to his use of French and Norwegian harbours, and thanks to the denial to us of the Irish bases – upon our shipping far out into the Atlantic. We have taken and are taking all possible measures to meet this deadly attack, and we are now fighting against it with might and main. That is what is called the Battle of the Atlantic, which in order to survive we have got to win on salt water just as decisively as we had to win the Battle of Britain last August and September in the air.

Wonderful exertions have been made by our Navy and Air Force; by the hundreds of mine-sweeping vessels which with their marvellous appliances keep our ports clear in spite of all the enemy can do; by the men who build and repair our immense fleets of merchant ships; by the men who load and unload them; and need I say by the officers and men of the Merchant Navy who go out in all weathers and in the teeth of awful dangers to fight for the life of their native land and for a cause they comprehend and serve. Still, when you think how easy it is to sink ships at sea and how hard it is to build them and protect them, and when you remember that we have never less than two thousand ships afloat and three or four hundred in the danger zone; when you think of the great armies we are maintaining and reinforcing in the East, and of the worldwide traffic we have to carry on – when you remember all this, can you wonder that it is the Battle of the Atlantic which holds the first place in the thoughts of those upon whom rests the responsibility for procuring the victory?

It was therefore with indescribable relief that I learned of the tremendous decisions lately taken by the President and people of the United States. The American Fleet and flying boats have been ordered to patrol the wide waters of the Western Hemisphere, and to warn the peaceful shipping of all nations outside the combat zone of the presence of lurking U-boats or raiding cruisers belonging to the two aggressor nations. We British shall therefore be able to concentrate our protecting forces far more upon the routes nearer home, and to take a far heavier toll of the U-boats there. I have felt for some time that something like this was bound to happen. The President and Congress of the United States, having newly fortified themselves by contact with their electors, have solemnly pledged their aid to Britain in this war because they deem our cause just, and because they know their own interests and safety would be endangered if we were destroyed. They are taxing themselves heavily. They have passed great legislation. They have turned a large part of their gigantic industry to making the munitions which we need. They have even given us or lent us valuable weapons of their own. I could not believe that they would allow the high purposes to which they have set themselves to be frustrated and the products of their skill and labour sunk to the bottom of the sea.

U-boat warfare as conducted by Germany is entirely contrary to international agreements freely subscribed to by Germany only a few years ago. There is no effective blockade, but only a merciless murder and marauding over wide, indiscriminate areas utterly beyond the control of the German sea power. When I said ten weeks ago, 'Give us the tools and we will finish the job', I meant, give them to us: put them within our reach – and that is what it now seems the Americans are going to do. And that is why I feel a very strong conviction that though the Battle of the Atlantic will be long and hard, and its issue is by no means yet determined, it has entered upon a grimmer but at the same time a far more favourable phase. When you come to think of it, the United States are very closely bound up with us now, and have engaged themselves deeply in giving us moral, material, and, within the limits I have mentioned, naval support.

In order to win this war Hitler must either conquer this island by invasion or he must cut the ocean lifeline which joins us to the United States ... Wonderful exertions have been made by our Navy and our Air Force ... by the men who build and repair our immense fleet of merchant ships, by the men who load and unload them, and need I say, by the officers and men of the Merchant Navy, who go out in all weathers and in the teeth of all dangers to fight for love of their native land and for a cause they comprehend and serve. Still, when you think how easy it is to sink ships at sea and how hard it is to build and protect them, when you remember we never have less than 2,000 ships afloat and 300 to 400 in the danger areas, when you think of the great armies we maintain ... and the world-wide traffic we have to carry, can you wonder that it is the Battle of the Atlantic which holds the first place in the thoughts of those upon whom rests the responsibility for procuring the victory?

After the attack on HX.117 on 9 April there was a further pause in attacks on Atlantic convoys until 28 April, when three ships were sunk from HX.121 (followed by two more on 1 and 2 May) as a result of the first submerged daylight attack by a pack of U-boats. The shipping losses to U-boats in April were about the same as in March, with forty-one ships of 240,000 gross tons sunk. However, only about 30 per cent of the tonnage sunk by U-boats was in convoy in April, as compared with 60 per cent in March.

On 28 April Dönitz, reviewing the 'Situation in the U-boat War', noted British shipping had dispersed itself widely in the Atlantic and anti-U-boat measures had increased. U-boats were now experiencing particular difficulties in locating convoys. German airforce co-operation had been of little use to the U-boat offensive. Aircraft numbers were insufficient, position reports given by aircraft uncertain and their range too short. For the present, U-boats would have to attempt to intercept convoys around the limits of the blockade area, where they would find concentrations of shipping. The greatest problem was reconnaissance and location of enemy convoys, which could only be solved with greater numbers of U-boats or more intensive air reconnaissance.

During April three Atlantic convoys had been attacked, with a total of fourteen merchant ships sunk. Despite these results, the BdU War Log for 2 May noted the lack of success in locating enemy convoys for attack by U-boats, particularly in the 'rendezvous' area north-west of Ireland, and this led to an enquiry into whether the Royal Navy had changed its convoy tactics. The subsequent report issued by the Intelligence Section of the Kriegsmarine War Staff on the British convoy system had established no drop in enemy convoy traffic; the problem remained unresolved.

As a result of the heavy attack on SC.26 on 1 April at about 28° west, the Iceland routing scheme was adopted in May earlier than was originally intended. Escorts were now based on Iceland, making it possible to meet convoys where the escort from Britain had to leave, and then to escort the convoys out to about 35° west, the escort there picking up an incoming convoy and then turning it over to an escort group from Britain. Sunderland and Hudson aircraft were also moved to Iceland to provide air coverage for convoys in areas which could not be covered by aircraft based in Britain.

Churchill, speaking in the House of Commons Debate on the War Situation on 7 May[7] and turning to a description of progress in the Battle of the Atlantic, said:

> Now we come to the Battle of the Atlantic. *It is a mistake to say that the Battle of the Atlantic is won.* First of all, how is it won? It would be quite easy to reduce our losses at sea to vanishing point by the simple expedient of keeping our ships in harbour or to reduce them markedly by overloading them with precautions. The Admiralty, on whom the first burden rests, naturally measure their struggle by the ships which they bring safely into port, but that is not the test by which those responsible for the highest direction of the country have to be guided. Our test is the number of tons of imports brought into this island in a given quarter or a given year. At present we are maintaining great traffic, although with heavy losses. We try to meet these losses by building new ships, repairing damaged ships, by repairing them more speedily and by acceleration of the turn-round of our ships in our ports and in foreign ports. We have made great progress in these spheres since the beginning of the year, but there is much more to do in that field.
>
> With the continued flow of assistance already given to us and promised by the United States, we can probably maintain our minimum essential traffic during 1941. As for 1942, we must look for an immense construction of merchant ships by the United States. This is already in full swing, and since I last mentioned this subject to the House a month ago, I have received

assurances that the construction of merchant vessels by the United States, added to our own large programme of new building and repair, should see us through the year of 1942. It may be that 1943, if ever we have to endure it as a year of war, will present easier problems. The United States patrol, announced by President Roosevelt, on which the American Navy and Air Force are already engaged, takes a very considerable part of the Atlantic Ocean, in a certain degree, off our hands, but we need a good deal more help, and I expect we shall get a good deal more help in a great many ways.

In an attempt to address and resolve the difficulties in locating convoys, and pending more successful methods of locating enemy convoys by greater numbers of U-boats or more extensive air reconnaissance, the Chief of the German Naval Staff suggested on 8 May that all U-boats adopt complete radio silence while in the operational area, and that research be undertaken to determine whether W/T could be used to cause confusion to convoys in the U-boat-patrolled areas.

Despite these ongoing difficulties, Dönitz now had enough U-boats to coordinate wolfpacks; but almost immediately there was an important unexpected development which would have a major impact on future wolfpack operations. This involved convoy OB.218, first attacked on 7 May, when two merchant ships were sunk. Three more were sunk and one damaged on 9 May, two more were sunk and one damaged on 10 May, and finally two were sunk after the convoy dispersed on 23 and 27 May. In the second attack, at midday on 9 May, U-110 sank two merchant ships but was then counter-attacked and depth charged by the corvette Aubretia and destroyers Broadway and Bulldog. The U-boat, seriously damaged, was forced to the surface, and the crew abandoned ship. However, when U-110 failed to sink, a boarding party from Bulldog was able to retrieve the U-boat's Enigma coding machine, code books, rotor settings and charts, whilst the destroyer Broadway stood by. An attempt to salvage the U-boat itself failed when she sank two days later while being towed to Iceland. Knowledge of the capture had been withheld from the crew, and Lieutenant Commander Lemp had died at the time of the boarding. Capture of the Enigma material was a significant intelligence coup. Once in the hands of the code-breakers at Bletchley Park, it provided the means to decode ULTRA signal messages, which disclosed details of U-boat tactics and deployments, enabling convoys to be re-routed around known U-boat patrol lines. The BdU War Log for 10 May simply read: 'U 110 gave no report of position as requested. She must be considered lost.' A report on U-boat radio devices dated 14 May expressed great anxiety about the proven superiority of the British locating systems.

Attacks on independent merchant ships continued to increase. Only about 20 per cent of the shipping sunk by U-boats in May was in convoy, and the focus of U-boat activity continued to move further west. On 19 May *U-94* located HX.126 at about 41° west before the escorts joined late on 23 May. The convoy was attacked by eleven U-boats of wolfpack *West*. Nine merchant ships were sunk over the following three days before the convoy was forced to disperse. Churchill noted this attack in his Memoirs but interestingly did not mention the intervening convoy OB.318, attacked between 7 and 10 May (also by wolfpack *West*), which also lost nine ships sunk and two damaged but was notable for the capture by the destroyer *Bulldog* of *U-110* and seizure of the Enigma machine.

As late as May 1941, Royal Navy escort groups could still only provide cover for the convoys from their UK bases out to 18° west, and from Iceland in the mid-Atlantic gap out to 35° west. The sinkings continued. After HX.126 lost seven out of thirty-three merchant ships on 20 May, and two more in the forty-eight hours after the convoy dispersed, it became imperative to increase the level of convoy protection across the North Atlantic. This was finally achieved following the establishment of the Royal Canadian Navy Escort Force base at St John's, Newfoundland on 27 May. This ensured complete surface escort cover could be provided on the North Atlantic convoy routes, but until adequate air cover and better detection and counter-measures were introduced, the Allied convoys remained extremely vulnerable to U-boat attack. HX.129 of fifty-nine merchant ships (departed Halifax 27 May) became the first of the UK-bound convoys to be escorted across the entire route. Convoys now assembled at Bedford Basin, Halifax. HX.129 was not attacked and reached Liverpool on 12 June. During May fourteen Atlantic convoys were attacked, with thirty-seven ships including stragglers sunk.

In his radio address to the American people on 27 May President Roosevelt declared:

> The war is approaching the brink of the Western Hemisphere itself. It is coming very close to home ...
>
> The Battle of the Atlantic now extends from the icy waters of the North Pole to the frozen continent of the Antarctic. Throughout this huge area, there have been sinkings of merchant ships in alarming and increasing numbers by Nazi raiders or submarines. There have been sinkings even of ships carrying neutral flags. There have been sinkings in the South Atlantic, off West Africa and the Cape Verde Islands; between the Azores and the islands off the American coast; and between Greenland and Iceland. Great numbers of these sinkings have been actually within the waters of the Western Hemisphere itself.
>
> The blunt truth is this – and I reveal this with the full knowledge of the British Government: the present rate of Nazi sinkings of merchant

ships is more than three times as high as the capacity of British shipyards to replace them; it is more than twice the combined British and American output of merchant ships today.

We can answer this peril by two simultaneous measures: first, by speeding up and increasing our own great shipbuilding program; and second, by helping to cut down the losses on the high seas.

Attacks on shipping off the very shores of land which we are determined to protect, present an actual military danger to the Americas. And that danger has recently been heavily underlined by the presence in Western Hemisphere waters of a Nazi battleship of great striking power.

At the conclusion of his speech Roosevelt declared an Unlimited National Emergency.[8]

In June U-boats were now operating out to 45° west, south-east of Cape Race, Newfoundland. Total U-boat strength was now over a hundred, with thirty operational and the rest undergoing training or trials. Most were active in the North Atlantic.

Speaking in the House of Commons on 10 June during the Debate on the Defence of Crete,[9] Churchill said:

> The Battle of the Atlantic is also being well maintained. In January, Herr Hitler mentioned March as the peak month of his effort against us on the sea. We were to be exposed to attacks on a scale never before dreamed of, and there were rumours of hundreds of U-boats and masses of aircraft to be used against us.
>
> These rumours were spread against us in the world, and a very alarming impression was produced. March has gone, April has gone, May has gone, and now we are in the middle of June. Apart from the losses incurred in the fighting in the Mediterranean – which were serious – the month of May was the best month we have had for some time on the Atlantic. Prodigious exertions were made to bring in the cargoes and to protect the ships, and these exertions have not failed. It is much easier to sink ships than to build them or to bring them safely across the ocean. We maintain our whole world-wide traffic, with never less than 2,000 ships on the seas or less than 400 in the danger zones on any day.

Atlantic convoys suffered multiple attacks throughout the month. Four were attacked during the first two weeks alone, with sixteen ships sunk and one damaged. There were no significant attacks between 10 and 24 June. Wolfpack *West* was disbanded on 20 June, having sunk thirty-two merchant ships and the AMC *Salopian*.

The westward movement of U-boats into the Atlantic was reported in the press on 21 June:

LOWEST SHIP LOSSES FOR THREE MONTHS

LONDON, Saturday

It is officially announced that mercantile losses for May were 98 ships, totalling 461,328 tons. This is the lowest aggregate since February.

The worst losses were in the North Atlantic, where the enemy changed his tactics, sending U-boats farther afield. This brought the initial success that a change of tactics usually brings, but as a result of steps now being taken it is hoped that the June losses will be much lower.

At midday on 24 June OB.336 was attacked south-east of Cape Farewell, Greenland and one merchant ship was sunk. Two more were sunk the following day after the convoy dispersed. Also on 24 June, HX.133 came under attack. After leaving Halifax on 16 June the convoy had just sufficient time to form up when it ran into dense fog. This persisted for four or five days, resulting in several collisions and five ships having to return to port; progress was also slowed by gales. The convoy was attacked by a U-boat in the early hours of 24 June, with one merchant ship torpedoed and sunk. Later, in the early evening, a second was torpedoed and sunk. In two further attacks late in the evening of 26 June two more were sunk and two badly damaged. In what would be the final U-boat attack, in the opening minutes of 29 June one more merchant ship was torpedoed and sunk. Later that morning, an FW200 was sighted, but after circling the convoy it did not attack and subsequently flew away.

The U-boat division of the Naval War Staff reported on 26 June that U-boat numbers had reached 370 U-boats, with 48 on operations, 48 being used for training purposes, 231 being built and 52 engaged on acceptance trials. Areas of U-boat activity in June were further afield and wider spread than before, with reports of U-boats near Newfoundland and south of Greenland; twenty-one merchant ships were sunk by U-boats from Atlantic convoys in June. Despite the increasing number of U-boats at sea, four were sunk during June.[10] The U-boats continued to have difficulty in locating Atlantic convoys.

Five east- and westbound convoys were attacked during June – OB.327, OB.328, OB.329, OB.336 and HX.133 – with twenty-five merchant ships sunk. Three U-boats were sunk in the North Atlantic during the month.

In July, with the introduction of continuous escort for convoys to North America, two new convoy series were introduced – UK/North America 'Fast' (ONF) and UK/North America 'Slow', (ONS). Air cover from Ireland, Iceland

and Newfoundland was improving, but RAF Coastal Command still lacked the aircraft to cover the mid-Atlantic air gap.

On 9 July Churchill announced the United States' occupation of Iceland.[11] The sub-text was the urgent need for redeployment of the British garrison to meet pressing operational commitments elsewhere.

Dönitz informed Hitler at the Führer Conference on 9 July that the situation in the Battle of the Atlantic was unsatisfactory and prospects for future operations unfavourable. Submarine warfare would become more difficult due to the increasingly strong enemy defences as a result of the concentration of enemy naval forces along the supply routes in the North Atlantic and extensive US support. Air attacks against merchant ships would also become more difficult owing to the strong anti-air defence of the convoys. Within a short time, with American support, aircraft carriers and auxiliary aircraft carriers with strong fighter defence would accompany the convoys, making it more difficult for Luftwaffe bombers to approach. The German floating supply bases in the Atlantic would be liquidated; submarine warfare and warfare against merchant shipping by surface forces made more difficult; and operations by German surface forces in the Atlantic made impossible during the summer months by large-scale enemy patrol activity in conjunction with a very efficient enemy intelligence and agent service. The operation of surface forces would also be handicapped by the systematic and successful attacks made by the Royal Air Force against German surface forces in Brest. The USA was giving more and more assistance in the matter of supplies to Great Britain; besides the actual delivery of war materiel, the occupation of Iceland, and American escort service for British convoys attested to this fact.

The reduction in shipping losses during June was reported in a press release on 15 July:

LONDON, Tuesday (AAP)

Shipping losses for June, which were announced to-day, show that the number of ships sunk by enemy action during the month were lower than for any month during the last 12 months, with the exception of last January.

The sharp reduction is regarded as a direct result of United States naval patrols of the Atlantic.

The announcement today showed that a total of 79 British, Allied, and neutral ships were sunk, representing a tonnage of 329,296.

The total includes 52 British ships of 228,284 tons, Allied 19, totalling 82,727 tons, and neutral 8, of 18,285 tons.

The figures represent a reduction, compared with May, of 25 ships of a gross tonnage of 168,551 tons. The total number of ships lost by enemy action during the war to the end of June is now officially given as 1738 representing 7,118,122 tons. Of these 1078 were British and totalled 4,605,132 tons.

The monthly average of sinkings has thus been 334,000 tons.

The Germans claim that they sank 876,783 tons of shipping during last month.

Germany's shipping losses have been very severe, and it is estimated that up to July 10 sinkings amounted to 3,391.000 tons.

Further Afield Now

The Admiralty, in presenting the figures announced that it did not propose after today to publish at regular intervals shipping losses due to enemy action because it gives valuable information to the enemy.

However, from time to time the Admiralty will consider publication of shipping losses as may be required.

Well-informed quarters explained that the enemy has gone further afield now in efforts to find new hunting grounds for our ships.

'The enemy continue to make such fantastic claims as ever in the hopes of finding out what really has happened, as reports from his U-boat commanders and airmen are necessarily inconclusive,' it was stated. 'We have obliged him by giving him monthly checks, but we do not intend to do so in future.'

The Germans claim that they sank during June 778,283 tons of merchantmen, and the Italians claim 98,500 tons. The total compared with actual losses represents a percentage exaggeration of about 165 per cent.

An authoritative spokesman in London commenting on British merchant shipping losses, said: 'We can assume that Hitler cannot be but disappointed at the results thus far of his maximum effort against our shipping in 1941.

'The better figures for June, though grievous and heavy, do give hope for decreasing figures in future.

'What must be the thoughts and the morale of enemy submarine crews and airmen who are engaged in the Battle of the Atlantic.

'Submarine crews have to look forward to ever increasing attacks; from the sea and from the air.'

The spokesman continued: 'This must produce a feeling somewhat akin to ploughing sand. Our staying power should indeed give us encouragement. I mean by staying power not only the wonderful staying power of merchant seamen but the constant increase in escorting vessels and the return to service on the high seas of damaged tonnage.

'The more our air force interrupts German railways communications by bombs, the more the enemy has to resort to the sea and, incidentally more difficult will be the transport of raw materials and stores to the east for his campaign against Russia.'

U-boats continued to experience difficulty in locating convoys, as confirmed in an update on the effectiveness of U-boat operations dated 22 July in which Dönitz once again stressed the main problem of U-boat warfare was location of enemy shipping concentrated in convoys on the high seas. Attempts to find enemy traffic farther to the west had not met with any success. An earlier statement, dated 21 July, had suggested the hunt should take place nearer the coasts of Britain, where air reconnaissance would be useful. Once again, the problem of reconnaissance could only be solved when there were more U-boats. To divide the numbers by using U-boats for special operations meant weakening the war against shipping.

The problem of how to locate convoys in the mid-North Atlantic theatre of operations remained unsolved in the summer of 1941. In the search for shipping, the U-boat areas of operation were transferred westwards to the south of Greenland and northwards into the waters south of Iceland, then eastwards again into the sea areas north-west of Ireland.

Raeder considered the output of U-boats inadequate and made representations to Hitler at their 25 July Conference on Naval Affairs for an increase in production. He showed Hitler graphs which illustrated that the monthly output of U-boats ought not to fall below twenty-five; the target of 300 operational boats, on the basis of a monthly increase of only twenty-one and five per cent losses (i.e. fifteen boats per month), could not be attained before 1 July. At that rate, the net monthly increase would be only six boats, whilst if losses reached 10 per cent (thirty boats), that would mean a monthly reduction of nine boats. With forty-two boats the losses had worked out at about 6 per cent; but from the end of 1941, the monthly output would be only about fourteen. The need for more workers was therefore very great (about 25,000 were needed at present). Hitler promised that after the end of the war in the east, the navy would get the necessary number of workers.

In the subsequent discussion of a report on the general situation in naval warfare against Britain, Hitler declared there was absolutely no reason for Raeder to be concerned that he (Hitler) had changed his view as to the great importance of the blockade of Britain by submarines and the Luftwaffe. He would, however, like to avoid the USA declaring war while the Eastern Campaign was still in progress, out of consideration to the Army which was involved in heavy combat; but he would never call a submarine commander to account if he torpedoed an American ship by mistake. After the Eastern Campaign, he reserved the right to take severe action against the USA.

An Annex to the report reviewing the status of the Battle of the Atlantic described it as

> proceeding unfavourably as the enemy was countering all German measures for warfare against merchant shipping with the strongest possible defences. With the help of the USA Britain had built up in the North Atlantic, its main supply area, a defence network and a convoy system which gave the greatest possible protection against German attacks by surface forces, submarines, and aircraft and thus greatly reduced the number of ships sunk by German forces. The whole situation in the Atlantic had become more unfavourable for all our forces following the occupation of Iceland and increasing effect of US support.
>
> British convoy and supply traffic was now as before the weakest and most vulnerable point of British war strategy. The aim of German war strategy against Britain must therefore be a war of destruction against British supplies in the North Atlantic. The strength of the enemy defences made it necessary to concentrate all available forces on this one target.
>
> The situation in regard to submarine warfare was unsatisfactory. Successes had decreased greatly reflecting the effect of strong British escorts and US patrols. It was of decisive importance to increase successes, and it is possible to do this.
>
> Air attacks against supplies were very promising, but here too successes had greatly decreased. It is necessary to increase substantially the number of operations.

Dönitz (perhaps not surprisingly given previous representations) in assessing the results and prospects of the submarine war noted the main problem lay in locating convoys over a wide area. The attempt to find a convergence of routes further to the west had not brought any results; fog and bad weather had been essentially responsible. The new patrol line of 21 July would attempt to intercept traffic nearer to the British coast. This new line was possible because of the increasingly long nights, in which boats could evade pursuit if necessary. At the same time, a renewed attempt at direct cooperation with air reconnaissance was possible. Once again, Dönitz argued the problem of reconnaissance could only be solved by a larger number of submarines. He continued:

> Any withdrawal of boats for special duties therefore diminishes the chances for success in the war against merchant shipping more than the actual number of boats withdrawn would indicate. Although increasingly

noticeable predominantly new submarines with inexperienced crews were out on operations, the successes in June and in the first ten days of July had been satisfactory.

Churchill by now seemed a little more optimistic, commenting during the 29 July Commons debate on War Production[12] that 'The Battle of the Atlantic, although far from won, has, partly through American intervention, moved impressively in our favour.'

A number of changes were made to the convoy system during this period. The minimum speed for HX convoys was raised from nine to ten knots, the minimum speed for SC convoys remaining at seven and a half knots. In July 1941 a rule was introduced requiring ships of less than fifteen knots crossing the Atlantic to sail in convoy (rather than independently). The designation of the OB convoys (outward-bound from Britain) was changed to ON for the northbound convoy heading for Halifax and to OS for the southbound convoys heading for Freetown. July 1941 also saw the introduction of CAM ships in convoys.

No North Atlantic convoys were attacked during the month of July, U-boat effort being focussed on the Gibraltar to UK convoy route. The reasons were varied – evasive convoy routing and more effective aircraft deployment as a result of the 'Ultra' work, introduction of radar and high frequency direction finding (HF/DF), the availability of more escorts, and introduction of continuous escort. Also, as the BdU War Log repeatedly complained, the U-boats although active were simply having difficulty locating the convoys.

By August 1941 the average number of U-boats at sea in the Atlantic had steadily increased from around eighteen in April to about thirty-six. The main feature of U-boat tactics during this third period would be the increasing use of wolfpack attacks, forced upon the Germans by the evasive routing of British convoys and the scarcity of experienced U-boat commanders

In the House of Commons debate of 6 August on 'The War Situation',[13] the Lord Privy Seal, Clement Attlee, reported:

During the past two months the enemy has continued his efforts to achieve success in the Battle of the Atlantic. He was able with the coming of spring to put an increasing number of U-boats into the water against us, and we in our turn had made early provision to meet this danger by providing more anti-submarine craft.. In the course of the last two months, owing to the heavy' scale of our defence in home waters, the enemy has tended to range further and further afield, so that the sea battle is now fought over an immense area, extending far into the Atlantic towards the coasts of the United States of America, and far south in the tropical seas of North

Africa. In this battle we have, of course, suffered severe losses, and we shall not be satisfied while those losses continue; but we can look back on the last two months with reasonable satisfaction. No one of any judgment will contend that we have yet won the Battle of the Atlantic. But we can say that in this vital part of the battle we are holding our own and that the enemy has up to now failed to prevent the ordinary transport of food and munitions across the sea to this country. It is worth remembering that the war at sea is not just a question of defending our own ships and our trade routes against the enemy; it has also its offensive side. The more enemy ships we can destroy, the less is the chance of successful invasion and the more is the enemy hampered in all his operations.

There was news of some improvement in the situation in Pan-American waters when the War Cabinet Minutes[14] for 19 August noted:

By 1 September the American Navy will have a convoy system in full operation between their coasts and Iceland. This will afford great relief to our naval vessels engaged on convoy duties. This procedure will present the enemy with a dilemma. Either he can attack the convoys, in which case his U-boats will be attacked by the American Naval forces; or he can refrain from attack, which will be tantamount to giving us victory in the Battle of the Atlantic.

The accompanying Cabinet Secretary's note reported:

Full agreement had now been reached on the scheme whereby the American Navy would have their convoy system in full operation between their country and Iceland by the 1st of September. This would release no less than 52 British destroyers and corvettes now based on Halifax for convoy duty on other routes. Each of our North Atlantic convoys would be escorted by 5 US destroyers, together with a capital ship or a cruiser. The President's orders to these escorts were to attack any U-boat which showed itself, even if it were 200 or 300 miles away from the convoy. Admiral Stark intended to carry out this order literally, and any Commander who sank a U-boat would have his action approved. Everything was to be done to force an 'incident'. This would put the enemy in the dilemma that either he could attack the convoys, in which case his U-boats would be attacked by American Naval forces, or, if he refrained from attack, this would be tantamount to giving us victory in the Battle of the Atlantic. It might suit us, in six or eight weeks' time, to provoke Hitler by taunting him with this difficult choice.

On 20 August Churchill, ever optimistic, told General Hastings Ismay, 'I am inclined to think that the corner has been turned in the Battle of the Atlantic and that the drop in the rate of sinkings might be maintained.'[15]

As the record of the discussion at the 22 August Führer Conference shows, Dönitz remained frustrated by Hitler's decisions to transfer U-boats to the Mediterranean, where in his opinion they could not be effectively employed, rather than concentrating on disrupting the Atlantic convoy routes, yielding yet another advantage to Churchill in sustaining the convoy programme. Dönitz argued that since enemy convoys were more and more heavily escorted, success could be achieved only if they were attacked not by just a few U-boats, but by a large number simultaneously. The transfer of enemy traffic to more distant and remote areas also necessitated the use of a very large number of submarines merely to locate the enemy convoys. Even with the gradual increase in the numbers of operational submarines, therefore, all available boats would have to be concentrated in the Atlantic. Only in this way could decisive successes be achieved. Submarines should be transferred to other theatres of operation and to other tasks only in cases of great emergency. Dönitz ordered the withdrawal of four submarines from Finland and four from the outlets of the Belts and the Sound (connecting the Baltic and North Sea), in order that the numbers of Atlantic submarines should not be reduced further; he believed no submarines should be transferred from the Atlantic to the Mediterranean until there were forty operational submarines in position in the Atlantic. With U-boat operations focussed, despite Dönitz's objections, on the Gibraltar and West African convoys, no North Atlantic convoys were attacked during August.

In the August 1941 retrospective 'Review of U-boat Operations', Flag Officer U-boats yet again complained of continuing difficulties in finding enemy convoys in a wide area. The attempt to concentrate attacks on a knot of convoy routes further to the west had been unsuccessful, with fog and bad weather largely responsible. The problem of reconnaissance could be solved only by using considerable numbers of U-boats; therefore diversion of boats for special tasks reduced the prospects of success in the merchant shipping war. It became more and more noticeable that the majority of boats on operations were new, with inexperienced crews. Yet successes in June and the first quarter of July were reassuring. The present lack of results in the U-boat war, he noted, had to be regarded as a temporary phenomenon.

Finally, at the beginning of September, U-boats returned to the Atlantic with the deployment of wolfpack *Seewolf* (2 to 15 September). On 9 September, Churchill in one of his periodic reports to the House of Commons on the progress of the Battle of the Atlantic[16] announced:

Since we last met, the Battle of the Atlantic has been going on unceasingly. In his attempt to blockade and starve out this Island by U-boat and air attack and the very formidable combination of U-boat and air attacks, the enemy continually changes his tactics. Driven from one beat, he goes to another. Chased from home waters, driven from the approaches to this Island, he proceeds to the other side of the Atlantic. Increasingly hampered by United States patrols in the North Atlantic, he develops his malice in the South. We follow hard upon his track, and sometimes we anticipate his tactics. But it is not desirable to give him too precise or, above all, too early information of the success or failure of each of his various manoeuvres, and it was therefore decided that the publication of our shipping losses at regular monthly intervals should cease. Accordingly, no statement of losses has been published for July and August, and I do not think the time has come to give the actual figures yet. The public, and indeed the whole world, have however derived the impression that things have gone much better in those two months. I cannot deny that this is so.

The improvement in the sea war manifests itself in two directions. In the first place, there is a very great falling-off in the sinkings of British and Allied ships, with a corresponding increase in the tonnage of invaluable cargoes safely landed on our shores.

He later added:

Although, as I have admitted, there has been a very great improvement in our losses at sea in July and August, it would be a very foolish mistake to assume that the grave dangers which threaten us are at an end. The enemy has been employing a greater number of U-boats and a larger number of long-range aircraft than ever before, and we must expect further increases. In the meanwhile, let us hear no vain talk about the Battle of the Atlantic having been won. We may be content with the successes which have rewarded patience and exertion, but war is inexhaustible in its surprises, and very few of those surprises are of an agreeable character.

The major attack on Atlantic convoys in September was suffered by slow convoy SC.42. From 28 August, wolfpack *Markgraf* (27 August to 16 September) of fourteen U-boats, reinforced days later by five more, was deployed south-west of Iceland across the North Atlantic convoy route. The Admiralty detected the deployment by Ultra, and convoys ON.10, ON.11, SC.41, HX.146 and HX.147 were re-routed around the U-boat concentration. SC.42 was less fortunate. It was weakly escorted, and the more frequent sailing of smaller SC convoys had not yet commenced. The summer practice of sailing HX and SC convoys together, in order to provide for a larger combined escort, had also been abandoned. SC.42 was routed north, through the Strait of Belle Isle then directly towards Cape Farewell, Greenland, which it passed on 7 September in an effort to avoid the U-boats. Aware that SC.42 was being shadowed, the Admiralty ordered it even further north, closer to the east coast of Greenland. On the afternoon of 9 September SC.42 was sighted and reported by *U-85*, and nineteen U-boats vectored onto the convoy. *U-85* then made an unsuccessful attempt to sink a straggler, whose report of torpedo tracks coupled with the burst of U-boat signal traffic alerted Allied naval intelligence. One straggler was sunk early on 9 September.

The following day, the main body of the convoy was attacked. Six merchant ships were sunk and two damaged (one sank later). Fourteen U-boats continued to pursue the convoy, sinking seven more merchant ships and damaging two the following day, before SC.42 came in range of air cover from Iceland. Two stragglers were sunk on 16 and 19 September. SC.42 was only saved from further attacks by the sea mist which descended on the night of 12 September. Over a period of forty-eight hours a total of thirteen merchant ships were torpedoed and sunk and two damaged. Another was sunk on 16 September. A total of sixteen merchant ships – a quarter of the convoy – were lost. This was the worst loss from an Atlantic convoy since the attack on SC.7 the previous year, although two of the attacking U-boats were destroyed.

Important lessons were learned from this encounter, which came to be known as the 'Battle of Cape Farewell'. First, stronger escorts, particularly long-range aircraft, were needed. Even though the escorts showed initiative and courage throughout, they were badly outnumbered, and their crews became exhausted. Second, more emphasis had to be placed on improved escort group training and technology, and specially equipped rescue ships had to be provided.

The US Navy announced on 15 September 1941 that it would provide protection for ships of every flag carrying land-aid supplies between the American continent and the waters adjacent to Iceland, where a US base had been established in July 1941. On 17 September the US Navy began to escort HX and ON convoys between Newfoundland and the Mid Ocean Meeting Point (MOMP), south of Iceland, where the Royal Navy took over. HX.150, with forty-four merchant ships underway from Halifax on 16 September, was the first to use US escorts, which relieved Canadian escorts 350 miles east of Halifax the following day. No U-boats were encountered to the point in mid-ocean where British destroyers took over.

The increased number of U-boats available to Dönitz (approaching 200, with 30 operational) now allowed him to establish patrol lines in the Atlantic.

Churchill in one of his periodic 'Review of the War'[17] reports to the House of Commons on 30 September, referring to Hitler's speeches earlier in the year, remarked:

The House will have noticed how very silent the Nazi leaders have fallen. For seven months Hitler has said nothing about his war plans. What he blurted out in January and February certainly proved helpful to us.

'In the spring,' he said, 'our submarine warfare will begin in earnest, and our opponents will find that the Germans have not been sleeping. The Luftwaffe and the entire German defence forces will, in this way or that, bring about the ultimate decision.'

He reported Hitler as saying, 'In March and April naval warfare will start such as the enemy never expected', and continued:

We were, therefore, led to expect a crescendo of attacks upon our lifeline of supplies. Certainly the Germans have used an ever-larger force of U-boats and long-range aircraft against our shipping. However, our counter measures, which were undertaken in good time on the largest scale, have proved very successful. For reasons which I have explained very fully to the House, we have since June abandoned the practice of publishing statements at regular monthly intervals of our shipping losses, and I propose to continue this salutary practice. But, apart from anything that may happen during this afternoon, the last day of the month, I may make the following statement to the House. The losses from enemy action of British, Allied, and neutral merchant ships during the quarter July, August and September have been only one-third of those losses during the quarter April, May, and June. During the same period our slaughter of enemy shipping, German and Italian, has been increasing by leaps and bounds. In fact, it is about one and a half times what it was in the previous three months. So we have at one end a reduction in average monthly losses of about a third and a simultaneous increase in the losses inflicted upon the enemy of half as much again.

These important results enable us to take a more expansive view of our important programme. Very few important ships carrying munitions have been lost on the way. Our reserves of food stand higher than they did at the outbreak of war, and far higher than they did a year or 18 months ago.

We are now within measurable distance of the immense flow of American new building, to which, together with our own construction, we look to carry us through and on progressively till the end of the war.

We must expect enemy U-boat warfare, now conducted by larger numbers of U-boats than ever before, supported by scores of Focke wolves [sic], will be intensified.

The U-boats will be beaten, and kept beaten, only by a corresponding intensification of our own measures and also, to put it very plainly, by that assistance which we are receiving in increasing degree from other quarters. We must not, I repeat, relax for an instant; nevertheless, the facts that I have stated must be regarded as not entirely unsatisfactory, and certainly they are most stultifying to Hitler, who so obligingly warned us of his hopes and plans. This is, I think, an apt illustration of the dangers which should prevent those who are engaged in the high conduct of the war from having to make too many speeches about what they think is going to happen or would like to happen or what they intend to try to do. All the more is this habit important when we have to deal not only with our own affairs but with those of other great Allied or associated nations.

The only transatlantic convoy attacked in September was ON.127, which encountered wolfpack *Vorwärts* between 10 and 14 September. Seven merchant ships and an escort were sunk, and five merchant ships damaged out of the total of thirty-two. After the attack on ON.127, U-boats were temporarily withdrawn from the Atlantic to cover operations in the Mediterranean theatre. It would be February 1942 before the wolfpacks returned.

Efforts continued to improve the application of radar technology to the detection of U-boats operating on the surface, particularly through increased training and greater experience in its use. The installation of the Type 271 shortwave (10cm) set on corvettes enabled radar contact to be made on a U-boat at much greater range. Coastal Command was also experimenting during this period with a searchlight carried in a Wellington aircraft, to provide illumination for night attacks on U-boats.

By October 1941 arrangements for convoy escort and protection in the North Atlantic were becoming well established, with the rapidly growing Royal Canadian Navy contribution and involvement of the US Navy. The RCN now provided escort for UK-bound convoys from Halifax to the Western Ocean Meeting Point (WOMP) south of Newfoundland. From there, as far as the Mid Ocean Meeting Point (MOMP) at 22° west, the USN escorted HX, and joint RN/RCN groups the slower SC convoys. RN ships based in Iceland then took over until the convoys were met by the Western Approaches escorts operating out of Londonderry and the Clyde. US Navy and Army Air Force aircraft were now adding to the efforts of the RAF and RCAF by flying escort and patrols from Newfoundland and Iceland.

There were few attacks on Atlantic convoys during October. Between 1 and 2 October three stragglers including a CAM ship from ON.19 were sunk south-east of Cape Farewell. Between 15 and 18 October convoy SC.48 was attacked by five U-boats, which claimed to have sunk eight freighters, three tankers, two destroyers and damaged two more merchant ships. In fact, nine merchant ships, two escorts and the USN destroyer *Kearney* were torpedoed and damaged by *U-568* in what was the only major attack on an Atlantic convoy during the month. During the remaining weeks of October fewer U-boats were available and they achieved little success.

After the Americans reported one of their destroyers had been torpedoed, the BdU requested U-boats report details of their encounters with destroyers. With the US not being at war with Germany the circumstances had to be investigated, since any such attack would have been contrary to standing orders. In the end no blame could be attributed since the *Kearney* had actively participated in the action, firing star shell and dropping depth charges on ASDIC contacts, making it impossible for the U-boats to distinguish between the RN escorts and the USN destroyer. On 31 October the USN destroyer *Reuben James* was torpedoed and sunk while escorting convoy HX.156, the first warship of the US Navy lost in the Second World War.

The estimated number of U-boats on 1 November was 216, of which 81 were operational. During the first week of November the scale of the U-boat effort was probably the greatest and the scope of their patrol areas at their widest spread in the Atlantic up to that time. SC.52 was attacked on 3 November by wolfpack *Raubritter* (fourteen boats) and lost four merchant ships. Dönitz continued to seek ways of making the U-boat arm more effective and on 6 November repeated his demands for an increase in the numbers of boats, arguing the most effective place to attack enemy convoys was the North Atlantic, rather than areas off the ports of destination or ports of departure; but the great problem remained reconnaissance and detection of convoys, for which many more U-boats were required. In addressing the withdrawal of U-boats from the Atlantic Dönitz admitted some were required to operate in subsidiary theatres of war but deprecated the withdrawal of boats from the Atlantic and from their task of attacking enemy supplies there. Following the attack on SC.52, convoy SC.53 was attacked between 11 and 14 November and lost two merchant ships. There was then a marked reduction in U-boat activity for the remaining weeks of the month.

During the 'Debate on the Address' in the House of Commons on 12 November[18] Churchill provided an update on the progress of the war at sea:

The House will remember the very good reasons which were given for leaving off publishing monthly figures of sinkings by enemy action and how those precise periodical statements, made at too frequent intervals, gave the enemy valuable information as to how his varying tactics were succeeding; but there is no objection to giving exact figures for longer periods, and I take this occasion to give figures of the last four months, ending with October, without dividing them into months, and compared with the figures, already published, of the four preceding months ending with June. They are certainly well worthy of mention. I am speaking in round numbers.

In the four months ending with June, we lost just over 2,000,000 tons, or an average of 500,000 tons per month. In the last four months, ending with October, we lost less than 750,000 tons, or an average of 180,000 tons per month. 180,000 contrasts very favourably with 500,000 tons. However, we must not count at all that the danger is past, but the facts are more favourable than are represented by the reduction on the four-monthly period from 500,000 to 180,000, because, from the point of view of keeping alive our power to wage war at sea and of increasing it, you have to take account not only of what is lost but of new building. You have to deduct the new building and see how the position stands. I do not intend to give exact figures about new building, but, making allowance for new building, the net loss of our Mercantile Marine, apart altogether from captures from the enemy and United States assistance, has been reduced in the last four months to a good deal less than one-fifth of what it was in the previous four months. That is an impressive fact. This has been done in spite of the fact that there were never more U-boats or more long-range aircraft working than there are now. While that fact should lead us to increase our successful exertions and should in no way favour an easy habit of mind, it does, I think, give solid and sober assurances, that we shall be able to maintain our seaborne traffic until the great American shipbuilding promised for 1942 comes into service. The United States are, of course, building new merchant ships on a scale many times what we are able to do in this Island. Having regard to the many calls upon us, our new shipbuilding is confined to a certain proportion of our resources, but the United States are embarking on an output of ships incomparably greater than what we can produce and far surpassing the enormous efforts they successfully made in the last war. If we are able to get through this year, we shall certainly find ourselves in good supply of ships in 1942. If the war against the U-boats and the enemy aircraft continues to prosper as it has done – about which there can be, of course, no guarantee – the Freedom Powers will be possessed of large quantities of shipping in 1943, which will enable overseas operations to take place utterly beyond British resources at the present time.

The fact that our shipping losses have so remarkably diminished and diminished at the very time when Hitler boasted that his sea war would be at its height must be taken in conjunction with our greatly increased production of food at home. I have always held the view that the British people, especially the heavy workers, must be properly fed and nourished if we are to get the full results from our war effort, and at the beginning of the year, when it looked as if we should have to choose to some extent between food and munitions imports, I asked the Cabinet to approve a minimum of food imports to be maintained, if necessary, even at the expense of munition materials. There is no doubt that the dietary of our people has been severely curtailed and has become far less varied and interesting. Still, at the rate we are now going, it is sufficient for our physical health, although I am hoping that we shall be able to give a somewhat larger share of the available supplies of meat to the workers who need it most. This will be done by a rapid expansion of canteens, which will supply meals off the ration to the workers they serve at places where those workers are actually gathered. I am glad to say that the figure which we prescribed for minimum food imports will now probably be achieved, and even a little surpassed, and that the Minister of Food has been able to make certain minor relaxations during the winter months in the severity of his restrictions. As a precaution, we have amassed stocks of bulky articles of our diet which amount to double what we had in September 1939. We are going to make a job of this war, and those who are working on the job must have their strength fully maintained, because although much has been asked of them in the past, we are going to ask them for more as the struggle deepens.

The same day, the First Sea Lord provided the War Cabinet[19] with a review of the naval position:

Dealing first with the Battle of the Atlantic ... the German U-boats are now working right across the whole ocean. At one time we had thought that after the Americans had assumed responsibility for the defence of the Western half of the Atlantic, the German U-boats would not operate in that sphere. We now had some indication that while German U-boats would not take aggressive action against United States warships except to facilitate their own escape, there was no sign that they would not attack convoys in this area,, At one time we had hoped that we should be able to bring back all our Corvettes from the other side of the Atlantic. Under the present arrangement, however, we retained responsibility for the SC convoys. We had therefore had to keep some Destroyers and Corvettes based on Canadian ports.

The U-boats' present tactics were that some of them operated independently, and others in large groups. Those acting independently gave notice of movements of our convoys to the larger groups. Attacks were made at night, at considerable range, after which the U-boats made away from the convoy. It was therefore difficult to establish contact with them in order to attack them. This was being dealt with by fitting new apparatus.

There was further speculation in the Australian press the following day on the progress of the Battle of the Atlantic:

BATTLE OF THE ATLANTIC

Tide Turning in Britain's Favour

In his review of the war situation in the House of Commons yesterday, the British Prime Minister (Mr. Churchill) revealed that British shipping losses for the four months ending October 1 were less than 75,000 tons, compared with 2.000,000 tons in the previous four months.

Mr. Churchill made it clear, however, that despite this great improvement it should not be assumed that all danger had passed. Nonetheless, it is a remarkable fact that British shipping losses in the last four months are considerably less than the Axis losses for the same period, which amounted to nearly 1,000,000 tons sunk or seriously damaged.

Further, the general position will greatly improve from Britain's point of view in 1942 when the vast United States shipbuilding programme may be expected to increase greatly the amount of tonnage at the disposal of the democracies. Though the battle for the Atlantic has not yet been finally won; all indications are that the tide is now running strongly in Britain's favour. This does not, of course, mean that the democracies can in any way afford to relax their present efforts. On the contrary, the present situation imperatively demands the utmost efforts of which they are capable.

At the 13 November Führer Conference it was announced submarine warfare on British imports in the Atlantic would be greatly reduced for a time after the boats now at sea had completed their missions, since tasks in the Arctic Ocean and Mediterranean were more urgent. The German High Command was endeavouring to commit all remaining boats wholly to the war on merchant shipping. Forces were tied down, however, by urgent escort and defence assignments in connection with returning prizes and blockade-runners. In addition, there were delays in carrying out repairs because of labour shortages, so that returning boats needed a very long time before they were ready for operations once more. Thus it was inevitable that fewer ships would be sunk and the enemy supply lines thus relieved. It was also reported that as of 10 November 1941 220 U-boats had been commissioned, eighty-four of which were operational, fifty-five training, and seventy-nine undergoing trials. Of those operational, fifty-seven were at sea; thirty-eight in the North Atlantic: of which twenty-two were in the zone of operations with three outward bound, and thirteen returning home. Twenty-seven of the operational boats were in port as follows: five at Kiel, ten at Lorient, seven at St Nazaire and five at Brest.

Only three convoys had been attacked during first two weeks of November – ON.27, SC.52 and SC.53, with a total of seven merchant ships sunk. After the attack on SC.53 there was no U-boat activity on the Atlantic convoy routes during the second half of the month. The following weeks brought the Germans no further successes, and the transfer of U-boats to the Mediterranean brought this phase of U-boat operations to an end. As the BdU War Log for 22 November confirmed:

U-boat warfare in the Atlantic had practically ceased owing to the concentrations in the Mediterranean; the only boats from which any result might be expected were the boats of Group *Steuben* which were to operate off Newfoundland. Although this fact was regrettable, it was nevertheless necessary of course to put every effort into dealing with the dangerous situation in the Mediterranean.

The following day, the BdU announced:

The decision to send in also the 'Steuben' boats to operate in the Straits of Gibraltar means a complete cessation of U-boat warfare in the Atlantic. This must be accepted.

Between 29 November and 2 December the six U-boats of *Steuben* sank no ships from Atlantic convoys.

Dönitz, unhappy with the decision to withdraw U-boats from the North Atlantic, suggested to the Operations Division of the Naval War Staff on 1 December that all large U-boats unsuited for the Mediterranean, all medium U-boats not needed in the Eastern Mediterranean or in the Gibraltar area and some of the U-boats stationed in northern waters be released for Atlantic operations. One week later, the BdU War Log noted:

Japan has started hostilities against England and USA – an event of great importance which must also, in a very short time, affect the former restriction of U-boat warfare in the Atlantic.

The following day, Dönitz requested that the U-boat Division, Naval War Staff release twelve type IX U-boats to attack shipping off the American coast, as these were unsuitable for operations in the Mediterranean, the Gibraltar area or for attacking the strongly escorted Gibraltar convoys. Two days later, F.O. U-boats asked the U-boat Division, Naval War Staff to release twelve large U-boats to strike a heavy blow against shipping off the American coast. The U-boat Division released six but would not withdraw large U-boats from the area west of Gibraltar. F.O. U-boats was of the opinion that large U-boats in the Mediterranean were at a disadvantage, as their size rendered them more easily located and they were more vulnerable to depth-charge attacks

The lifting of all restrictions regarding American ships and the so-called Pan-American safety zone had been ordered by Hitler. Therefore, the whole American coast would become open to operations by U-boats, an area in which the assembly of ships took place in single traffic at the few points of departure of Atlantic convoys. There was an opportunity here, therefore, to intercept enemy merchant ships under conditions which had ceased almost completely for some time. Further, there would hardly be any question of an efficient patrol in the American coastal area, at least of a patrol used to U-boats. Attempts had to be made to utilize as quickly as possible these advantages, which would disappear very shortly, and to achieve a 'spectacular success' on the American coast.

On 10 December three ships of homeward-bound convoy SC.57 were torpedoed and sunk 300 miles west of Ireland. The next day, Churchill once again informed the House of Commons about the progress of the Battle of the Atlantic:[20]

When I last spoke on the subject, I said that in the four months ending with October, making allowance for new building but not for sea captures or United States assistance, the net loss of our Mercantile Marine had been reduced to a good deal less than one-fifth of what it was in the four months ending in June – a tremendous saving. As these were the very months when Hitler had boasted that his strangulation of our seaborne supplies would be at its height, we were entitled to rest with some solid assurance upon that fact. The House was right to treat the fact as of great importance because these matters of sea power and sea transport involve our lives. The month of November has now gone by, and, without revealing actual figures, I am glad to say that it fully maintained the great recovery of the previous four months. In the first 10 days of this month, we have also found that the progress and position have been well maintained. These are the foundations upon which we live and carry forward our cause.

Following the Japanese attack on Pearl Harbor on 7 December 1941, Hitler, having promised Japan he would do so, declared war on the US on 11 December. At this point, all restrictions preventing U-boats attacking Allied merchant shipping in American waters were lifted. The following day, Dönitz launched Operation *Paukenschlag* ('Drum roll') off the east coast of America. U-boat commanders would now enjoy their second 'Happy Time',[21] especially against the unescorted merchant ships sailing in what were, in effect, peacetime conditions off the United States' east coast.

Dönitz correctly identified the Western Atlantic as the weakest segment in the supply system that kept Great Britain fighting, later stating in a report to Hitler on 14 May 1942 on the U-boat Operations:

> U-boat warfare is a fight against enemy merchant tonnage ... The use of boats in the American area is right according to this standpoint of economic deployment ... America is the largest enemy ship builder. The shipbuilding industry area lies in the eastern states and it, and the industries connected with it, relies considerably on oil fuel ... For each tanker which is shot up the Americans lose not only the oil transport but it affects their new construction adversely. Therefore the sinking of this American transport tonnage seems to me especially important.[22]

Dönitz was acutely aware of the strategic conditions along the eastern seaboard of the United States. It would take the Americans some time to organize convoys, build ships and be able to effectively combat U-boats in their waters, so the decision was made to exploit these weaknesses. Dönitz was also aware time was crucial, since these circumstances were unlikely to persist, stating it was of primary importance to 'take full advantage of the favourable situation as quickly as possible and with all available forces, before the anticipated changes occurred'.[23]

U-125 reached the east coast of the USA on 13 January, two days before the other four boats departed Brest and Lorient. Each boat carried sealed orders to be opened after passing 20° west and directing them to different parts of the North American coast. No charts or sailing directions were available – *U-123* was reportedly provided with two tourist guides to New York, one of which contained a fold-out map of the harbour. Each U-boat made routine signals on exiting the Bay of Biscay, which were picked up by the British Y service and plotted at the Submarine Tracking Room (part of the Operational Intelligence Centre, OIC) in London, allowing the Admiralty to follow the progress of the U-boats across the Atlantic and cable an early warning to the Royal Canadian Navy. Working on the slimmest of evidence, the Submarine Tracking Room correctly deduced the target area and passed a detailed warning across the

Atlantic to Admiral Ernest J. King (Commander-in-Chief of the US Fleet and, from 18 March, Chief of Naval Operations) of a 'heavy concentration of U-boats off the North American seaboard', including the five boats already on station and more in transit, making a total of twenty-one.

In his second address of the year to the Joint Session of Congress on 26 December Churchill thanked the US for its help in the Battle of the Atlantic 'upon which all depends, and which has in consequence been successfully and prosperously maintained'.

One initiative adopted to improve convoy protection was the introduction of auxiliary aircraft carriers, the rationale for which was outlined in a memorandum by the First Lord of the Admiralty[24] dated 29 December 1941:

1. Since June 1940, when the enemy obtained the French Atlantic coast in addition to the Norwegian it became apparent that we should be unable to deny U-boats free access to the Atlantic trade routes. Owing to the limited number of escort and hunting craft available we have had to base our trade protection on a policy of evasion. The trend of shipping losses in the last few months showed this policy to be justified, but meant the number of U-boats sunk, although by no means inconsiderable, has not had so damaging an effect on Germany's resources in this arm as could be desired. The German submarine strength is estimated to be increasing by about 20 a month and it is becoming increasingly difficult for convoys to avoid being sighted. Once the convoy has been sighted, the U-boat has a sufficient excess of speed over the convoy to maintain touch without difficulty, and then 'home on' all other U-boats in the vicinity. The thread is bound to become much more serious as the number of operational U-boats increases, and in the end it may be necessary for convoys to fight their way through.

2. The Germans had developed a very effective technique, using long range aircraft to direct U-boats onto convoys. The chances of successful evasion therefore largely depended on the degree of vigour with which the enemy air reconnaissance could be countered. This could be done to a limited extent by single aircraft carried on the merchant ships themselves; but the protection afforded would be much greater if the convoy escort included an aircraft carrier able to operate a number of aircraft.

3. Moreover, experience had demonstrated most clearly the role of aircraft in convoy protection was by no means limited to the frustration of enemy air reconnaissance. They were recognized as invaluable for direct attack on U-boats at sea. With the development of the antisubmarine patrols

of Coastal Command the U-boats had been driven further and further away from the shores of the United Kingdom. In the North Western Approaches during October 1940, the U-boats were operating regularly to within 100 miles of the coast; by now they were rarely operating within 400 miles. It had become evident convoy protection would be immeasurably improved if each convoy could have with it aircraft capable of effective attack on any U-boats sighted. Such aircraft could only be operated usefully from a carrier accompanying the convoy. A mobile air umbrella of this kind might well be the chief means of preventing disastrous losses in convoys which have to fight their way through U-boat concentrations.

The months between September and December 1941 had seen the lowest number of U-boats in the Atlantic, with a lull in activity towards the end of November following the transfer of boats to the Mediterranean and sea area to the west of Gibraltar. Only three U-boat attacks took place in the North Atlantic: on 6 December, when one straggler from SC.56 was sunk; on 10 December, when three ships were sunk from SC.57 west of Rockall; and on 31 December, when a straggler was sunk from HX.166.

The War Cabinet Weekly situation report for 25 December to 1 January recorded no activity in the South Atlantic and little evidence of movements in the North Atlantic, although latest reports indicated a possible recrudescence of activity in this area. This was reflected in the BdU War Log entry for 29 December, which noted:

The war in the Atlantic has been suspended for weeks now – the first objective must be to resume it with new forces as soon and thoroughly as possible.

As Admiral Dönitz would later comment:

The year 1941 presented the U-boats with almost insoluble tasks as far as the finding of merchant shipping was concerned. The number of U-boats was still limited. The building programme ordered at the beginning of the war had as yet no effect on the fighting group. There was no longer any question of attacks near the coast. The disposition of forces had to take place in the open sea. Yet the number of U-boats was too small for the complete surveillance of the open sea. Its disposition could only succeed through surprise, almost deprived of every accepted principle.

The enemy had recognized that the best protection for his convoys was in taking advantage of the wide spaces of the open sea by a continually varying routing. So, for example, the U-boat successes were small in the months of July and August 1941 because of the failure to find convoys in the North Atlantic. Already, to some extent, long-range British aircraft began to locate and attack the U-boat dispositions, so that, as far as possible, the U-boat patrols were detected by the enemy and then avoided by the convoys. After an unsuccessful search for convoys in July and August, at last in the beginning of September 1941, a convoy was detected near the coast of Greenland and attacked with good results. This shows how very greatly the wide ocean spaces favoured the enemy, with the dispersal of his convoys from Greenland and Iceland down to the Azores and the resulting difficulty on the part of the U-boats to find anything.

Once contact was made with the convoy the attack succeeded every time. The difficulty lay in the finding and not in the attacking. The limited sinkings for many a month resulted from the searching and waiting, lasting for weeks.

With its own extensive, long-range air reconnaissance, the outcome of the U-boat war in the year 1941 would have been quite different. The lack of an extensive naval air arm proved to be a decisive disadvantage for the German conduct of the war at sea.

The attitude of the United States of America was a further stumbling block in the U-boat war. The United States had declared the Western Hemisphere to be their zone of protection and, although neutral, announced they would attack any German warships in this area. In fact, German U-boats were actually depth charged by American destroyers. In spite of this contravention of international law, the German U-boat officers had definite orders from the political leaders to avoid, under any circumstances, any incident with American warships and merchant ships. As a result, the U-boat officers had to prohibit, in this western area, any attack on English destroyers, since at night or through periscopes it was quite possible to confuse them with American destroyers.

A situation most unfortunate for the captains was the decision of the political leaders to forbid U-boats to proceed west of Newfoundland because they wanted to prevent any incident in this area. This was with a view to avoiding war with the United States of America. The U-boat officers were unable, therefore, to search out the convoys proceeding to England near their point of departure and in the areas of strong concentration (e.g., near Halifax), but had to remain in the open spaces of the Atlantic, where, after passing Cape Race, a very great dispersal of the convoys was possible. Also the operations division of the naval staff required a detachment of U-boats in the Mediterranean. So, of necessity, the number of Atlantic U-boats was reduced, and the finding of merchant shipping was made more difficult. There was an even greater drop in the number of successes.

For all these reasons the successes of the year 1941 were moderate, the losses, at the same time, happily being low. The U-boat arm knew that they could fight and that their limited success lay only in the failure to make contact with the enemy. They further knew that this would improve as soon as greater numbers of boats were available for searching and so regarded future developments with confidence.

Chapter 7

Phase Seven: January to August 1942

The events of January 1942 would be dominated by U-boats attacks on shipping off the east coast of America. The BdU announced on 8 January that Type IXc U-boats becoming operational by the middle of January were to make a surprise attack in the Aruba-Curacao-Trinidad area – (see 16 February, below). Three days later (on 11 January), the BdU noted many independently routed ships could be expected off the coast of Canada making their way to the convoy collecting points off Halifax and Sydney. Type IXb U-boats could operate as far as Florida Straits and Type IXc as far as Trinidad-Aruba. Operations further afield could not be undertaken until a U-boat tanker was provided.

Operation *Paukenschlag* called for the first group of U-boats to be in position off the US east coast on 13 January and to co-ordinate an initial simultaneous attack. When the five U-boats assigned to the first attack started hunting targets in earnest late in the week of 11 January, their commanders were amazed to find coastal sea-lanes full of merchant vessels sailing independently without escort, few patrol aircraft, no US Navy warships patrolling the coast and their targets brightly silhouetted by the lights of coastal cities and seaports. The first attack took place a day earlier than planned, when on 12 January *U-123* sank the unescorted British merchant ship *Cyclops* about 125 miles south-east of Cape Sable, Nova Scotia. Two more ships were sunk the following day.

The westward movement of U-boats across the Atlantic continued during the second week of January, and the focus of U-boat activity was concentrated south of Newfoundland. A force of some twenty U-boats began to operate off the Atlantic seaboard of the United States and in the coastal area off Nova Scotia and Newfoundland. Their preferred targets were tankers and larger cargo ships sailing independently.

The initial deployment of U-boats was followed by the twelve boats of wolfpack *Ziethen*, which arrived singly off the Newfoundland Bank to the east of Canada to begin a programme of individual patrols as far south as Nova Scotia. Between 6 and 22 January they would sink eleven merchant ships and damage three more.

During the third week of January a concentration of U-boats operated off the North American coast from Newfoundland south to Virginia, with smaller groups still in the North-Western Approaches.

The War Cabinet Weekly Resumé reported by the end of the month that over forty U-boats were operating in the North Atlantic during the period; a large number were concentrated off the North American coast, with shipping casualties during the period heavier than in previous weeks. There were a number of attacks, particularly off the eastern seaboard of North America, where seventeen ships were torpedoed, one of which was in a convoy from the United Kingdom; ten had so far been reported as sunk.

The BdU War Log noted that by 24 January reports of U-boat successes in the American Area declared the situation should be exploited fully before enemy counter-measures increased.

With the entry of the United States into the war, Churchill later wrote:[1]

We might hope that in the war at sea the U-boats would soon be brought under control. But 1942 was to prove in the Atlantic the toughest of the whole war. By the end of 1941 the U-boat fleet stood at 250 with a 100 operational and fifteen new boats added each month. For six or seven months U-boats ravaged American waters almost uncontrolled.

And later:

By the end of January 1942 thirty-one ships of nearly 200,000 tons had been sunk. The attacks then spread south off Hampton Roads, Cape Hatteras and down to the coast of Florida. At the time the merchant shipping sailing along this coast lacked any defensive protection; there was no convoy system. This was also the principal route for the many tankers sailing between the oil ports of Venezuela and the Gulf of Mexico.

The bulk of the merchant shipping losses in the Atlantic in January were due to the U-boat offensive off the eastern seaboard of North America. The total tonnage sunk in this area amounted to thirty-one ships of approximately 195,000 gross tons. Most ships sunk during the month were sailing unescorted, or were stragglers from convoys after they dispersed, there being no convoy protection in American waters. There were no attacks on convoys in the North Atlantic during the month.

By February 1942 organization of the North Atlantic convoy escorts had been formalized into American, British, and Canadian groups. The Royal Navy was primarily responsible for the Western Approaches to the UK; the US Navy protected the mid-Atlantic from its bases in Newfoundland and Iceland; and the Royal Canadian Navy protected the convoys as they departed or arrived off Newfoundland and Nova Scotia.

By the time the first U-boat group ended its operations on 6 February to return to base, twenty-five merchant ships totalling 156,939 tons had been sunk. The same day, Churchill wrote to Roosevelt's Special Adviser Harry Hopkins: 'It would be as well to make sure the President's attention has been drawn to the very heavy sinkings by U-boats in the western North Atlantic.'

The BdU announced on 7 February that five more U-boats were to be sent to the American area during the month. The first U-boat commander to return from the American east coast reported encountering many independently routed ships, also the clumsy handling of ships, slight, inexperienced sea and air patrols and defences so weak that conditions had to be described as almost completely of peacetime standard. There were more potential targets in the sea area south of New York to Cape Hatteras than he could attack – at times as many as ten ships in sight sailing with lights on peacetime courses. It was unfortunate that only six rather than the twelve boats requested had been released for the operation, limiting the success achieved.

The BdU War Log of 11 February set out details of the next phase of planned operations:

> Sailing of those large and medium boats in western France, and large boats in Germany, which were ready for patrol off the American coast. Medium boats would go to the northern area (south of Nova Scotia and Newfoundland), the larger ones to the coast of the USA between Florida Straits and New York, or important traffic points in the West Indies. On 16 February, three boats would be off Curacao and Aruba for the first time.
>
> The number of U-boats off the American coast was given as thirty-five, of which nine were operational there, fourteen returning to port and twelve en route (including six bound for the West Indies). The larger U-boats were employed off the American coast between Florida and New York or the important junctions for shipping in the West Indies.

U-boat losses from September 1939 to 11 February 1942 now totalled seventy-three. Losses in January were five, of which four were in the Mediterranean. The overall average loss since September 1939 was 2.5 boats per month. The War Cabinet Summary for week ending 12 February noted slightly fewer U-boats operating in the North Atlantic during the period, a large number concentrated off the American seaboard from Cape Race to Charleston and others north-east of Bermuda and in the North-Western Approaches. During the week, eight ships were torpedoed by U-boats, four off the eastern seaboard of North America, two north-east of Bermuda and two in the North-Western Approaches; of these, four were known to have been sunk

Press reports graphically described two of the U-boat attacks.

SEA SINKINGS

U-boat Attacks in Atlantic

NEW YORK, Feb. 11

The Navy today announced the sinking of the tanker *W. L. Steed* (6,182 tons) off the coast of New Jersey on February 2. Three survivors of the crew of 38 were landed here today. Three lifeboats are missing. A submarine hit the ship with one torpedo in pitch-black darkness. The submarine then fired 17 shells. The survivors were rescued after two days in a lifeboat, with the temperature below zero by a ship proceeding to another port.

Forty-seven survivors from a British freighter have been landed at an east coast Canadian port, the remainder of the crew being unaccounted for. The vessel was shelled for 31 hours and eventually sunk by a U-boat. The name of the ship and the time and location of the attack have not been disclosed.

Torpedoed Tanker Makes Port

LONDON, Feb. 11

The torpedoed tanker *Tahchee* (6.508 tons) with a cargo of oil worth over £250,000 struggled 592 miles into port after an attack in the Atlantic. The crew abandoned the *Tahchee* when she became on fire, but the captain and officers re-boarded her when they saw a chance of saving the ship. The corvette *Orilla* began towing the tanker, but finally the tanker's engineer got up sufficient steam to proceed slowly on her own power.

The results of the U-boat operation in Pan-American waters were reviewed at the 13 February Führer Conference, which noted:

Submarine warfare in the Atlantic produces good results at the present time. In the war against enemy shipping everything depends on the number of submarines available. Time and again Churchill speaks of shipping tonnage as his greatest worry. Britain and the U.S. are building 7,000,000 BRT [gross tonnage] in 1942, which means that Germany and Japan will have to sink a monthly total of 600,000 BRT to offset this increase. This will become possible once the Japanese war against enemy shipping in the Indian Ocean gets under way.

Two days later, Churchill gave a further radio broadcast on the state of the war which touched on the importance of the situation in the Atlantic:

> As for us, our British resources were stretched to the utmost. We had already been for more than a whole year absolutely alone in the struggle with Hitler and Mussolini. We had to be ready to meet a German invasion of our own island ... Above all, we had to bring in the food, raw materials, and finished munitions across the Atlantic in the teeth of the German and Italian U-boats and aircraft, without which we could not live, without which we could not wage war. We have to do all this still.

Operation *Paukenschlag* was extended on 16 February as far south as the Caribbean, with U-boats shelling oil installations and sinking tankers off Aruba, Curaçao, Trinidad and other oil ports. Churchill later wrote:

> On 16 February a U-boat appeared off Aruba and after sinking one ship and damaging another shelled the installations ashore – fortunately not causing serious damage. The same day, another U-boat sank three tankers at sea in the same area. Another entered the harbour at Trinidad and sank two ships.

However, U-boats remained active elsewhere in the Atlantic, and east of Newfoundland a pack of five attacked convoy ON.67 (thirty-six merchant ships) between 22 and 24 February, sinking eight, six of which were tankers.

The Royal Navy now suffered a major intelligence setback when U-boats in the Atlantic changed from the Enigma Hydra code to Triton, which would not be broken until December 1942 – a ten-month delay.

The War Cabinet Weekly Resumé for 19 to 26 February reported six U-boats were believed to have been operating in the Caribbean and two to the west of Trinidad. An outburst of activity in the Florida area indicated the presence of two and possibly three U-boats. Activity further north on the American coast had declined, and only isolated reports had come in from the area between New York and Newfoundland. During the week nineteen ships, nine of them tankers, were torpedoed in the West Atlantic and West Indies, of which only two were known to be still afloat. Eight from the slow westbound convoy ONS.67 (21 to 25 February) were sunk and one damaged in the sea area 420 miles south-south-east of St John's

In the 26 February House of Commons debate on the Navy Estimates for 1942[2] the First Lord of the Admiralty reported:

> The Battle of the Atlantic, which was our principal preoccupation for the greater part of the year, has now developed into what I may call the Battle

of the Seven Seas. U-boat construction is undoubtedly on an unprecedented scale, and the U-boat fleet expands month by month. The U-boat fleet have, as before, shown, and continue to show, ingenuity and organizing skill in their operations and great flexibility in their tactics.

During February the majority of merchant shipping losses occurred on the Atlantic seaboard of North America and in the Caribbean Sea and its approaches, where forty-five ships totalling 291,000 tons (including twenty-three tankers) were sunk, as the number of U-boats operating in the Western Atlantic increased and U-boat activity spread further south, with ships sunk off the coast of Florida and in the Caribbean. Tanker losses continued to be severe, with the tanker traffic to and from the West Indian and Venezuelan oil fields an objective, as illustrated by the attack carried out by several U-boats on 16 February on six tankers off Aruba and in the Gulf of Venezuela, with five sunk and one seriously damaged. A total of ten Atlantic convoys were attacked, with eighteen merchant ships sunk.

The BdU War Log for 7 March noted operations by U-boats off the coast of North America being temporarily hampered by bad weather, especially in the area east and south of Newfoundland as far as the coast of Nova Scotia, where very low temperatures prevailed, leading at times to heavy icing-up of submarines. Visibility was bad on the whole, with a lot of fog and stormy weather. Shipping, which at first continued to run as usual despite the sinkings, had almost ceased, and Type VIIc U-boats were not as successful as hoped. Stormy weather was also reported along the coast between New York and Cape Hatteras. The traffic, which at first continued to proceed regularly along the American coast and adjacent stretch of sea regardless of sinkings, now seemed to stop at intervals. The outlook for success by the medium boats (type VIIc) in American operations area was limited by these two facts, but was expected to improve as the presence of a submarine tanker would enable them to remain longer close to the coast in the exact operational area.

An average of about forty U-boats had been operating between 5 and 12 March, including those on outward and homeward passage. The main concentration continued to be in the Western Atlantic and Caribbean Sea. During the week twenty ships were attacked by U-boats, sixteen in the West Atlantic and West Indies. The rising toll of tanker losses with their valuable cargoes became a matter of concern for Churchill. On 12 March he wrote again to Hopkins:

1. I am most deeply concerned at the immense sinking of tankers west of the 40th Meridian and in the Caribbean Sea. In January eighteen ships totalling 221,000 dead-weight tons, were sunk or damaged; in

February the number rose to thirty-four, totalling 364,941 dead-weight tons; in the first eleven days of March seven vessels totalling 88,449 dead-weight tons have been sunk. Yesterday alone 30,000 tons were reported as sunk or damaged. Thus in little over two months, in these waters alone, about sixty tankers have been sunk or damaged, totalling some 675,000 dead-weight tons. In addition to this several tankers are overdue.

2. By rearrangement of Atlantic convoy routes a considerable number of American destroyers have been released from escort duties on the cross-Atlantic route for other services. We have handed over twenty-four anti-submarine trawlers of which twenty-three have now reached you.[3]

3. The situation is so serious that drastic action of some kind is necessary, and we very much hope that you will be able to provide additional escort forces to organize immediate convoys in the West Indies–Bermuda area by withdrawing a few of your destroyer strength in the Pacific until the ten corvettes we are handing over to you come into service.[4]

4. The only other alternatives are either to stop temporarily the sailing of tankers, which would gravely jeopardize our operational supplies, or to open out the cycle of Halifax–United Kingdom convoys (i.e. lessen the traffic), thus for a period releasing sufficient convoy vessels to make up the West Indies convoys. It must be realized, however, that not only will this further reduce our imports by about 30,000 tons per month but will also take some time to become effective.

5. I should like these alternatives to be discussed on the highest naval level at once. If through opening out the convoy cycle[5] we were forced to reduce our imports for a time, this would have to be taken into consideration by you in helping us out with new tonnage in the last half of the year.

The President replied at some length on 16 March to Churchill's cable to Hopkins. He welcomed the arrival of the trawlers and corvettes and proposed various economies in the transatlantic convoys, including 'opening out' i.e. extending the cycle of convoys until 1 July. Only the implementation of an effective convoy system would counter the threat.

Twenty-three anti-submarine trawlers arrived at the Brooklyn Navy Yard in late March for modification before entering patrol service in April. One was lost en route, another four in action or accidents. The survivors transferred to West Africa in October 1942.[6] Ten corvettes transferred between 10 March and 2 May would remain in USN service until May 1945.

Not surprisingly, the BdU was pleased with the outcome of the American operations. Flag Officer U-boats reporting on 15 March on the first two and a half months of operations in Pan-American waters noted sea defence in the area off Halifax and Cape Race was small, badly organized and untrained. American air defences in areas such as Aruba, Hatteras and Halifax were described as 'adequate' in number but inexperienced, and performed poorly compared with the British. A reduction in tanker traffic observed around Aruba, Port of Spain, and the Hatteras-Florida Straits was judged possibly the result of a momentary panic and not a considered policy. The presence of independent ships sailing on direct route America–Britain pointed to the Allies' difficulty in organizing a comprehensive convoy system. Finally, he observed a surprising number of tankers appeared to be engaged on purely American import trade, illustrating how short of oil America was and her difficulties in giving up tanker space to Britain. He went on to note operations in American waters had become more difficult, but the task might be lightened by a U-tanker, which would enable simultaneous attacks on many important traffic points; quicker deployment of boats to a temporarily favourable traffic junction; extension of attack to the most distant areas off Central and Southern America, not only by large, but also medium boats; and shallow-water and special missions. Sooner or later, the formation of convoys as defence must be expected, but long distances and lack of suitable vessels would impede this for some time.

Admiral Dönitz would not be slow to exploit these opportunities. However, as the BdU reported on 16 March, there were, as a result a result of the withdrawal of seven U-boats to the Hebrides-Iceland area, only four in American waters, although five more were expected to within the next few days.

Churchill now regarded the state of the Battle of the Atlantic with some concern, commenting in his address to the Central Council of the Conservative Party on 27 March:

> The Battle of the Atlantic, upon which all the time our power to live and carry on the war effort depends, after turning markedly in our favour for five or six months, is now for the time being – and only for the time being – worsened again.

During March 1942 the focus of U-boat operations was in the area between Charlestown and New York. Single U-boats operated throughout the Caribbean and Gulf of Mexico. Sinkings during the month of March rose to nearly 500,000 tons, 75 per cent of which was sunk within 300 miles of the American coast, with tankers accounting for almost half the tonnage lost.

By 1 April there were 288 U-boats, of which 125 were operational. Eighty-one were allocated to the Atlantic – forty-five at sea in the North Atlantic and off the US coast, two in the South Atlantic and thirty-four in bases on the western coast of France.[7]

Churchill later noted:

On 1 April 1942 the USN implemented a partial convoy system. This involved short routes of about 120 miles between protected anchorages by groups of ships under escort during daylight hours. This to avoid the night-time U-boat attacks.

The War Cabinet Weekly Resumé to 2 April noted activity had been considerable near Cape Hatteras and estimated with remarkable accuracy that the number of U-boats operating in the Atlantic remained fewer than fifty. During the following seven days U-boats continued to be active, though to a lesser extent than previously, in the area between Cape Hatteras, Bermuda and Nantucket. with some activity observed in the Caribbean.

The BdU War Log for 12 April, commenting on the appearance of increased American air patrols, referenced a report signed by Dönitz which noted that although counter-measures had been increased, U-boat successes remained at the same high level. American crews had proved inexperienced and unwatchful, and even depth charge attacks in shallow water had not caused any losses. Air attacks had, however, increased, and U-boats had been forced to remain submerged for days. In the full moon period the aircraft, because of their large number, were especially dangerous and had forced the U-boats to carry out their attacks further out to sea. When U-boat tankers arrived, the U-boats would have greater scope and should exploit this to the full in attacking along the whole length of the American coast before defences became fully organized.

An additional entry described the situation in the American area as contained in U-boat W/T messages and reports from commanders who had returned:

Anti-submarine activity immediately under the coast has increased. Destroyers, Coast Guard ships and escort vessels were patrolling the steamer routes, sometimes ships were escorted by escort vessels in particularly endangered areas (Hatteras). In spite of these measures, the successes of U-boats so far remained at the same level. Before the U-boat attack on America was begun it was suspected American anti-submarine activity would be weak and inexperienced; this conjecture has been fully confirmed. Anti-submarine vessels had no ASDIC, some were equipped with hydrophones. The crews were careless, inexperienced and little persevering in a hunt. In several cases escort vessels, Coast Guard ships and destroyers, having established the presence of a U-boat, made off instead of attacking. This could be the only explanation for the fact that so far no losses have occurred from D/C hunts in shallow water (20 metres).

Air activity had increased considerably, with boats forced to remain submerged by day near the coast. On full-moon nights it was dangerous owing to the numbers of aircraft involved, and boats were forced to transfer their attacking areas further out to sea.

On the whole, however, the boats' successes were so great as to justify their operation near the coast and this would continue.

Their range and operational endurance of the boats would be extended when they had been supplied by a U-tanker and the number of boats in operational areas would increase.

President Roosevelt's representative Harry Hopkins was in London at the time and on 14 April reported back to the President that in the preceding three months Allied losses had totalled 1,200,000 tons, over half of which was represented by tankers. The First Sea Lord had informed the Prime Minister that the tanker losses for the preceding week 'had been frightful'. 'We are', said Hopkins prophetically, 'going to need all these ships desperately in the next few month. I doubt very much that anything short of convoy is going to do this job ... They [the British] whose island is so dependent on imports realize full well the significance of these sinkings to the future of the war.'

Meanwhile Dönitz, reporting on 15 April on the results of the first three months of U-boat attacks off the east coast of America since the focal point of attacks was shifted to that area, claimed 229 ships of 1,521,882 G.R.T. sunk and twenty-three of 82,566 G.R.T. damaged, apart from the sinking of several destroyers and corvettes. These figures, he claimed, demonstrated it was better to use the U-boats off the American coast than in the Central Atlantic, despite the long journey which this entailed; and, he added, not a single U-boat had yet been lost off the American coast. The focal point of U-boat attack should therefore remain off the American east coast, so long as the weak defences and good chances of success remained. Only prompt, effective action to introduce a convoy system could thwart Dönitz's strategic objectives, but the USN still seemed for a variety of reasons unwilling or unable to implement it.

The release of escorts from the mid-ocean convoy escort groups was under constant review, and on 16 April the Halifax convoy cycle was increased from six to seven days to allow two escort groups to be sent to the east coast of America.

The operations of U-boats in the Western Atlantic now extended into the Gulf of Mexico. No ships were lost from Atlantic convoys during April; those sunk in the western Atlantic and off the American coast were sailing independently or dispersed from convoys. Sixty-five of seventy-seven sunk during the month were lost in American and Caribbean waters.

Eighty-five U-boats were operating in the Atlantic on 1 May. The War Cabinet Minutes of 3 May[8] noted:

> There were indications U-boats were beginning to fight back from the surface against air attack; this development was likely to prove expensive for the U-boats.

The same day, the BdU War Log emphasised the advantages of employing U-boats in the Atlantic rather than in Arctic waters:

> U-boats of Greater Value in Atlantic than in Northern Waters. F.O. U-boats stated to the U-boat division his view that U-boats should be employed in the war on merchant shipping in the Atlantic rather than on operations in Northern Waters as U-boats operating in Northern Waters were very much hampered by the long daylight hours in summer, while attacks would still be possible in the Atlantic by night.

The War Cabinet Summary for the week 30 April to 7 May estimated twelve U-boats were operating in the Florida Strait, Gulf of Mexico and Caribbean. Activity had been less in Northern American waters, with none in the Atlantic. There had been a considerable increase in the number of ships attacked by U-boats. Twenty-two ships (seven of them tankers) were known to have been torpedoed, all of them in the West Atlantic and the Caribbean. The majority of the casualties occurred in the northern Caribbean and off the Florida Coast. Six of the ships were known to have sunk.

Churchill had, some weeks previously, indicated an intention to write to Stalin about the size and frequency of the Arctic convoys, but he had not yet done so; now, on 9 May, he wrote at some length:

> I have received your Telegram of May 6 and thank you for your message and greetings. We are resolved to fight our way through to you with the maximum amount of war materials. On account of the *Tirpitz* and other enemy surface ships at Trondheim the passage of every convoy has become a serious fleet operation. We shall continue to do our utmost.
>
> No doubt your naval advisers have pointed out to you the dangers to which the convoys are subjected from attack by enemy surface forces, submarines, and the air from various bases in enemy hands, which flank the route of a convoy throughout its passage.
>
> Owing to adverse weather conditions the scale of attack, which the Germans have so far developed, is considerably less than we can reasonably expect in future.

We are throwing all our available resources into the solution of this problem, have dangerously weakened our Atlantic convoy escorts for this purpose, and as you are no doubt aware have suffered severe naval casualties in the course of these operations.

While these events were taking place in the west, the North Atlantic had been fairly quiet. No planned wolfpack attacks had taken place since the previous November. After the disastrous encounter with Gibraltar convoy HG.76 between 19 and 23 December 1941 which resulted in the loss of five U-boats, the BdU had temporarily abandoned operations against convoys. Most of the available U-boats had been sent to the unprotected coasts of America, or to Norway to operate against the convoys to northern Russia. As the defences off the American coast became better organized and the opposition tougher, the BdU planned to resume attacks again the vital North Atlantic convoy routes.

Early in May, a group of six boats allocated to the western Atlantic wolfpack *Hecht* (8 May to 18 June) was ordered to move north and attack the convoys after the B-Dienst department of Naval Intelligence deduced from intercepted wireless traffic that convoys were again using the shorter 'great circle' route across the North Atlantic. The first convoy attacked by wolfpack *Hecht* between 12 and 13 May 1942 was ONS.92, which lost seven merchant ships overnight. A seventh, a straggler, would be sunk on 18 May.

In the afternoon of 14 May at the Führer Conference on Naval Affairs Dönitz reported to Hitler his latest assessment of the progress of the U-boat campaign:

Submarine warfare is war against enemy merchant shipping. Since American and British ships are under unified command, they have to be regarded as one. Therefore we must sink ships wherever the greatest number of them can be sunk at lowest cost to us, i.e. where we lose the least number of submarines. We should not concentrate in one certain area if that means sinking fewer ships. From the point of view of operational cost, our submarine actions in the American area are justifiable. Sinkings from 15 January to 10 May amounted to 303 ships or a total of 2,015,252 BRT. However, submarine operations in the American area are also justifiable in attempting to offset the merchant vessel construction programme of the enemy. America is producing the largest number of merchant ships. Her shipbuilding industry is located in the eastern States. Shipbuilding and other allied industries depend mostly on oil for fuel, and the most important American oilfields are found near the Gulf of Mexico. Consequently, the greater part of American tankers is used in coastal traffic, transporting oil from the oil region to the industrial area. From 15 January to 10 May 1942 we sank 112 tankers or a total of 927,000 BRT. About two thirds of these ships were employed in the above mentioned American coastal traffic. The Commander-in-Chief, U-boats, intends to operate submarines in the American waters as long as it is profitable. He closely watches the monthly results of submarine warfare; it means that the average of ships sunk by each submarine is calculated for every day at sea.

This daily average amounted to 209 BRT in January, 378 BRT in February, 409 BRT in March and 412 BRT in April. The figures indicate that the average is still increasing slightly. Therefore we are still justified in operating submarines in the American zone. But the calculation of this daily potential also shows how much we are losing by operating submarines in the Norwegian zone.

One of these days the situation in the American zone will change. Even at this time everything points to the fact that the Americans are making strenuous efforts to prevent the large number of sinkings. They have organized a considerable air defence and are likewise using destroyers and PC boats off the coast. However, all these are manned by inexperienced crews and do not constitute a serious threat at present. In any case, the submarines with their greater experience in warfare are mastering these countermeasures. The American fliers see nothing, the destroyers and patrol vessels are travelling too fast most of the time even to locate the submarines, or they are not persistent enough in their pursuit with depth charges. As such, the shallow American coastal waters make it very easy to safeguard and protect shipping.

Dönitz was however realistic about future prospects, stating:

I believe the Americans would choose to organize all shipping into convoys. This method will probably be chosen, and the convoys will be led along the coast in shallow waters. The daily traffic will then become lighter, and our chances of success will become fewer. However, as long as their escorts are inexperienced, I believe that we will be able to attack the convoys in the usual manner even in shallow waters. It is due to our tested medium-sized type of submarines that we are able to do this at all.

If operations in the American area prove unprofitable, we shall resume warfare against the convoys in the North Atlantic with a large number of submarines. Up to this time, locating the enemy was always the most difficult part of this warfare. The Commander- in-Chief U-boats believes that the larger number of submarines will make this easier in the future. More convoys will be located due to the large number of submarines, and it will be easier to maintain contact with them and to attack them.

It will then become more important again to work hand in hand with the Commander, Air, Atlantic Coast. This cooperation with the Luftwaffe used to cause difficulties because no integrated training covering large areas was carried out. Such cooperation cannot be improvised. More recent stages were, however, more successful. Powerful long-range planes must be assigned to Atlantic operations soon.

The large number of submarines which we expect to have available in the near future will enable us to attack shipping in additional and more remote areas, which are now brought within our reach through the existence of submarine tankers. Thus the tankers enable us to operate a 517-ton submarine for two weeks in the Gulf of Mexico and off Panama.

The Commander in Chief U-boats feels that the outlook in regard to submarine warfare is promising in view of the large number of submarines soon available and the variety of operations possible.

The defence situation must also be taken into account when the possibilities of submarine warfare are considered. Our submarine losses are extremely light at this time. There is no doubt that the number of losses will rise again once attacks on convoys are resumed and the defences in some zones become stronger. Therefore we must strive with all means at our disposal to improve submarine weapons in order to keep the submarine abreast of defensive devices of the enemy.

On 14 and 15 May the US Navy began to introduce what was to become a fairly complete system of coastal convoys between Norfolk, Virginia, and Key West, Florida. The U-boats were now concentrating in the Caribbean and Gulf of Mexico, where they could now spend more time on station assisted by 'Milchkuh' (milk cow) supply boats.

By 17 May the BdU War Log was noting:

Attacking conditions on the N. coast of America from Cape Fear to New York had become extremely unfavourable since 20 April. Boats lying immediately under the coast and off the main ports reported no traffic. It appeared the traffic had temporarily ceased or been so re-organized that the boats had not been able to pick it up. A complete cessation, even for a short time, was unthinkable, as America could not stand the loss. Most of the sinkings during the month had been in the Caribbean, the Gulf of Mexico and the Florida Straits.

The War Cabinet Weekly Resumé for 14 to 21 May reported a recrudescence of attacks by U-boats on the convoy routes in mid-Atlantic and to the north of the Cape Verde Islands. Attacks continued in the West Atlantic and in the

Caribbean Sea, and in addition, U-boats had been reported in the Gulf of St Lawrence and the Gulf of Mexico. And the following week, it was reported United States convoys were now operating between Key West and Hampton Roads.

The German Naval Staff was now faced with a conflict of priorities in the allocation of U-boats, between operations against the PQ convoys to northern Russia and operations in the Atlantic. The War Log recognized the primary importance of the former at the expense of withdrawing U-boats from Atlantic operations, but rejected the proposal to increase the numbers to the level requested.

Churchill later wrote: 'In May 1942 Dönitz shifted the focus of U-boat operations to the eastern Atlantic and the waters off the Portuguese Atlantic Islands and West Africa'; and in further commenting on this phase of the war at sea in his memoirs and on the German Navy's conflicting priorities, he added:

> The U-boat attack was our worst evil. It would have been wise for the Germans to stake all upon it. Just as Goering repeatedly shifted his air targets in the Battle of Britain in 1940, so now the U-boat warfare was to some extent weakened for the sake of competing attractions. Nevertheless, it constituted a terrible event in a very bad time.[9]

In May 1942 the total merchant shipping losses reached the second highest monthly total of the war at 681,000 gross tons, with the bulk occurring in the western North Atlantic, including the Caribbean and Gulf of Mexico, where the U-boats were particularly active. Some 124 of 126 ships sunk were lost in American waters and the Caribbean, most of them independently routed or dispersed. Only eleven ships were lost from transatlantic convoys.

Eighty-eight U-boats were deployed in the Atlantic on 1 June. The Chief of the BdU Operations Branch continued to express concern over the imposition of conflicting priorities, complaining on 7 June:

> The increasing need for boats to meet the tasks in Arctic waters, to attack convoys, and act as anti-invasion defence could only be met at the expense of the warfare in the Atlantic Ocean.

It was only on 10 June that Admiral Ernest J. King, the US Navy's Commander-in-Chief, finally accepted the need to introduce a full convoy system throughout the Caribbean, aided by the British escort groups withdrawn from the Atlantic convoys and the deployment of a squadron of RAF Coastal Command Lockheed Hudson anti-submarine aircraft to operate from Trinidad.

The War Cabinet Resumé for week ending 11 June reported:

Now for the first time since U-boats began to operate in United States waters, they attacked escorted shipping when BX.23A was attacked in the Gulf of Maine on 9 June with two ships damaged,[10] and a convoy from Trinidad to Aruba lost two ships. The number of U-boats operating in the Atlantic remained at the same level (about forty-five), but a considerable number were on passage to or from their operating areas.

Wolfpack *Hecht* was still at sea and, after a relatively unsuccessful period of three weeks during which only one small Portuguese sailing ship was sunk, found ONS.94 and ONS.96, but lost contact due to the proximity of land before in the evening of 8 June making contact with ONS.100 again. Over the following four days the U-boats sank four merchant ships and one corvette from this convoy.

The conflicting operational priorities between Hitler, the German High Command and the BdU were again reflected in the minutes of the Führer Conference of 15 June, at which Hitler proposed an operational group of submarines be held in readiness for the purpose of quick intervention in case the enemy should suddenly strike at such points as the Azores, Madeira or Cape Verde. Dönitz pointed out that at this time he could not afford to divert a considerable number of submarines for such a purpose alone. All available submarines had to be used in the war against enemy merchant shipping. It might be possible, however, to form such a group within the framework of present submarine warfare. For instance, the Commander-in-Chief U-boats had eight submarines patrolling the convoy lanes to and from the US via the Azores. In an emergency, these boats could be used as suggested.

The chief development during the week of 11 to 18 June was the renewal of attacks on convoys by groups of U-boats in the North Atlantic. Elsewhere, the main area of activity continued to be the West Indies and the Caribbean, extending to the north of the Gulf of Mexico. There appeared to be little change in the number of boats off the east coast of Canada and the United States

Dönitz's reaction to Hitler's proposal is recorded in the BdU War Log for the same day, in which he noted:

> The Führer had ordered an operational U-boat group be held ready against a possible landing on Madeira and the Azores. This made heavy demands on the conduct of the U-boat war. I informed the Naval War Staff that the most important function of the U-boats was to sink enemy tonnage and, in view of the enemy's vastly increased new construction programme for the next year, to sink enemy tonnage quickly.
>
> All other requirements should, unless it is a question of overcoming an acute danger which might involve the loss of the war, be subordinated to operations They can only be met if the number of boats and the situation in

general permits the withdrawal of U-boats without serious consequences to the war on merchant shipping.

It is assumed that an operational group of U-boats to act as defence against enemy operations against Madeira and the Azores has been asked for in ignorance of the present U-boat situation.

A Joint Memorandum submitted by the First Lord of the Admiralty and the Minister of War Transport to the War Cabinet on 22 June 1942 entitled 'North Atlantic, United States Coast, and Gulf and Caribbean – Extension of Convoy System' provides a useful analysis of the outcome of U-boat attacks in American waters:

When U-boat attacks began off the east coast of the United States, the Americans were completely unprepared to deal with this form of attack. At that time our homeward-bound convoys were receiving escort throughout their voyage, but our outward-bound convoys were dispersing about 500 miles short of Halifax. The new attacks created an urgent need for all-through escort and for anti-submarine forces on the United States seaboard, and United States agreement to the necessary reorganization was achieved early in February. The desirability of a convoy system on the United States coast was also represented to the United States authorities, but on the 10th of February the Admiralty Delegation in Washington reported that anti-submarine forces on the American coast were quite inadequate for this purpose. It was therefore decided to lend 24 large anti-submarine trawlers to the United States. Arrangements had previously been made to hand over 10 corvettes, under construction or repair, to the United States.

Owing to U-boat attacks in the Caribbean in the middle of February it then became necessary, since the United States were unable to afford adequate protection, to cut down tanker sailings. The routeing of the remainder was made the subject of continuous study by the Admiralty and the Ministry of War Transport.

We continued to press for the institution of the United States coastal convoy and offered to open out the cycle of the Atlantic convoy so as to make two escort groups, as well as other reinforcements possible, to assist them. This entailed accepting a loss of imports estimated at 30,000 tons a month and was implemented as soon as the United States plans were ready. The coastal convoys started on the 14th of May.

Early in May the advent of fine weather made it possible to withdraw one more group from the trans-Atlantic convoy escorts in order to start a tanker convoy between the Dutch West Indies and Trinidad.

On 21 May Commander-in-Chief, United States Fleet, requested the loan of a further 15–20 corvettes to deal with the serious situation which had arisen in the Gulf of Mexico and the Caribbean. The proposals we made in reply were not acceptable to the United States, and Canadians and the United States authorities finally decided to start a convoy between Halifax and Aruba as soon as possible, and a further convoy between Key West and Trinidad on the 1st of July.

This is how the matter stands at present, but certain modifications will be made later. Although convoy arrangements and protective measures in the Western Atlantic are the responsibility of the United States, the matter is constantly studied on this side with a view to securing the most advantageous employment of available forces to meet shipping needs and making recommendations to this end.

Review of the Anti-U-boat Campaign and Air Offensive

It is believed we are approaching another of the turning points in the German U-boat campaign. Since January the main weight of attack has been in the Western Atlantic and until recently attacks on our other convoys have more or less been abandoned, with the exception of the attempt to interrupt the flow of supplies to Russia. The slowly increasing potency of the anti-submarine effort on the Atlantic seaboard has led to an increased scale of attack in the Caribbean and to the south and east of the Antilles and to the development of the U-boat threat in the Gulf of Mexico. Convoy and escort should start in the Caribbean on 1 July and should thereafter increase in this connection we have drawn the attention of the United States to the importance of providing a strong air effort to the eastward of Trinidad. The above measures may be expected to encourage the dispersal for the concentrated U-boat effort in the Western Atlantic. There are already signs of a renewed threat to our north–south convoys in the Eastern Atlantic, and it may be that the easing of the situation in the Western Atlantic will be followed by a renewed onslaught on our cross-Atlantic convoys. The further extension of U-boat efforts in the South Atlantic must also be expected.

Dönitz stated on 30 June that U-boat successes in June had been unexpectedly high, due to U-boats on passage to North America and the Caribbean having met a number of independently routed ships in the open sea, those in the Caribbean sinking a large number of ships, and the resumption of convoy traffic in the Cape Hatteras area; the situation in the Caribbean was more favourable than the North American area and to be exploited. By the end of the month six ships had been sunk from four Atlantic convoys. The majority of other sinkings were of unescorted ships in American and Caribbean waters.

On 1 July the Change of Operational Control (CHOP) line was introduced for Atlantic convoys. Shipping sailing to the east of 26° west (approximately south of Iceland) after that date was to be controlled by the British Admiralty and that to the west by the US Navy from Washington. (In November 1942 the line would be moved to 47° west, approximately south of Greenland.)

The BdU War Log for 2 July contained an explanation for the reduction in sinkings off the American coast:

After America's entry into the war, U-boats operated in the North American area which yields good results, isolated boats of type IXc in the Caribbean area. The traffic situation in North American coastal waters began to deteriorate at the end of April 1942.

Here, the fact must be taken into account that the figures for June are adversely affected by the large number of returning boats (about thirty) and a medium number of outward-bound boats which have a fairly long voyage to their field of operations. The potential was in fact as high as that of May if not higher. It would still be wrong, then, to start purely anti-convoy operations again with medium forces. The traffic situation must be exploited as long as it yields numerous isolated successes with the minimum number of losses. Furthermore, attention is drawn to the fact that operations in coastal waters with for the most part strong aerial protection and medium if inexperienced sea defence is an excellent training for anti-convoy operations.

In a follow-up, a U-boat Command War Log entry 10 July noted:

Traffic in the American area was again reported to have ceased since about 3 July, probably as a result of heavy losses at the end of June. While this means the Americans are suffering great difficulties, to the U-boat it means a drop in sinkings.

Nine days later, on 19 July, following the introduction of the convoy system along the American east coast and into the Caribbean, Dönitz transferred the main focus of operations to the mid-Atlantic, where convoys sailed out of range of land-based air cover and where, he later wrote, 'Wolfpack tactics could be employed without any interference in all phases of surface operations and that we could in consequence achieve the maximum possible success.'[11] (The offensive would continue until September in the north of the Gulf of Mexico and off Trinidad, where the largest number of independently routed ships would be found.) Dönitz ordered the last two U-boats near Cape Hatteras to shift their patrol areas to waters off Newfoundland.

The BdU War Log entry for the same date read:

In the sea area off Hatteras successes have dropped considerably due to the formation of convoys and increased defence measures. Two U-boats have been lost and two badly damaged, and this state of things is not justified by the amount of success achieved. The remaining boats (*U-754* and *U-458*) will therefore be removed. Occasional operations by single boats and mine-laying operations in harbour entrances and areas along the east coast of America will come under consideration as before. [*U-754* was sunk on 31 July south of Nova Scotia with depth charges by a Canadian Hudson aircraft.]

Churchill remained ever-optimistic that the rate of American shipbuilding output would offset the sinkings. In his Memorandum of 21 July 1942 entitled 'A Review of the War Position'[12] commenting on the importance of seaborne tonnage, i.e. numbers of merchant ships, he wrote:

We can only get through this year by running down our stocks heavily. At the cost of much internal friction and disturbance, we may, by 'tightening the belt', save perhaps a million tons. Whether this should be done as a moral exercise should be carefully weighed. It can, however, have no appreciable effect upon the problem of maintaining our war effort at home and abroad. There is no reason to assume that we cannot get through the present year or that the tonnage position in 1943 will not steadily improve as a result of the prodigious American shipbuilding. But we must be careful not to let our position deteriorate to an unmanageable degree before we have a clear understanding with the United States as to the future. With this object we must now in the next few weeks come to a solemn compact, almost a treaty, with the United States about the share of their new building we are to get in 1943 and 1944. Up till the time when the United States entered the war, we had pretty well recouped ourselves for our losses by acquiring control of the shipping of Continental States as they were successively subjugated by the enemy. No more windfalls can be expected from this source. We can only expand our own building sensibly at dire expense to our war effort. There is nothing we can do to change our minimum import requirements appreciably. The tonnage needed to guarantee these must be a first charge. We ought, therefore, to ask the United States to deliver to us during sufficient tonnage to occupy fully our available merchant crews. As it would be foolish to have large numbers of British life-trained merchant seamen and officers standing idle without ships while in the United States crews will have to be trained specially, our desire should not be deemed unreasonable.

On no account must we run our stocks down to a dangerous level for the sake of getting through 1942, without knowing where we stand in 1943. And the minimum stocks needed must not be written down unduly. Serious bombing of our ports might well hamstring our intake for considerable periods when we should be lost without something in the larder. Moreover, we should not start on the basis that the British should make a greater sacrifice of their pre-war standard of living than the American people. We should point out that any further curtailment of imports taking 1942 and 1943 together can only be made through a definite curtailment of our munitions output. Already nearly three quarters of British and British-controlled shipping is primarily employed on the war effort, and only one-quarter is exclusively engaged in feeding and supplying this island.

It might be true to say that the issue of the war depends on whether Hitler's U-boat attack on Allied tonnage, or the increase and application of Allied Air power, reach their full fruition first. The growth of U-boat warfare and its spread to the most distant waters, as well as improvements in U-boat design, in a formidable degree must be expected. Against this may be set the increase of Allied anti-submarine craft and improvement in methods. But here is a struggle in itself.

The War Cabinet Weekly Resumé for week ending 30 July reported a U-boat had been sunk in the Atlantic; otherwise there had been no outstanding events at sea during the week. Shipping losses reported had been lighter than of late. An Atlantic convoy[13] had been repeatedly attacked, and U-boats were active off Trinidad.

Convoys ON.113 and ON.115 were attacked by wolfpacks *Pirat* and *Wolf* between 25 July and 3 August. ON.113 lost three merchant ships sunk, with one damaged, and ON.115 had three sunk and one damaged. One U-boat was sunk by the escort in the attack on ON.115. Bad weather hampered U-boat operations.

The Atlantic convoys would now come under increasing threat of attack as forecast in newspaper reports of an interview given by Dönitz on 27 July and published between 3 and 7 August:

U-BOAT WARFARE

Interview with Nazi Chief

STOCKHOLM, 3 Aug

'Contrary to general opinion, fighting in American waters is not simple,' Admiral Dönitz, U-boat Chief, declared in an interview with the *Svenska*

Dagbladet. 'Americans have rapidly created a defence which inspires respect and also inspires a positive conclusion on the fighting spirit of American crews.'

'Anglo-Saxon leaders lack ideas,' he continued. 'Our wolfpack tactics are successful. U-boat commanders are actually pleased that the enemy has introduced the convoy system.'

Admiral Dönitz ridiculed stories of U-boat bases in neutral territory and also mother ships. 'The secret of our long-range U-boats,' he said, 'is that we sacrifice comfort for range and for fighting qualities. RAF bombardments of U-boat bases in 1940 could have been unpleasant. U-boats are now operating from absolutely bomb-proof concrete sheds.' 'Our intention is to meet new American defences with new hordes of U-boats,' Admiral Dönitz concluded.

Dönitz would later write:

This warning I felt had been necessary to counteract the exaggerated hopes that had been raised among the German people by speeches and by press and radio accounts of the tremendous U-boat successes of the previous months. A correct sense of proportion had to be restored in the public mind.

We now know that my statement to the press was carefully scrutinized by the British admiralty and was regarded as a 'tip straight from the horse's mouth'. My indication of heavier U-boat losses to come was regarded as proof of my intention to resume my attacks once more against the Atlantic convoys.[14]

In early August the international press carried reports of the fresh challenges presented by U-boats and measures to counter these. Their source was an interview given by Dönitz reported in the Swedish newspaper, *Svenska Dagbladet*, published in Stockholm on 2 August 1942. The interview was widely reported in various formats in a range of international newspapers on 3 and 4 August. A typical article which appeared on 4 August 1942 read:

U-BOATS' CHALLENGE

Although Admiral Dönitz's threat to send out new hordes of submarines to counter the latest American defence measures was doubtless calculated to serve a propagandist purpose, especially in South America, the Nazi U-boat chief can claim some notable successes for his counter-blockade since last December. America's inability so far to defeat the U-boats in the Western Atlantic and Caribbean Sea is still hampering the Allied war effort. Not until this menace is under control can we look forward confidently to a great and sustained offensive which will crush Germany and Japan. Armaments are pouring out of American and British factories at a prodigious rate, but until we have reasonably safe sea lanes for their transportation to the overseas theatres of war, this production will remain largely a potential war-making power. Sinkings by submarine in the North Atlantic and around the British Isles have been reduced to almost negligible figures, and now that the United States Navy has put into effect a similar convoy policy we may expect to see a marked reduction of losses in American waters. No computation, of course, can leave out of account the German submarine commanders, who have proved their daring and efficiency.

If current American proposals are developed for a vast fleet of air transport-carriers, the Allies may come to rely on air-transport to combat the U-boats, but this offers no early solution of the problem. For the present we must depend on water-borne transport, and that means that we must beat the U-boat in its own element. There is no need for pessimism on this score. After all, it was only in May that the United States instituted convoys on the eastern seaboard between Florida and Maine; the good results achieved thereby have been off-set by increased sinkings in the Caribbean, where many ships have been working out of convoy, and where, it is strongly suspected, the Germans have secret bases for supplying their submarines. The experience has persuaded the United States Navy Department to revise its earlier opinions against the convoying system, which the British have made so effective that only one out of every 200 convoyed ships has been sunk.

It has also accepted British representations about the value of the corvette for anti-submarine work. Before long, with the sea Powers fighting this enemy on common lines, the improvement in protection of their vital shipping lanes should be made apparent.

Another article dated Tuesday, 4 August 1942 referred to the same interview:

US SEA DEFENCES INSPIRE NAZI RESPECT

STOCKHOLM, Monday (A.A.P.)
Contrary to general opinion, fighting in American waters is not simple, as the Americans have created a defence which inspires respect. Admiral Dönitz, U-boat chief, in an interview with the Swedish newspaper *Svenska*

Dagbladet, said that it also inspired the positive conclusion that the fighting spirit of American crews was high and that Anglo-Saxon leaders lacked ideas.

'Our wolf pack tactics have been successful and U-boat commanders are actually pleased that the enemy introduced the convoy system,' he said. Admiral Dönitz ridiculed the stories of bases in neutral territories; also the claim that the secret of long-range U-boats was sacrifice of comfort for fighting qualities. R.A.F. bombardment of U-boat bases in 1940 could have been unpleasant, but U-boats were now operating from absolutely bomb-proof concrete sheds. 'It is our intention to meet the new American defences with new hordes of U-boats,' he concluded.

One inference to be taken from the final paragraph is that aircraft could not successfully attack U-boats in this particular context. Various published sources, however, directly cite or paraphrase Dönitz as stating during the interview, 'an aeroplane could no more attack a submarine than a crow a mole' or 'an aircraft can no more kill a U-boat than a crow can kill a mole', representing this as a claim that the U-boat generally was invincible to air attack – sometimes in the context of the lack of an effective anti-submarine bomb. Much of this seems speculation, with no primary source for the quote ever cited. However, Stephen Flower in his book *The Dam Busters: An Operational History of Barnes Wallis' Bombs* claims, I would suggest quite correctly, that the words refer to the unsuccessful RAF attempts to destroy the French U-boat pens. Otherwise we are left with another example of a wartime myth.

The first Atlantic convoy to feel the weight of Dönitz's new offensive was SC.94. By the time it was attacked by eight U-boats of wolfpack *Steinbrinck* on 5 August about 450 miles south of Cape Farewell, it consisted of thirty-three ships with seven escort vessels in company, sailing in foggy weather with no air cover. In the first attack one merchant ship was sunk. The next day, in a series of actions, the Canadian destroyer *Assiniboine* rammed and sank *U-210* but was damaged and had to return to base. Two other U-boats were damaged, but the reduced escort repelled all further attacks (including those by the substantial reinforcements sent by Dönitz), until the afternoon of 8 August, when five merchant ships were lost. In the resulting confusion the crews of three others abandoned ship under the impression they had been torpedoed; two crews quickly returned on board, but the third refused to do so, and their ship, though still undamaged was abandoned, to be sunk later by a U-boat. The corvette *Dianthus* rammed and sank *U-379*, and another U-boat was damaged.

On 9 August Dönitz ordered more reinforcements to the scene, but in the afternoon Liberators of No. 120 Squadron from Northern Ireland arrived to escort the convoy at a distance of nearly 800 miles from their base, supported by the US Navy's Catalina flying boats from Iceland. The surface escort and continuous air cover during the day deterred the U-boats. Just after noon, before the first Liberator had arrived, four merchant ships were torpedoed, with three sunk and one left abandoned and burning to sink later. From noon till dusk the air escort was almost continuous, and no more ships were lost. Though many U-boats were attacked by the Liberators and Catalinas, none was damaged; but it was largely the presence of the air cover and the onset of fog which forced the U-boats to abandon the operation. Of the eighteen U-boats taking part, two were sunk and four others damaged.

The War Cabinet Resumé for the week 6 to 13 August noted the general trend of U-boat activity now appeared to be away from the US coasts and West Indies area towards the North-Western Approaches and the African convoy routes. Sixteen ships were reported to have been attacked by U-boats during the week; of these, thirteen were known to have been sunk. The homeward-bound convoy from Canada, in which one ship was reported sunk on the 5th in the previous week's Resumé, was followed by eight U-boats and attacked again on the 8th and 10th. Eight more ships were sunk, including the Commodore's vessel, and one damaged. One tanker was attacked in the Caribbean; two ships, one of which was a tanker, were sunk and two attacked in the Western Atlantic. Groups of U-boats were reported in the following week's Resumé to be disposed on the North Atlantic convoy route, and there had been considerable activity against convoys between Key West and Trinidad. Twenty-nine ships were reported to have been attacked by U-boats during the week; of these, twenty-two were known to have been sunk.

The BdU War Log for 21 August assessed the outcome of the attack on SC.94:

The following report must be made on the subject of the enemy air situation in the East Atlantic:

Number of enemy aircraft have increased, a great variety of aircraft types have appeared, aircraft are equipped with an excellent Radar set against U-boats: all these factors have made the conduct of the U-boat war in the East Atlantic very difficult. Apart from heavy losses (total losses from aircraft in the approach routes in July and August, probably four boats so far), several boats have suffered severe damage and a number slight damage. The enemy's daily reconnaissance covers as far as about 20° west, and U-boat dispositions have therefore to be made far out to the centre of the Atlantic, as, if the dispositions were discovered, the convoys would be re-routed. Besides daily air reconnaissance, it is now known that there are some types of aircraft of particularly long range which are used for convoy escort. Air escort has been flown over convoys chased by U-boats nearly 800 miles away from English bases and England itself. As the War Log of 20 July shows, this has made the operation of boats very difficult and in some cases no longer worthwhile. If development continues at the present rate these problems will lead to irreparable losses, to a decline in successes and consequently to a decline in the chances of success of the U-boat war as a whole.

In view of this situation, I must once more demand the use of the only aircraft which has a range and fighting power capable of combating the enemy aircraft (HE 177) in Biscay and in the Atlantic against convoys.

As a defensive measure against enemy Radar, the fitting of Radar interception gear seems to be successful, as far as can be seen at present. Further experiences will however have to be collected.

In a general view of the operation against Convoy No. 40, radio messages received from U-boats show positively that convoy operations are perfectly possible even against heavily escorted convoys in the Atlantic, and a verbal discussion with several C.O.s who took part has confirmed this to the full.

The BdU War Log summary at 24 August of U-boat losses between September 1939 and August 1942 listed:

Total of boats put into operation since beginning of war	304
Total losses since beginning of war	105
Monthly average loss	2.9
Monthly average ratio of losses to number of operational boats	4:9

The attempts to intercept Atlantic convoys continued. The BdU, anticipating the sailing of ONS.122, deployed wolfpack *Lohs* in a 300-mile-long patrol line directed to search to the north, since earlier ON convoys had all been re-routed closer and closer to Iceland and Greenland. C-in-C Western Approaches, alerted to the movement by decrypts of the BdU signal traffic, attempted to divert the convoy to the south of the patrol line. Unfortunately, as a result of a decryption error, the movement was miscalculated, and *U-135*, which had not followed the other U-boats to the north, sighted the convoy on a south-westerly course on 22 August. The convoy was pursued intermittently over three days, with skirmishes between U-boats and escorts. In the early hours of 25 August three U-boats attacked and sank four merchant ships. These encounters took place in thick fog with visibility at times reduced to less than 330 yards. At noon on 26 August the BdU ordered all U-boats to break off the operation against the convoy after contact was lost in the fog, which persisted throughout the day. In fact, none of the fourteen participating U-boats (ten on their first war patrol) were lost, but eight were damaged; two of these had to abort their patrols and two more were ordered to return to base low on fuel and no longer fully operational.

The Führer Conference of 26 August, assessing current and planned operations in American waters following the introduction of the convoy systems and the need for better air support for U-boats in the Atlantic, concluded:

> The enemy transportation system in American waters underwent great changes, as the *Seekriegsleitung*[15] predicted and expected even sooner. The Americans abandoned individual ship movements off their eastern coast and adopted convoy formation. They have considerably strengthened their defences, particularly in the air. Only occasionally will submarines operate and mine harbour entrances in this area. Some individual ship traffic still takes place in the Caribbean Sea and the Gulf of Mexico; the enemy has just started to organize convoys there. He has increased his defences there too, however. Accordingly, submarine attacks in these areas must be focused on points where the largest number of ships, not sailing in convoys, has been observed; and where ships are expected to sail alone.

British aircraft operating from bases in Newfoundland, Iceland or Northern Ireland still could not protect the convoys over their entire route, and U-boat attacks in the mid-Atlantic air gap continued.

The main body of convoy SC.97 sailed from Halifax on 22 August to be joined by ships from Sydney, Cape Breton and St John's, Newfoundland – a total of sixty-four in all, planned to terminate in Liverpool on 7 September. Six merchant ships returned for various reasons. They were the more fortunate, since nine days later, when the convoy entering the apparent safety of UK waters on 31 August, it was attacked by *U-609*, which torpedoed and sank two merchant ships. The remainder of SC.97's passage was uneventful, with no more U-boat attacks; the remaining merchant ships would reach Liverpool on 7 September.

With the return of the U-boats to the North Atlantic during August, five Atlantic convoys had been attacked by the end of the month, with thirteen ships sunk and four damaged. The coastal waters of the Atlantic from Nova Scotia to the tip of Florida remained free from attacks by U-boats during the entire month, at the end of which the coastal convoy system was further extended, with New York as one of the ports in the system.

Chapter 8

Phase Eight: September to December 1942

Admiral Dönitz wrote in his War Log that aircraft patrols, by forcing U-boats to submerge, frustrated their ability to launch mass attacks. He refers to this in his description of the attack on SC.97 which appeared in the BdU War Log for 3 September, accompanied by yet another appeal for U-boats to be provided with their own effective air cover:

> The early appearance of enemy aircraft to protect their convoys has had a restricting effect on convoy operations, and this fact has forced me again to demand an effective aircraft to combat the enemy air force protecting convoys.
>
> This demand has been made to Naval War Staff, giving the following reasons:
>
> The use of enemy aircraft to escort convoys has again severely restricted convoy operations and caused the total failure of the operation against Convoy No. 49.
>
> The convoy was picked up on 31 August on an east course and during the first day two ships were sunk and two others torpedoed.
>
> Air escort appeared over the convoy already at 0900/1/9 (800 miles from England, 450 miles from Iceland). Air escort was reinforced towards evening. Systematically forcing the U-boats to submerge made them lose contact at evening twilight and thus spoilt all the boats' best chances to attack during the first four moonless hours of the night. The enemy made clever use of the boats' loss of contact to make a sharp leg, so that contact was not regained until 0300 and it was no longer possible to get the boats of the Group (except 2) near to the convoy. The convoy operation had to be broken off on 2.9 in the morning, as it no longer seemed possible for them to haul ahead in the face of the strong enemy air activity expected, and in view of poor visibility they were also exposed to too great a risk from aircraft with radar. Altogether 3 boats had been more or less severely bombed on 1.9.
>
> The English have succeeded in gaining air control of a large sector of the North Atlantic by increasing the ranges of their shore-based aircraft and have thus narrowed down very much the area in which U-boats

can operate without danger from the air. In this connection it has been noticed so far that air patrol is stronger in the east half of the Atlantic than in the west. Reasons for this are probably the small number of air bases in Newfoundland and Greenland and the fact that fewer U-boats have operated in this area. It is to be expected, however, that if U-boats were transferred to the West Atlantic, there would shortly be a stronger air patrol there and conditions would become the same as in the East North Atlantic.

Apart from the serious effects enemy aircraft have so far had on U-boat warfare, i.e. total losses and the large number of boats badly and slightly damaged; enforced shifting of U-boat operations far into the Atlantic and the consequent higher fuel consumption and short operational periods (final result: fewer U-boats in operations areas); greater difficulty in finding the enemy in the open Atlantic.

The BdU is gravely concerned at the prospect of the same unfavourable air situation over the convoys extending to almost all parts of the North Atlantic, the main battleground of U-boats; this will undoubtedly be the case if things develop at their present rate. Unless suitable counter-measures can be taken, prospects of success by U-boats will be reduced to an unjustifiable extent.

The urgent need to counteract enemy aircraft protecting convoys must therefore be emphasized once more. The BdU therefore requests every emphasis be laid on the development of an effective aircraft with long range, in the interests of continued effective U-boat warfare.

Fortunately for Dönitz, it would still be another seven months before the Allies achieved almost total air cover. Indeed, during those seven months U-boats would achieve their greatest successes against convoys in the air gap. It is no surprise, then, that Dönitz began concentrating his U-boats in the air gap in 1942, noting:

We did our utmost to attack convoys in mid-Atlantic, where they were beyond the range of land-based aircraft, and where we could be sure of finding them with no cover at all.

The ongoing importance of the Battle of the Atlantic was emphasised in a speech given by the First Lord of the Admiralty on 3 September and reported in the press two days later:

Importance of Atlantic Battle

LONDON, 3 September

The First Lord of the Admiralty (Mr A. V. Alexander), in a speech at the War Anniversary lunch, said the Battle of the Atlantic remains of the highest possible importance. July and August were our most successful months of the war for the numbers of U-boats destroyed. We also damaged a large number of U-boats, putting them out of action for varying periods. If the U-boats found conditions dangerous last year they will find them doubly dangerous now. New methods have been developed and new devices are in action to combat them. Apart from other losses, the Italian submarine fleet was now little more than half the size with which it entered the war. Despite our losses in the Far East we have built up a powerful fleet in the Indian Ocean.

The *Express* naval correspondent says Mr. A. V. Alexander's statement must mean that more than 28 U-boats were destroyed In July and August. Previous records announced in the early months of the war an average of 31 U-boats sunk weekly.

He adds: 'It is doubtful if Germany, even with the help of building resources in occupied countries, is producing more than 14 ocean-going U-boats monthly.'

Five days later, Churchill addressed the House of Commons on the Progress of the War.[1] Commenting on anti-U-boat warfare, he said:

The losses at sea are still very heavy, but I am glad to say that the months of July, August, and September so far as it has run, are a definite improvement on those which preceded them. This is due largely to the continued development and completion of the convoy system off the American coast, and this improvement has been effected in spite of heavy losses in war operations, such as the Russian and Malta convoys.

In September, New York became the main western terminus for the transatlantic convoys, with HX and SC convoys beginning and ON convoys terminating their passage there. The first HX convoy, HX.208, sailed from New York on 17 September, and the first SC convoy, SC.102, two days later. The first ON convoy, ON.125, arrived in New York on 12 September.

Five North Atlantic convoys were targeted during September 1942. The first, ON.127, was attacked between the 10th and 14th by twelve U-boats of wolfpack *Vorwärts*. Over a period of five days seven merchant ships and one escort were sunk and four merchant ships damaged. The second convoy attacked, slow convoy SC.100, had departed Halifax on 12 September. It had been scattered by a violent storm when U-boats found it on 18 September. Two wolfpacks – *Lohs* (nine boats) and *Pfeil* (eight boats) – were deployed, sinking five stragglers between 20 and 24 September before losing contact the following day. The BdU account of the operation read:

> The B-Dienst was able to decode a course instruction concerning convoy SC.100. Wolfpack *Lohs* was deployed and the convoy of 24 merchant ships detected on 18 September. The contact-keeping U-boat was, however, immediately shaken off by evasive movement, and the U-boats were unable to attack in the night. A gale prevented the U-boats attacking the following day and made it difficult to approach; but also some merchant ships had trouble keeping up with the convoy. After the failure of the boats of *Gruppe Lohs* to re-establish contact in the previous night, the *Gruppe Pfeil* was also thrown into the pursuit.
>
> The weather was deteriorating rapidly and made further attacks impossible. The operation was temporarily broken off on the 22nd and resumed on the 23rd, when two ships were sunk; two more were sunk on the 24th.
>
> Further attacks had no success, and the operation was finally broken off on the 25th.

In the week between 17 and 24 September ninety U-boats were estimated to be operating in the Atlantic. Between 24 and 29 September merchant ships from three other convoys were attacked. ON.131 lost one straggler on the 24th, HX.209 had one damaged on the 29th and SC.101 suffered one straggler sunk the same day.

In his conference with Hitler on 28 September to review the state of the Battle of the Atlantic, Dönitz confirmed that he had, following the lack of successes of U-boat operations on the American coast, shifted the focus of the struggle to combating convoys in the North Atlantic. He was confident the greater number of U-boats now operating would make discovery of the enemy more likely, as convoys were now normally proceeding on the direct 'Great Circle' routes, it being thought roundabout routes were being avoided to maximize tonnage. This was not without risk; convoys were strongly guarded, with escort vessels stationed around the convoy as close defence, a certain number remaining inside the convoy, and a distant screen of destroyers which hampered the approach of U-boats.

Once again Dönitz emphasised the main challenge now for the U-boat was the menace of enemy aircraft, increases in the range of which between 1940 and 1942 had shifted the area of intensive attack by U-boats out into the central

President Roosevelt with Special Adviser Harry Hopkins, September 1938.

Churchill as First Lord of the Admiralty, 3 September 1939.

SS *Athenia*. (*National Archives of Canada, PA-056818*)

Lend-Lease Destroyers HMS *Castleton* (ex USS *Aaron Ward* (DD.132)) and HMS *Clare* (ex USS *Abel P. Upshur* (DD.193)) at Devonport, September 1940. (*IWM A 724*)

Convoy ON.34, December 1940. (*IWM A 6637*)

SS *Beacon Grange*, 27 April 1941.

U-110 and HMS *Bulldog*, 9 May 1941.

HMS *Vanoc*. Atlantic Convoy Escort, July 1941. (*IWM A 4581*)

HMS *Vanoc* on escort duty with Atlantic convoy. (*IWM A 4586*)

St John's, Newfoundland. Convoy assembly point, c. August 1941. (*NH 86946*)

HMS *Banff* (ex USN Coastguard Cutter *Saranac*). (*IWM FL 1381*)

CAM ship *Empire Spray*, 22 October 1941. Convoy ON.28. (*IWM C 0450*)

Battle of the Atlantic, October 1941. Convoy escort. (*IWM A 5668*)

Officers on the bridge of a destroyer, escorting a large convoy of ships, keep a sharp look out for attacking enemy submarines during the Battle of the Atlantic. (*IWM A 5667*)

CAM ship SS *Novelist*. Convoy ON.34. (*IWM A 6638*)

HMS *Kingston Cyanite* (sister ship to *Kingston Ceylonite*). (*IWM FL 14415*)

Convoy HX.188 leaving Halifax. (*Canadian War Museum*)

German U-boat commander tracking a British merchant ship through his periscope during an attack on a convoy, 10–20 June 1942. (*IWM HU 40239*)

North Atlantic convoy of twenty-four ships steaming south of Newfoundland, Canada, on 28 July 1942. (*NARA, 80-G-21187*)

Tanker *Pennsylvania Sun* burning after attack by *U-571*, 15 July 1942. (*NMUSN, 80-G-61599*)

Convoy being protected by corvette, December 1942.

German battleship *Admiral Scheer*, 1942.

U-442 in front of what is believed to be burning tanker *Empire Lytton* of convoy TM.1 on 9 January 1943. Bound to North Africa from Aruba, the convoy lost eight of its nine tankers. (Photo taken from *U-578*). (*Naval History and Heritage Command, NH 111257*)

HMS *Scylla* in the North Atlantic, February 1943. (*IWM A 15365*)

HMS *Lagan*, 4 February 1943. (*IWM A 14733*)

Convoy rescue ship *Zamalek*, Convoy ON.165. (*IWM A 13378*)

Escort Carrier HMS *Archer*, 18 February 1943. (*IWM A 14602*)

German U-boat *U-118* attacked and sunk 12 June 1943 by aircraft from USS *Bogue* (ACV-9). (*Naval History and Heritage Command, 80-G-68694*)

Stalin, Roosevelt, and Churchill (the big three) at the Tehran Conference, 28 November 1943.

A British convoy under the protection of Royal Air Force Coastal Command, 1943. (*IWM C 2644*)

A depth charge explodes astern of HMS *Starling*. (*Wikimedia Commons*)

On 4 June 1944, the US flag flies over the German naval ensign on *U-505*, with the German submarine's periscope serving as the flagstaff. The photo was taken soon after the submarine's capture. USS *Guadalcanal* (CVE-60) in the background. (*Naval History and Heritage Command, 80-G-324800*)

Hedgehog anti-submarine mortar. (*IWM A 31000*)

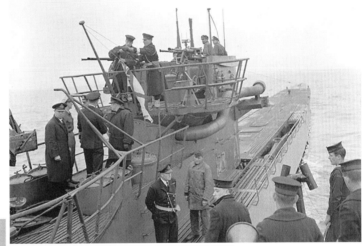

Surrender of *U-889* near Shelburne, Nova Scotia, 13 May 1945.

Canadian seamen raise the White Ensign above a German submarine in St John's, Newfoundland, 1945.

An RCN crew handles the surrendered *U-889* off Shelburne, Nova Scotia, as a Royal Canadian Air Force (RCAF) Canso flying boat passes overhead.

Hudson A/C over convoy. (*IWM CH 2859*)

Short Sunderland Flying Boat. (*IWM CH 7504*)

Leigh Light. (*IWM CH 13997*)

FW200 Condor.

An RCAF B-24 Liberator flies patrol over an Atlantic convoy. Safeguarding the sea lanes between North America and Europe was central to the Allied strategy in the Second World War. (*Archives of Canada*)

An Atlantic convoy underway as seen from a Royal Air Force Short Sunderland flying boat. (*Dennis Richards and Hilary St. George Saunders:* Royal Air Force 1939–1945. Volume II: The Fight Avails; *London, HMSO, 1953*)

Grand Admiral Karl Dönitz. (*Bundesarchiv, Bild 146-1976-127-06A*)

USN Fleet Admiral King.

Atlantic. Dönitz then announced the U-boat and its weapons were undergoing technical improvements, to counter the strengthened enemy defences, priority being given to measures to increase the speed of boats when submerged – this would be the 'Walter' U-boat. Other measures were designed to improve the ability of U-boats to dive to greater depths to evade enemy ASDIC location and minimize the effect of depth charges. The acoustic torpedo was to be introduced to help eliminate the escorts, which prevented the U-boats from taking up firing positions; and owing to the growth of the air menace it would be necessary to strengthen the U-boat's AA armament.

Hitler reiterated his belief in the decisive importance of the U-boat war, regarded by the Naval Staff as a 'Tonnage War' on the working principle of 'sink, anywhere, whether laden or unladen', a policy which had great success, especially in 1942. The aim of the Naval Staffs of all three Axis Powers, Hitler stressed, must be to attain and keep the figure of enemy tonnage sunk above that which the enemy could build. At present the only way of pursuing the war against Britain was by means of the Kriegsmarine, whose best weapon of attack was the U-boat, and it must be used to the best advantage; but no war in history had yet been won by using only one weapon. It was far more effective to use all available weapons to attack the enemy's weakest spot, and the Luftwaffe and surface vessels must be used to intensify and reinforce the U-boat war.

By 30 September Dönitz had 367 U-boats, of which 199 were available for operations, 112 were engaged on trials and final tests and fifty-six were being used for training. Up to 1 September 1942, cumulative losses had reached 105 boats.

The BdU assessment for 30 September of the convoy situation in the North Atlantic reflected Dönitz's brief:

> Contrary to convoy methods during the first six months of 1942, convoys are now scattered over a wider area. Even so, the spacing out was not nearly so great as in autumn 1941 and remains within certain limits on either side of the Great Circle. Information gathered through radio intercept intelligence and experience gained on the timing of convoys has made it possible to track down convoys, especially when westbound. Prospects are still considered favourable in this respect. The successes scored against the convoy from 9–13.9 and the failure from 20–22.9 clearly shows the decisive role played by the weather. When operating against North Atlantic convoys the medium-sized submarines have the advantage.

By October it had become evident that U-boats were returning to the North Atlantic in force to attack Atlantic convoys in the mid-ocean gap beyond the range of land-based reconnaissance aircraft. This would give them freedom to operate on the surface in wolfpacks – often of ten or more and occasionally as many as thirty to forty U-boats. Their numbers also now reached the point at which Dönitz was able to permanently operate two large wolf packs in the mid-ocean air gap, one on its eastern edge, the other on the western.

Notwithstanding this increase in numbers, the BdU War Log of 2 October complained that, anti-submarine conditions being as they were (large number of enemy destroyers and corvettes, surface radar sets, and the Kriegsmarine's own developments not keeping pace), it was essential to have the necessary large number of U-boats to effectively combat convoys, split up enemy anti-submarine forces and maintain continuous shadowing. The convoy routes were so uncertain and sea areas so extensive that the few U-boats available had to be disposed in very shallow patrol lines. With weather conditions being on average bad, it took a very long time for U-boats to come up on a convoy once it was sighted. Experience of several convoy operations had shown a successful action could only be fought, as a rule, in sea areas outside the range of the enemy air force, after early detection of the convoy on the side of the Atlantic from which it set out. As result, U-boats leaving home ports and western France were to be deployed against ON convoys; after picking up a convoy they were to proceed south-west, operating against it but breaking off the operation (in the area of the Newfoundland Bank) to pick up SC or HX convoys.

The different experiences of convoys SC.104 and HX.209 illustrated the value of effective air cover in preventing concentrated U-boat attacks from developing and disrupting convoy formations. The BdU War Log noted that attempts to attack H.209 between 1 and 6 October again proved how difficult it was to fight convoy actions in areas with strong air patrols. The early appearance of enemy aircraft indicated there were now air bases in Greenland. The BdU hoped, as winter went on and the Greenland coast iced up, that the flying boats would not be able to take off, allowing the U-boats to operate further east without the threat of enemy aircraft. The results of the convoy operation confirm the opinion expressed in the War Log of 2 October, i.e. that convoys must be picked up on the side of the Atlantic from which they started. As Dönitz later recognized, violent storms had ruined operations against the two convoys.

The Admiralty estimated over a hundred U-boats were operating in the Atlantic during the first week of October, with concentrations on the convoy routes outside the effective range of aircraft based on Ireland (R)[2] and Canada and considerable activity east of Trinidad.

Churchill did not underestimate the severity of the U-boat threat. On 12 October, in a speech in Edinburgh on being made a Freeman of the City, he said:

The U-boat warfare still remains the greatest problem of the United Nations, but there is no reason whatever why it should not be solved by the prodigious measures of offence and defence and of replacement on which Britain, Canada, and above all the United States are now engaged.

The months of August and September have been, I will not say the best, but the least bad months since January. They have seen the new building of merchant ships substantially outweigh the losses.

The first serious attack of October centred on convoy SC.104 en route from Sydney, Cape Breton to Liverpool, sighted and reported by a U-boat on 11 October, when ten U-boats of wolfpack *Wotan* were vectored onto its route. By 13 October three were shadowing the convoy, to be joined during the day by five more. In the first attack in the very early hours of 14 October four merchant ships and the whale factory ship *Southern Empress* were sunk. The wolfpack continued to shadow SC.104 but was unable to mount any successful attacks that night. The following day, *U-661* was detected in fog, rammed and sunk by the destroyer *Viscount*, and the destroyer *Fame* rammed and sank *U-353*. On 16 and 17 October SC.104 came within range of anti-submarine air patrols by long-range Liberators and Catalina flying boats, which were able to disrupt any further attacks. On 17 October Dönitz terminated the operation against SC.104, which reached Liverpool on 21 October. SC.104 lost eight merchant ships and ten landing craft (carried as deck cargo), with two destroyers damaged. In counter-attacks by the escort two U-boats had been sunk and two damaged.

Despite the pressing need for VLR (Very Long Range) aircraft to deter and attack U-boats in the mid-Atlantic air gap, Churchill continued to prioritize the bombing offensive over Germany. In his Memorandum of 24 October to the War Cabinet on the Policy for the Conduct of the War[3] he wrote:

There preys upon us as the greatest danger to the United Nations, and particularly to our Island, the U-boat attack. The Navy call for greater assistance from the Air. I am proposing to my colleagues that we try for the present to obtain this extra assistance mainly from the United States, and that we encroach as little as possible upon our Bomber effort against Germany, which is of peculiar importance during these winter months. I have, on the contrary, asked for an increase in the Bomber effort, rising to 50 squadrons by the end of the year. Thereafter our bombing power will increase through the maturing of production. It may be that early in 1943 we shall have to damp down the Bomber offensive against Germany in order to meet the stress and peril of the U-boat war. I hope and trust not, but by then it will be possible at any rate to peg our bomber offensive at a higher level than at present. The issue is not one of principle, but of emphasis. At present, in spite of U-boat losses, the Bomber offensive should have first place in our air effort.

After the attack on SC.104, *Wotan* was relieved by wolfpack *Puma* of thirteen boats, which attacked three convoys between 22 and 29 October The first, ON.139, lost two merchant ships on 22 October, the second, ONS.136, a straggler the next day. The third convoy, HX.212, was sighted by *U-436* on 26 October. Heavy seas made it difficult for the escorts to use their radar to detect and deter the U-boats, and a British whale factory ship was sunk late on the 27th. The following day, two more merchant ships were sunk and one damaged. In the first few minutes of the 29th a straggler and two merchant ships from the convoy were sunk. Later on the 29th, the air escort drove off the U-boats and the wolfpack operation was terminated.

The following day, a BdU assessment of the 'Convoy Situation in the North Atlantic' speculated on the reasons for possible changes to convoy routing and future expectations:

If pressure from U-boats continues, it is to be expected convoys on the N. Atlantic route will in principle adopt a more scattered formation by comparison with their present sailing directions on this traffic route, but such a formation has not been observed so far.

When two westbound convoys [probably ON.131 and ON.133] were encountered in September much further north than hitherto mentioned in the previous reference, this was probably due to the fact that from the middle of September [starting with ON.131] the centre of ON traffic was transferred north.

Nevertheless, after this, of eleven convoys picked up, three still used the southern sector of the North Atlantic route. It was not clear whether this was the beginning of wide scattering of the whole of ON traffic, or whether the enemy was routing this traffic according to an unknown plan (perhaps based on speed or time of sailing) in order to have a part in the north and a part in the south sector of the main route.

Eastbound convoys, however, had not been diverted north of the routes established in June and July, and wider scattering than hitherto in the formation of these convoys has not been observed.

The U-boats' efforts were also frustrated by extremely stormy weather during the month.

Towards the end of October, convoy SC.107 came under sustained attack by a large number of U-boats after it passed out of the range of air cover from Newfoundland. Wolfpack *Veilchen* of thirteen U-boats was formed on 24 October and stationed east of Newfoundland to intercept eastbound

Atlantic convoys. On 30 October SC.107 of forty-four ships, which sailed from New York on 24 October, was detected by *U-522*, and all thirteen U-boats of wolfpack *Veilchen* plus *U-520* and *U-521* were ordered to attack. Their radio transmissions were detected and left the Admiralty in no doubt the convoy was in imminent danger. Two destroyers of the Western Local Escort were ordered to remain with the convoy, and an air escort was provided. The latter sank two U-boats on 30 October. On 1 November SC.107 entered the 'black pit', the area devoid of air cover. In the early hours of 2 November the escorts were overwhelmed by the U-boats, which sank nine merchant ships and damaged another. Two more merchant ships were sunk on 3 November and a further four the next day. The following day, Liberators of 120 Squadron RAF arrived and drove off the wolfpack. With fifteen merchant ships sunk, SC.107 suffered the heaviest loss of any trans-Atlantic convoy in the winter of 1942–43.

Churchill later wrote:

In September and October the Germans reverted to the earlier practice of submerged attack by day. With the larger numbers now working in the 'wolf packs', and with our limited resources, serious losses in convoy could not be prevented. It was now that we felt most acutely the lack of sufficient numbers of very long-range (VLR) aircraft in the Coastal Command. Air cover still ranged no more than about 600 miles from our shore bases, and only about 400 from Newfoundland.

Naval escorts alone, although providing reasonable protection against attacks launched in the traditional manner by submerged U-boats in daylight, could never range widely from the convoys and break up the heavy concentrations on the flanks. Thus when the 'wolf packs' struck they could deliver a combined blow in numbers sufficient to saturate the defence. We realized that the remedy lay in surrounding each convoy not only with surface escorts, but also with a screen of aircraft sufficient to find and force any U-boats nearby to dive, thus providing a lane through which the convoy might move unmolested. This purely defensive measure was not in itself enough. To overcome the U-boats we must seek out and attack them vigorously wherever we could find them, both by sea and air. The aircraft, the trained air crews, and the air weapons needed were not yet numerous enough to have a decisive influence, but we now made a start by forming a 'Support Group' of surface forces.[4]

Meanwhile, on 4 November, barely a week and a half after releasing his Memorandum of 24 October, Churchill made an abrupt volte-face after becoming aware of the extent of the October shipping losses. U-boats, largely operating in the air gap, had sunk ninety-four merchant ships – forty-one from

North Atlantic convoys alone. Realizing that a continuation of losses at this rate would seriously endanger British imports and preparations for an Allied invasion of Europe, Churchill reconstructed the Battle of the Atlantic Committee in a new form and with a somewhat different grouping of Departments, under the title of the 'Anti-U-boat Warfare Committee',[5] the first meeting of which would be held on 4 November. Chaired by himself, the new committee consisted of those 'who were responsible for the conduct of the war at sea' with as a main priority the remit to discover 'how to bring about first quick relief then achieve a solution' to the U-boat threat.

At the Committee's first meeting on 4 November, members immediately tackled the air gap issue. In a telling memo, the First Lord of the Admiralty stressed that 'The air had been of great help in meeting the U-boat menace; but there was a blind spot in the centre of the North Atlantic where no air cover was provided, and it was here that our heaviest losses occurred. Aircraft with an overall range of 2,500 miles would be needed to cover this area.' At that very moment in the air gap, a battle was raging around SC.107, an engagement which provided a crucial example of both the need to close the air gap and the effectiveness of VLR aircraft in the defence of convoys. It was only on 5 November that 120 Squadron was able to provide coverage for SC.107, 650 miles south-east of Iceland, driving off the remaining-boats and causing Dönitz to break off the attacks.

The second meeting of the Committee on 12 November decided the only solution was to remove thirty-three Liberators from the Bay of Biscay air offensive, convert them to VLR and allocate them to serve with 120 Squadron and the recently created No. 86 VLR squadron.

Hitler was advised at the Führer Conference on Naval Affairs of 13 November that a group of fourteen U-boats was in the North Atlantic, reinforced mainly by U-boats from German bases. Attacks on North Atlantic convoys were judged especially successful at this time when enemy escorts were weak. The remaining available U-boats would be used in the North Atlantic and current zones of operations to exploit the weakness of enemy escort forces and inflict the largest possible losses on enemy shipping. Hitler ordered that opportunities in the Atlantic resulting from the reduction in enemy escort forces be exploited.

The Lord Privy Seal took steps on 18 November during the Debate on the Address[6] to assure the House of Commons every effort was being made to combat the U-boat threat:

> The most serious problem of those which have been mentioned by Hon.
> Members in the course of the Debate which faces us today is that of the
> U-boat. The fact that we do not widely advertise the steps that are being
> taken to cope with this menace must not lead Hon. Members to think that

we are doing nothing in the matter. In fact very special measures are being taken to make effective both our offensive and our defensive operations in this important field – that is, as effective as the skill of our scientists and the courage of our seamen and airmen can make them. The country indeed owes a very deep debt of gratitude both to our navy and to our merchant seamen for the endless resource and courage they have shown in fighting the U-boats over three years of war. The skill and endurance of the men of the Coastal Command have also done very much indeed to assist in securing for us those vital cargoes of food and raw material which have kept our war effort not only alive but ever-growing throughout that period. Sea power remains the vital key to our success and a first charge upon our resources.

The 18 November estimate of the U-boat situation found the BdU clearly convinced the bulk of the U-boat war must be carried out in the Atlantic; only the war against tonnage would be effective, and any deviation from this fundamental concept would damage the total war effort. The same day, in London, the Anti-U-boat Warfare Committee in their third meeting finally sanctioned a change in strategy, placing the defence of trade above the bomber offensive and the Bay of Biscay offensive in the list of priorities. It had only taken three years for the British to give adequate precedence to this defensive measure. The Second Sea Lord observed, 'Our fight with the Air Ministry becomes more and more fierce as the war proceeds. It is a much more savage one than our war with the Huns, which is very unsatisfactory and such a waste of effort.' There were two options available. The first was to increase the number of shore-based VLR aircraft, which had the advantage of not requiring protection. However, Britain did not produce any, and the available US models needed modification, which delayed delivery by a few months. The second option was coverage by aircraft carriers. The Royal Navy had several at the beginning of the war, and America had shared some with Britain, but these had been deployed to the Mediterranean theatre. The Navy had begun building smaller carriers for convoy escort, but their construction was delayed while their design was modified to include increased capabilities, postponing the availability of an asset which could have reduced shipping losses.

  Wolfpack *Kreuzotter*, the only wolfpack left to operate against the North Atlantic convoy routes between 8 and 24 November after the withdrawal of all other available boats to oppose the Allied landings in North Africa, sighted convoy ONS.144 on 15 November, but lost contact until two days later, when two merchant ships were sunk, followed by three more merchant ships and an escort the following day. On 19 November the escort was reinforced and the U-boats driven off.

A BdU situation report for 19 November on 'Disposition of U-boats and Intentions' noted fifty-seven boats and two U-tankers were in the operational area in Atlantic, thirty-three being outward- or inward-bound. A group of fourteen boats from Germany was in the North Atlantic; attacks on North Atlantic convoys were at present very successful owing to weak enemy escorts.

Convoy ON.145 was attacked by a single U-boat about 200 miles south-east of Sydney, Cape Breton. One merchant ship was sunk and two damaged. The merchant ship sunk – the *Empire Sailor* – carried 2,700 tons of general cargo, including 270 tons of phosgene bombs, 60 tons of mustard gas, 100 tons of commercial cyanide and 300 tons of mail. The explosion of the torpedo released a quantity of phosgene gas which killed seventeen crew members and three gunners. A report to the Admiralty by the Commander of the escort *Wanderer* contained these remarks:

> No precautions had been taken onboard, apparently only the senior officers being aware of the nature of the cargo. If the crew had carried ordinary service respirators they would have been adequately protected. These respirators were not even carried on board. It is submitted that these facts should be made the subject for a full enquiry, as it seems that there are some who do not realize that our merchant navy have enough to put up with without having to die horrible deaths caused by their own cargo. The effect of this occurrence on the morale of merchant seamen in Halifax can readily be imagined.

The rate of shipping losses to U-boat attacks now reached the point that, on 22 November, the First Sea Lord told Churchill the situation in the North Atlantic could not be allowed to continue. The Minister of War Transport had represented that if the convoys continue to be 'knocked about in the Atlantic as at present', there were signs that merchant seamen might refuse to sail. In order to tackle the rate of losses, approval had now been given for very long-range aircraft to be provided, but the numbers required would not be available for some considerable time, and in any case the First Sea Lord did not feel air protection could be relied on entirely to deal with this dangerous situation in the Central Atlantic, as there were so many days on which aircraft might not be able to fly. It was essential, therefore, that the escort situation be improved. Owing to Operation TORCH (the Allied invasion of North Africa), it was quite impossible at the present time to strengthen all the escorts, and the situation must be dealt with as best it could by using reinforcing groups. Certain proposals put to the Canadians and Americans for temporarily augmenting the escorts over the western portion of the mid-ocean voyage had been agreed to, although it seriously weakened their escorts on the run west of Newfoundland

and would have to be cancelled if the U-boats moved again in strength to that area. Two reinforcing groups were required to deal with the western half of the dangerous area. The Royal Navy could just scrape together one of these groups from ships returning from TORCH, and the First Sea Lord, explaining to the Americans the urgency of the requirement, requested them to release a group of the British escorts operating on the convoy route between Guantanamo and New York. Despite these concerns, the week between 19 and 26 November proved remarkably quiet, reflecting the withdrawal of some twenty to twenty-five U-boats from the Atlantic trade routes for operations in the Gibraltar approaches and western Mediterranean.

In the War Cabinet discussions of 28 November on Manpower Requirements for 1943,[7] Churchill focussed on shipbuilding and ship-repair priorities:

> The greatest danger which now confronts us is the U-boat peril. We must expect attack by increasingly large numbers and spread over wider areas. The highest priority must therefore be accorded to vessels and weapons for use against the U-boat. No construction of merchant shipbuilding below 1,100,000 tons or slowing down of repair work can be accepted.

By November forty-two U-boats were deployed between Greenland and the Azores, and thirty-nine active elsewhere in the Atlantic. Although by 1 December 154 U-boats were assigned to Atlantic operations, the month saw fewer attacks on the Atlantic convoys. Three convoys – ONS.146, ON.149 and HX.217 – were attacked between the 3rd and the 9th, with nine merchant ships (including one straggler) sunk.

In a highly significant development in the intelligence war on 13 December, after a ten-month gap, the cryptologists at Bletchley Park finally broke the U-boat 'Triton' code used for Atlantic operations. Now, and for the remainder of the war, U-boat radio transmissions would be intercepted and read, and the intelligence gained used to route convoys away from the wolfpacks.

No convoys were attacked after 9 December until on 16 December ON.153 was attacked by wolfpack *Raufbold*, with three merchant ships sunk; a destroyer escort was sunk the following day and a straggler on 20 December. ON.152 lost two stragglers, one each on 18 and 21 December. Most convoys passed through the danger area without incident, including HX.219, otherwise notable for the ramming and sinking of *U-357* by the destroyer *Hesperus* on the night of 26 December about 30 miles astern of the convoy. The convoy experienced severe weather conditions, with several ships suffering storm damage.

Weather conditions in the North Atlantic were described in the BdU submarine situation report for 19 December:

The weather during December made refuelling of U-boats in the North Atlantic almost impossible. Most of those out in the North Atlantic would shortly have to return to base.

As an example of the effect caused by boats being withdrawn, only three boats could at first be sent against 'HX219', about which excellent radio intercept intelligence was available. Had more boats been on hand, successes would have been far greater.

Total reported U-boat strength on 24 December approached 400, compared to 250 in January, despite eighty-six submarines being lost during the year. Of the total, over 200 were operational. Many were on passage, but the numbers on patrol were still large and growing, with most operating in the North Atlantic or west of Gibraltar.

It frequently took some weeks for any reports on significant convoy battles to appear in the press, but on 28 December reports appeared of the attack on SC.104:

U-BOAT ATTACKS

NORTH ATLANTIC ACTIONS

LONDON, 26 December

In a series of actions extending over four days and nights, escorts of a North Atlantic convoy, bound for Britain, fought off repeated attacks by U-boats. The convoy did not escape but two U-boats were destroyed, and several others were damaged.

Describing the attacks the Admiralty states that 'escorts were under Commander R. Heathcote, in the destroyer HMS *Fame*. Several escort vessels were corvettes of the Royal Norwegian Navy.'

One October morning in very heavy seas U-boats were reported. One broke the surface ahead of HMS *Viscount* which attempted to ram it, but the U-boat succeeded in clearing the destroyer's bow. The destroyer turned and again attempted to ram it, but the heavy seas obscured the U-boat which altered its course rapidly and dived. Depth charges were dropped, and a large patch of oil was seen. The U-boat probably was severely damaged.

Repeatedly sighted

For the next three days and nights U-boats were repeatedly sighted. Numerous attacks were carried out. At least two U-boats were damaged by depth charges in the dark. Towards the dawn of the fourth day the

Viscount sighted a U-boat and closed at full speed to ram it. The enemy boat increased its speed and attempted to escape, but the destroyed manoeuvred so swiftly that she rammed the U-boat aft of the conning tower. The *Viscount*'s stem struck the U-boat squarely, then lifted and crashed down on top, pinning her under for 15 seconds.

The following day, the *Fame* carried out a depth charge attack on a U-boat. Large bubbles were seen, and the U-boat broke the surface. The *Fame* opened fire and closing at full speed the U-boat stopped on even keel and the *Fame* rammed it, dropping depth charges as she broke clear. The enemy crew abandoned the U-boat, which later sank.

Only one convoy, ONS.154, suffered heavy losses in the North Atlantic during the month. Sailing on a more southerly route, as it drew out of the range of air cover it was persistently attacked between 26 and 30 December by the nineteen U-boats of wolfpacks *Spitz* and *Ungestum*, which pursued the convoy for four days. Between 27 and 30 December they sank thirteen merchant ships, damaged two more and sank the special service ship HMS *Fidelity*, which had fallen behind with engine trouble. One straggler from ONS.156 had been sunk on 29 December.

The German Admiralty was clearly disappointed not to have sunk more merchant ships, as revealed in a press report dated 31 December:

NAZI ADMIRAL ADMITS U-BOAT
SINKINGS LOWER

LONDON, Wednesday

Allied shipping losses have fallen this month, according to the German Admiralty's spokesman, Admiral Lutzow.

Speaking over Berlin radio, he said that this was due to Britain naturally using her sea routes in the Atlantic, which was ten times the size of Europe, also to the weather, which in autumn and winter was rough, and visibility, which was usually bad.

'In addition,' he said, 'the enemy has been working to improve defences against U-boats. The temporarily low figures of shipping losses do not indicate that the enemy has mastered the U-boat threat.'

Six Atlantic convoys had been attacked during the month for the loss of twenty-seven merchant ships. By the end of December 1942, Coastal Command still had only one squadron of VLR aircraft capable of patrolling the mid-Atlantic.

Chapter 9

Phase Nine: January to June 1943

On 1 January 1943 there were 164 operational U-boats in Atlantic The month opened with extremely stormy weather which, combined with the adoption of wider evasive routing of convoys, disrupted attempts by U-boats to locate and attack convoys and brought about a dramatic reduction in the rate of merchant ship losses.

A BdU War Log entry for 8 January criticised the results being achieved in the North Atlantic as being currently unsatisfactory:

> The thirteen boats of *Falke* (28 December to 9 January) formed the only operational wolfpack in the area. The assembly of a second wolfpack *Jaguar* of eleven U-boats was being delayed by weather conditions (until 10 January). The lack of high priority radio intercept intelligence led to great uncertainty about the dates of departure and routes of 'ON' and 'ONS' convoys. It was difficult to pick up one of these convoys with only one group of submarines operating in the eastern area of the Atlantic. Since hardly any independents were now met with in the North Atlantic, the fact that 'ON' convoy was missed (31.12– 2.1.1943) meant no successes for eight days. Thirteen boats were not sufficient to track down the convoy when data was scanty. The convoy may have passed the patrol strip to the east or north-west, or it may even have sailed right through the patrol during the bad weather between 31.12.42 and 2.1.43 without being sighted.
>
> The failure to contact the convoy meant greater uncertainty about the route. This could be clarified when more boats were available to extend the patrol line with boats stationed closer together. Time will show whether the thirteen boats would succeed in tracking down the 'ONS' convoy expected between 7 and 9 January. On this occasion it was not possible for the boats to cruise to the west each night to cover the night-run, as this would leave the boats insufficient space for attack in the west.

Western Allied leaders, meeting at the Casablanca Conference attended by Roosevelt and Churchill and held between 14 and 24 January 1943 to plan the conduct of the next phase of the war, faced the very real possibility that failure to secure the main Atlantic convoy routes would seriously threaten any attempt to open a Second Front in mainland Europe. The Combined Chiefs of Staff therefore declared, 'The defeat of the U-boat must remain a first charge on the resources of the United Nations' and agreed to provide eighty VLR aircraft to close the mid-Atlantic air gap. As the leaders were meeting, further press reports appeared on 14 January:

SEA WOLVES

There have been recent unpleasant and even tragic reminders that the U-boat menace is still with us, and that the Battle of the Atlantic has yet to be won. The outlook improved – up to that time it had been nothing short of alarming – when, a few months ago, the rate of Allied shipbuilding overtook the rate at which our merchantmen were being sunk; but the recent discovery that Germany is building submarines, as we are building surface craft, faster than they can be destroyed, is not indicative of any early or decisive defeat for the Axis to the ugly type of sea warfare by means of which, despite the Kaiser's eventual failure as an under-water pirate, Hitler still hopes to starve and subdue the hated English. The U-boats that now infest the seaways are bigger, stronger, faster and in every sense more formidable than those of the last war; and. like wolves, they have learned to hunt in packs. They will be mastered, in their turn; but there is still a grim struggle in prospect.

On 15 January the BdU War Log complained:

Neither the 'SC' nor the 'HX' convoys were contacted by wolfpack *Jaguar*. Delays in refuelling reduced the wolfpack to six boats. Probably 'SC' and 'HX' passed to the north of the submarine disposition. These two convoys brought the total up to four missed since 31 December. It was assumed the enemy had left the convoy routes he had been sailing for nearly five months and was again scattering his convoy routes. This development was a great drawback to attacks by our boats, but only to be expected.

   Probably the convoy routes to the north have been moved into the patrol areas of the Greenland and Iceland units. The next step for us to take is to make long dispositions with numerous boats so as to find out exactly what detours the enemy is making. Wolfpacks *Falke* and *Habicht* had been given a disposition for 16 February to operate against the 'ONS' convoy. If this operation is again unsuccessful, it will be necessary to patrol farther to the north, preferably in the area south-east of Greenland.

A further assessment, four days later, reflected continuing disappointment but also some optimism:

Wolfpack operations up to 19 January only intercepted one convoy for a short period on the 17th but could not attack. [We have] concluded convoys were being sent along more widely dispersed routes to outmanoeuvre the wolfpack patrol lines by a long disposition in the area south-east of Cape Farewell. It is possible here to fight to the south-west and north-east with some chance of success and to bring pressure to bear on ON, ONS, HX and SC convoys.

Of the five westbound and nine eastbound convoys at sea during the month only four lost any ships – SC.115 on 11 January, HX.222 on 17 January, SC.117 between 22 and 25 January and HX.223 on 26 January, losing seven merchant ships in all. On 30 January 1943 Dönitz replaced Raeder as Commander-in-Chief of the Kriegsmarine but retained his position as Head of the U-boat service.

During February U-boats made constant and persistent attempts to locate both eastbound and westbound Atlantic convoys. There were now 178 U-boats allocated to the Atlantic theatre. Over 2 and 3 February convoy HX.224 was intercepted by *U-456* and *U-632*, with one merchant ship sunk on the 2nd and two tankers the following day. The second of the latter was the unescorted motor tanker *Cordelia* – a straggler from the convoy. *U-632* rescued the Chief Engineer, the sole survivor of the *Cordelia* who, when taken prisoner, informed his captors that a large, slow convoy (SC.118) was following astern of his own faster one, by the same route. Eastbound SC.118 and westbound ON.166 were then heavily attacked by packs of about twenty U-boats. SC.118, attacked between 5 and 8 February by thirteen boats of wolfpack *Pfeil*, five boats of wolfpack *Haudegen* and two other U-boats, lost twelve merchant ships, seven being sunk during a period of three hours. However, at least two U-boats were sunk and six damaged during this action. ON.166, attacked between 21 and 26 February, suffered the loss of fourteen merchant ships over a period of five days as a result of U-boat attacks whilst out of range of shore-based aircraft. Of the eleven ships sunk, seven had been torpedoed by *U-602*; only three other U-boats managed to carry out successful attacks. Of the twelve, four were stragglers; only two U-boats managed to penetrate the escort screen. The correct offensive use of HF/DF and radar made U-boat attacks on the surface difficult. This would lead to a future change in tactics: instead of attacking on the surface during the night and making submerged attacks during daylight, as had been done in the past three years, the U-boats were ordered to distance themselves from the convoy during the day and make frontal attacks while submerged at night. Three U-boats were sunk and four damaged in the encounter with SC.118 which Dönitz later described as having been 'perhaps the hardest convoy battle of the war'.

There was then a reduction in U-boat activity in the Atlantic, the BDU War Log noting on 6 February:

In a few days' time the number of boats operating in the North Atlantic will be considerably reduced. An attempt was made to facilitate the finding of convoys by having as many boats as possible, and boats were therefore ordered to defer their return passage until they had only the minimum possible fuel left, or to remain in their operations area and refuel on the way back. These boats will now shortly be forced to return owing to lack of fuel. This means that in a few days group operation against convoys will in practice no longer be possible unless a corresponding number of fresh boats are sent out from home and Western France. It will therefore be necessary to send all Type VIIc boats sailing in the near future to the North Atlantic, as well as the boats from Group *Hartherz*, so that there will be at least one or two strong groups. In order to have an effective disposition to intercept convoys, a lot of boats are required. U-boat operations on a large scale both in the North Atlantic against America–England traffic and in the area of the Azores against America–Africa traffic are not possible.

Attacks on the sixteen North Atlantic convoys north of 43° N were prioritized over attacks on convoys bound for the Mediterranean, with the aim of sinking as much enemy tonnage as possible after forming two strong groups in northern waters, to send further boats to the Azores area to relieve 'Delphin' boats which have to return owing to lack of fuel.

The BdU 8 February War Log entry for the operation against SC.118 read:

Boats were constantly forced to dive by strong air activity by land-based planes and could not get ahead. The boats were ordered to move away from the convoy by first light on the 9th, as air activity by land-based planes was likely to be very strong off the North Channel

Operations Control knew this was a particularly important convoy, part of which was destined for Murmansk. There are said to have been fifty-six ships, almost all above normal size, including twelve tankers. A captured ship's officer from the HX convoy which crossed some days before this one had stated that this convoy was to follow the same route as the preceding one. Operations Control had already suspected this, and Group *Pfeil* had been disposed along the route of the HX convoy. This group picked up the convoy, two days behind schedule, but it was known afterwards from radio intelligence that this actually was the scheduled SC.

Because of the size and importance of the convoy, all possible boats were operated against it, altogether twenty-one.

The escort was unusually strong, in accordance with the importance of the convoy. During the first two days the boats had a difficult task with the destroyers, which were giving close- and long-range escort. Only a few boats got anywhere near the convoy. The unusually calm weather certainly made things easy for the enemy vessels, as it favoured surface and underwater location. By the 6th the convoy had a strong air escort. Several boats were attacked and damaged by bombs. Above all, the boats could not get ahead as they constantly had to dive. On the 7th there were fewer aircraft with the convoy, and only towards evening were planes reported in any numbers. But boats' reports showed that the air escort had given them a lot of trouble. On the 8th, land-based aircraft picked up the convoy and finally drove the boats off. These difficult conditions account for the fact that so many boats achieved such little success, and always the same ones.

The enemy's knowledge of U-boat dispositions was of increasing concern to Dönitz. At the 8 February Führer Conference he showed Hitler charts demonstrating enemy awareness of U-boat dispositions, not only their positions, but sometimes the actual number in each locality. This surprising fact might, he said, be due to (a) treason or (b) location of boats by undetected ASV (Air to Surface Vessel radar) aircraft. Everything possible was being done with regard to (a). If (b) were the case, U-boats must in future be dispersed widely, at considerable distance from each other.

Churchill, speaking in the House of Commons debate of 11 February 1943 on the 'War Situation',[1] referred to the discussions at the Casablanca Conference:

U-boat warfare takes the first place in our thoughts. There is no need to exaggerate the danger of the U-boats or to worry our merchant seamen by harping upon it unduly, because the British and American Governments have known for some time past that there were these U-boats about and have given the task of overcoming them the first priority in all their plans. The losses we suffer at sea are very heavy, and they hamper us and delay our operations. They prevent us from coming into action with our full strength, and thus they prolong the war, with its certain waste and loss and all its unknowable hazards.

Progress is being made in the war against the U-boats. We are holding our own, and more than holding our own.

Very serious depredations were committed by the U-boats off the east coast of America until the convoy system was put into proper order by the exertions of Admiral King.

The number of U-boats is increasing, but so are their losses, and so also are the means of attacking them and protecting the convoys.

Even if the U-boats increase in number, there is no doubt that a superior proportionate increase in the naval and air escort will be a remedy.

On the offensive side the rate of killing U-boats has steadily improved. From January to October 1942, inclusive, a period of 10 months, the rate of sinkings, certain and probable, was the best we have seen so far in this war, but from November to the present day, a period of three months, that rate has improved more than half as much again.

At the same time, the destructive power of the U-boat has undergone a steady diminution since the beginning of the war. In the first year, each operational U-boat that was at work accounted for an average of 19 ships: in the second year, for an average of 12, and in the third year for an average of 7½. These figures, I think, are, in themselves, a tribute to the Admiralty and to all others concerned.

Provided that the present intense efforts are kept up here and in the United States, and that anti-U-boat warfare continues to hold first place in our thoughts and energies, I take the responsibility of assuring the House – and I have not misled them so far – that we shall be definitely better off, so far as shipping is concerned, at the end of 1943 than we are now, and while it is imprudent to try to peer so far ahead, all the tendencies show that unless something entirely new and unexpected happens in this well-explored field, we shall be still better off at the end of 1944, assuming that the war continues until then. Meanwhile, let the enemy if he will, nurse his vain hopes of averting his doom by U-boat warfare. He cannot avert it, but he may delay it, and it is for us to shorten that delay by every conceivable effort we can make.

By mid-February the North Atlantic routes were well covered by four wolfpacks formed or forming, but their next operation was not a success. The slow outward convoy ONS.165 located about 350 miles east of Newfoundland was attacked in very stormy weather on 19 and 20 February. Two merchant ships, both stragglers, were sunk, while the escorts sank two U-boats. Fog, storms and atmospheric interference severely restricted U-boat operations, and owing to fuel shortages, the operation against ON.165 was broken off at dawn on the morning of 20 February.

During the month Ultra intelligence decrypts were used by the Admiralty to guide convoys around U-boat concentrations. Coincidentally, B-Dienst was able to decode some or most of the messages concerning convoy routes. So when B-Dienst discovered the route of the following convoy ON.166 and the BdU deployed wolfpacks *Ritter* and *Neptun* accordingly, the convoy was re-routed to the south. When the re-routing was discovered, wolfpack *Knappen* was formed on the south-east of the *Ritter* patrol line. The convoy was pursued across 1,100 miles of sea between 21 and 25 February, fourteen merchant ships were sunk and two were damaged. One U-boat was sunk. The U-boats then lost contact with the convoy during the evening, and in the morning of 26 February the operation was broken off.

The BdU War Log noted the operation against ON.166 was made difficult in the final two days by very poor visibility, with partial fog. During the whole operation the weather was comparatively calm, so that the convoy on one occasion was able to get away; and conditions were favourable for the location of U-boats by the escort. It was particularly pleasing that thirteen of the nineteen boats operating fired successfully; over half of the boats participated equally in the sinkings. Twenty-three ships in all were claimed to have been sunk and a further seven torpedoed (i.e. damaged).[2] One boat, *U-606*, was lost in the operation, ten were depth-charged by escorts and four had to break off operations on account of damage. In spite of the strong escort and unfavourable conditions for the U-boats, success had been made possible by stubborn shadowing and continued pursuit of the convoy. Demands made on the boats were particularly high. However, the Commanding Officers were for the most part experienced older men.

Despite these successes, the U-boats continued to experience difficulty locating convoys, as recorded in the BdU War Log for 26 February:

Dönitz reported February had been a typical month for the North Atlantic: fourteen days out at sea, nothing sunk because nothing was sighted. There were three reasons: bad weather and therefore bad visibility, possibly discovery of U-boats by radio-location, and above all a lack of own reconnaissance. Hitler promised to see whether at least three BV222 flying boats could be stationed in the west for U-boat reconnaissance

A secondary reason for this reduction in the tracking of convoys during the winter of 1942/43 may have been that, at this time, the enemy grasped the U-boat reconnaissance and patrol tactics and took avoiding action. If mobile operations employing the so-called wolfpack system of a number of submarines operating together on the surface were to be given up, it would be impossible to achieve the desired concentration on one convoy. In this respect, the same conditions apply to sea warfare as to warfare on land. There also, no decisive results can be obtained by static trench warfare, but only by mobile operations.

These successive attacks on three outward convoys (ONS.165, ON.166 and ONS.167) were made possible by the two milk cows[3] *U-460* and *U-462*. Operating between 400 and 600 miles to the north of the Azores, they replenished no fewer than twenty-seven U-boats between 21 February and 5

March. ON.167 was attacked on 27 February, with two merchant ships sunk. HX.227 was attacked on late on 28 February. One merchant ship straggling 8 miles behind the convoy, in order to secure her deck cargo and lifeboats in heavy weather, was torpedoed and sunk. Another straggler would be sunk on 2 March. By the end of the month six Atlantic convoys had been attacked and thirty-one merchant ships sunk.

On 1 March the 'Atlantic Convoy Conference' was opened between the United Kingdom, the US and Canada in Washington. The matters discussed included revision of the arrangements for the operational control of Atlantic convoys, provision of air and surface escorts and adjustment of the 'Chop Line' to coincide with the Western Ocean Meeting Point in 40° west. It became evident at an early stage in the discussions that the Americans wished to withdraw entirely from sharing the protection of the North Atlantic convoys (HX/ON and SC/ONS). The main reasons for the American proposal appear to have been Admiral King's dislike of escort groups of mixed nationality and a desire to focus his own ships on the more southerly Atlantic convoy routes, which supported US forces in the Mediterranean theatre. As a result, it was agreed that the USN would assume responsibility for escort of the tanker convoys (CU/UC) between the Dutch West Indies and Britain, and provide a support group, of an escort carrier and five destroyers, to work under British command with the North Atlantic convoys. It was decided that Britain and Canada would take complete charge of all convoys running between Britain and New York, or ports north of the latter; Canada would create a North-West Atlantic Command to exercise full control on her side of 47° west (to which meridian the 'Chop Line'[4] would be shifted), in the same way that the Commander-in-Chief, Western Approaches controlled all movements to the east of that line. In addition, new convoy cycles were agreed for the North Atlantic, and it was decided that the number of long-range aircraft in Newfoundland would be increased to four squadrons (forty-eight aircraft). The long-range aircraft, no matter of which country, were to work to the limit of their endurance without regard to the 'Chop Line'; and the support groups were also to have freedom to move wherever they might be needed, under the general strategic control of the command to which they belonged.[5]

The First Lord of the Admiralty, A. V. Alexander, in a statement to the House of Commons on 3 March[6] on the progress of the Battle of the Atlantic and shipping losses in particular, reported:

In the last half of 1941 the U-boat threat seemed to be under control. Shipping losses were less than in the two previous six-monthly periods, and we were killing U-boats faster. The whole position was altered overnight by the entry of Japan into the war, and some of the naval strength on which we had counted for escort work in the Atlantic had to be diverted. At the same time, the great flow of trade along the coast of Central and North America, mainly carried in American ships, was attacked by U-boats operating from bases on this side of the Atlantic. In the first half of last year the sinkings on the Eastern seaboard of America proved a grievous drain on the tonnage available to the United Nations; at times indeed the losses in that period in that area were as much as three-quarters of the total. With the adoption of the convoy system in that area the losses began to fall and declined rapidly until now they represent a small part of the whole. The Royal Navy and Dominion Navies contrived, at some sacrifice to protection elsewhere, to offer considerable help to the United States Navy in these waters. Many anti-submarine vessels, including corvettes, were sent. Other corvettes, under construction, were earmarked at once for the United States Navy; in addition, Coastal Command planes with special experience of U-boat hunting were despatched to the threatened area.

When the American coast offered a diminishing return, the U-boats appeared to have concentrated on the mid-Atlantic area, where convoys were furthest from friendly air bases, and extended their attack as far over the main shipping routes as possible. By the use of supply ships, and supply U-boats of great endurance, their packs seek to replenish themselves at sea and undertake patrols of long duration.

As the Prime Minister has told the House more than once, we must face a bitter struggle with the U-boats. There will be set-backs and periods of serious losses. On the other hand, I can say that from 1 December last to 28 February our tonnage losses have been much less than in the corresponding months of last winter. When they first fell, in the month of December, we felt we must take the weather as a factor, although that added to our marine risk losses, but now, taking three months, and comparing like with like, the result is encouraging, especially when it is remembered we have been competing against considerably larger forces of U-boats. I do not suggest to the House that the U-boats will not increase. There is still probably a larger output of U-boats than the total numbers killed, but the gap is being reduced. Already I can say that the results in that direction during the last four months have been the most encouraging of the whole period of the war, and in the month of February just ended, from the number and nature of the attacks we know have been carried out, we believe we achieved the best results against U-boats yet experienced.

The BdU War Log for 5 March noted that a systematic evaluation of the U-boat situation for the month of January and the beginning of February now led Dönitz to suspect the British had broken the U-boat codes or otherwise obtained exceptional knowledge of operations. He concluded they were able, with the help of aircraft radar, to intercept U-boat dispositions with sufficient accuracy to enable convoys to take successful evasive action.

SC.121, which sailed from New York on 23 February and was attacked by wolfpacks *Westmark* and *Ostmark* between 6 and 11 March after being scattered by a Force 10 storm, lost twelve ships sunk and one damaged out of fifty-seven, with just 76 of the sunken ships' crews of 275 rescued. The same day, the main body of convoy SC.122 of forty-eight merchant ships plus two LCTs (Landing Craft Tanks) sailed from New York for Liverpool on 5 March. The following day, off Cape Cod, three ships left to return to New York due to bad weather, and on 8 March another six abandoned the crossing and put into Halifax. SC.122 was joined on 9 March by nine merchant ships and a rescue ship (convoy HSC.122) from Halifax and on 12 March by one ship from St John's. Meanwhile, on 7 March wolfpack *Raubgraf* was stationed on the western edge of the mid-Atlantic air gap, with wolfpacks *Stürmer* and *Dränger* formed in a long patrol line through the air-gap centre. The B-Dienst signals intelligence group had given BdU notice of an eastbound convoy, and by the evening of 13 March had a location for SC.122. Dönitz directed *Raubgraf* to intercept, forming a new patrol line to the west. A westerly gale gave speed to SC.122, which passed through *Raubgraf*'s patrol area on the morning of 15 March, just twenty-four hours before the patrol line was formed.

HX.228 was attacked by wolfpack *Neuland* between 10 and 12 March. The convoy had been escorted by the carrier USS *Bogue* since 6 March. When poor weather and limited freedom to manoeuvre in the middle of the convoy restricted the carrier's air operations, *Bogue* was detached on the afternoon of 10 March. After the carrier departed, the convoy of sixty merchantmen suffered losses from U-boat attacks, with six merchant ships sunk and two damaged, and one escort sunk. Two U-boats, *U-432* and *U-424*, were sunk by surface escorts.

The Allied Cipher No. 3 used by the convoy escorts had now been broken by B-Dienst. This allowed Dönitz to position wolfpacks in the path of HX.229, which was following a similar course. It passed through *Raubgraf*'s patrol line during the night of 15/16 March in bad weather without being sighted. On the morning of 16 March *U-653*, detached from *Raubgraf* to return to base with mechanical problems, spotted HX.229 heading east and sent a sighting report. Dönitz immediately ordered *Raubgraf* to pursue and intercept, while *Stürmer* and *Dränger* were ordered west to form a line ahead of the convoy.

Nine U-boats were in contact with HX.229 by noon on 16 March. Meanwhile, SC.122 had been located some 120 miles ahead of HX.229. With the leading convoy the slower, the two convoys gradually closed up on each other, forming a large group of ships concentrated in a relatively small area of sea. *Raubgraf* caught up with HX.229 in the evening of 16 March and attacked that night. Three merchant ships were sunk and another five on the morning of 17 March, a total of eight in just eight hours. The naval escort was reported to be weak, as two ships had dropped out to pick up survivors. *U–338* encountered convoy SC.122 on 17 March at the north-eastern end of *Stürmer's* patrol line heading east, at about 120 miles from HX.229's position. After sending a sighting report *U–338* attacked, sinking four merchant ships in quick succession and damaging a fifth, sunk later in the day. Two more ships from HX.229 were lost in the following hours. Two boats from the *Stürmer* wolfpack were able to penetrate the defences around noon on 17 March but were driven off by the escorts, supported by brief visits from VLR aircraft flying at extreme range from Northern Ireland and Reykjavik and carrying out some of the first effective patrols into the air gap. SC.122 was able to resist further attacks until the evening.

News of the intensified U-boat campaign appeared in the press on 17 March:

NAZIS CLAIM NEW U-BOAT OFFENSIVE

LONDON, Tuesday (AAP)
Berlin radio quoted a Wilhelmstrasse spokesman as saying that Admiral Dönitz has launched the new U-boat campaign which was recently foreshadowed.

Sixty-seven ships, totalling 411,000 tons, have been sunk since the beginning of March. A special German communiqué claims that seven ships totalling 49,000 tons were sunk from a strongly escorted convoy off the east coast of South America.

RAF Liberators again reached SC.122 on 18 March, but were unable to find HX.229 only 70 miles away. U-boats torpedoed two more ships from HX.229 and another from SC.122. A freighter from HX.229, the *Matthew Luckenbach*, alarmed at the continuing loss of ships, 'romped' (left the convoy without authorization) to proceed directly to England at her best speed.

The War Cabinet Resumé for week ending 18 March reported that concentrated U-boat attacks on convoys in the North Atlantic had again caused heavy shipping losses. The U-boat situation in the North Atlantic continued to be serious. The main concentration was in the central gap between the air cover available from Newfoundland and Ireland (R). It was estimated that more than half of the 110 U-boats operating in the Atlantic were concentrated on the North Atlantic convoy routes. Two homeward bound Atlantic convoys had been heavily attacked in mid-ocean, out of range of air cover until the 17th, when it was provided from the United Kingdom. Weather conditions in Iceland (C)[7] prevented flying. Eleven ships were torpedoed in one convoy; five of these had sunk. In the other, seven ships were torpedoed and of these six had been lost.

The same day, the Prime Minister informed the War Cabinet[8] of the severe losses incurred in the Atlantic, about twenty merchant ships having been sunk in the previous two days. Our naval resources, he said, were stretched to the uttermost, and the strength of the escorts of Atlantic convoys inadequate to meet the enemy's concentration of U-boats.

After discussion, the War Cabinet agreed the convoys to northern Russia should be temporarily discontinued to concentrate all available escort forces on protecting the Atlantic convoys. Churchill then telegraphed Roosevelt on 18 March; the fifth paragraph of his message read:

Sinkings in the North Atlantic of 17 ships in convoys HX.229 and SC.122 are a final proof our escorts are evidently too thin. The strain upon the British Navy is becoming intolerable. If instead of carrying out the blind proposed in paragraph 3 above[9] it were definitely decided now not to run any more convoys to Russia until after HUSKY [the Allied invasion of Sicily], this would release one escort carrier, several ocean-going escort vessels and six other escort vessels for immediate service and enable us to form support groups in the Atlantic, which are vital, and to bridge the April–May gap before our reinforcements, particularly of air power, come into play. My mind therefore is turning to a blunt and complete cessation until after HUSKY. Here again I should be most grateful for your advice.

Meanwhile, the attacks on SC.122 and HX.229 continued. During the night of 18/19 March the convoys were running in tandem, though independently, on the same course. All attacks on both were repelled during the night, when six positive U-boat contacts were attacked without result. But during the day two merchant ships were sunk – one from SC.122, the second the 'romper' from HX.229, sunk as she ran into the concentration of U-boats around SC.122. Additional escorts and increasing numbers of air patrols reached the convoys on 19 March, and *U-384* was sunk by an RAF Flying Fortress. There were no further losses from the convoys that day; faced with stiffening resistance and sensing nothing further would be achieved without disproportionate losses, Dönitz called off the assault.

The double battle had involved ninety merchant ships and sixteen escorts (though not all were present at the same time). Twenty-two merchant ships were sunk (thirteen from HX.229 and nine from SC.122), a loss of 146,000 tons. More than 300 merchant seamen died. A total of thirty-eight U-boats had taken part (though not all had been in contact at the same time). One U-boat had been lost with all hands, and a number damaged. The operation was undoubtedly a success for the U-boats. The twenty-seven surviving merchant ships of HX.229 arrived at Liverpool on 23 March, and SC.122 with forty-two ships later the same day. This would later prove to have been the largest convoy battle of the Atlantic campaign. A Royal Navy report later concluded: 'It appeared possible that we should not be able to regard convoy as an effective system of defence.'

Dönitz later wrote, 'HX.229/SC.122 was the greatest success that we had so far scored against a convoy', and Roskill calls it 'a serious disaster to the Allied cause'. (S. W. Roskill, *The War at Sea 1939–45*, Vol. II, p.366.)

On 29 March the Combined Chiefs of Staff gave first priority to the modernization of Liberators to VLR standards and ordered that 'the greatest practicable number of existing VLR ASV-equipped aircraft ... now assigned to other duties be diverted to anti-submarine operations in the Atlantic.'

The U-boats' attempts to attack the next HX convoy (HX.230) between 27 and 30 March were frustrated by the increasingly severe weather, hurricane conditions presenting difficulties to the U-boats as well as the merchant ships. The convoy lost only one merchantman – a straggler on 29 March. On 30 March Dönitz ordered:

> Discontinue operation on convoy insofar as there is no contact with convoy or single ships. Move off westward in convoy lane and count on single ships. Stay tenaciously with these until they are sunk. (1048/30 March 1943)

The American escort carrier *Bogue* accompanied slow convoy SC.123, passing eastwards at the same time, as far as a position some 175 miles south-east of Cape Farewell, but she would be detached on 26 March, when rough seas prevented refuelling from her destroyer escorts, and she was forced to leave that afternoon. The convoy was not attacked.

In what may have been an example of German propaganda, the following press report appeared on 21 March:

ADMIRALTY CHIEF URGED TO RESIGN

BUENOS AIRES, 18 March (Domei – Japanese news agency)
The apparent inability of the British Admiralty to cope with the growing U-boat menace was the cause of a fierce concerted attack in the House of Commons against the Admiralty, climaxed by a demand for the resignation

of the first Lord of the Admiralty, Albert V. Alexander, according to a London report yesterday.

The Opposition hinted that the Admiralty was afraid to publish shipping losses because revelation of the truth would show inefficiency or neglect somewhere. It charged Alexander with having no time to attend properly to his duties because 'his time is taken up with speeches, inspections and social functions'.

The Opposition also asked for the meaning of the Washington U-boat conferences in view of Churchill's statement that no changes were planned in the present machinery for combating U-boats.

In answer to these charges, Alexander denied that the Admiralty was complacent, declaring that the situation was much too serious for that.

The War Cabinet was informed on 22 March that the sailing of the March convoy to northern Russia (JW.54) had been postponed; the escort vessels would now be redeployed to combat the U-boat menace in the North Atlantic, where Support Groups would be established to help the convoys fight their way through the U-boat concentration.

The main reason for the great increase in tonnage sunk in convoys was an increase in the number of convoys attacked, rather than a weakening in the effectiveness of the escorts. Five convoys lost a total of thirty-four merchant ships.

The first convoy to be attacked during April was HX.231, an eastbound convoy of sixty-one merchant ships pursued by wolfpack *Löwenherz* of fourteen U-boats from 4 to 7 April over a distance of 700 miles. Six merchant ships were sunk. The BdU War Log for 7 April reported numerous U-boats bombed and some unable to carry on further operations owing to damage sustained. The operation was broken off in the evening of 7 April, when the U-boats were increasingly threatened by aircraft as the convoy drew near to the coast. The Log noted *U-632* and *U-636* probably lost on operations against the convoy, it was assumed as a result of aircraft bombing. A further five were heavily damaged by aircraft bombs or by depth charges.

The extent of merchant shipping losses in the Atlantic during March was described in press reports which appeared on 8 April:

U-BOAT MENACE INTENSIFIED IN ATLANTIC

LONDON, Tuesday

The naval correspondent of the *Daily Mail* says that new German tactics in the Atlantic include the use of 21-knot interceptor U-boats, which shadow Allied convoys and guide U-boat packs to them.

Shipping losses in the Atlantic were considerably worse last month than in February, owing to the intensified operations. Interceptor U-boats are able sometimes to radio a rendezvous ahead to packs by a new under-water communications system. Interceptors attack a convoy only when there is little chance of arranging a meeting with a pack.

SITUATION SERIOUS

WASHINGTON, Tuesday

The Secretary for the Navy (Colonel Knox) stated at a Press conference that the submarine campaign had been greatly intensified. More submarines than ever were operating, and shipping losses in the Atlantic were considerably worse in March. The rise in sinkings had been accompanied by a change in submarine tactics. Colonel Knox said that U-boats were now concentrating in mid-Atlantic along shipping routes from the United States to Britain and to the Mediterranean. The situation was serious.

He disclosed that there had been a marked improvement in the production of destroyer escort craft, although this had been hampered by a shortage of engines, However, the launching rate was now very good.

The message was reinforced in a declaration by Dönitz which appeared in the international press on 9 April and gave some indication of what might be to come:

VITAL TASK OF U-BOATS
SPEECH BY DÖNITZ

Berlin radio states that the Commander-in-Chief of the German Navy, Admiral Dönitz, declared in a speech that Britain could be defeated only by sea. 'The British shipping lanes are her life-lines and must be cut by U-boats', he added. 'We must be tough and hang on to the enemy without giving him a respite.'

The announcer said that more U-boats were being used than ever before. Many enemy bombers were being used for the U-boat war. Thus the U-boats were contributing towards weakening the enemy air offensive against Germany.

The announcer added that a record number of U-boats were now at sea.

Submarine construction in the past few months had gone up by leaps and bounds. U-boat packs were now described as 'naval artillery directed by wireless'. Well informed Berlin sources state this most important arm of maritime warfare may be needed for other purposes than hitherto.

At the 11 April Führer Conference Dönitz reported submarine losses had amounted to nineteen in February, fifteen in March and six so far in April. These losses were high; submarine warfare was difficult. However, it was obvious that the aim of sinking merchant ships must be to sink more than the enemy could build. If this objective was not reached, the enemy would still continue to suffer severely through loss of material, but [Germany] would not be successful in bleeding him to death due to diminution of his tonnage. Dönitz feared the submarine war would be a failure if it did not sink more ships than the enemy was able to build. In this fourth year of the war the submarines were still fighting but, of course, many more submarines were now required to achieve what one U-boat could accomplish in 1940. Donitz argued for an increase in the submarine building programme so far as shipyard capacity permitted, so the ratio of losses to new ships did not become too unfavourable. Hitler agreed an increase in the submarine building programme must be effected.

On Wednesday, 7 April 1943 Berlin radio announced that Hitler had received Admiral Dönitz and decorated him with Oak Leaves to the Knight's Cross of the Iron Cross 'in recognition of his unique conduct of the U-boat warfare'.

There were further press reports on 10 April of the new tactics adopted by U-boats to intercept and attack convoys:

GERMANS EMPLOY NEW SUB TACTICS

BUENOS AIRES, 8 April (Domei)
New tactics of German submarine warfare include the use of 21-knot interceptor U-boats which shadow anti-Axis convoys and guide U-boat packs to them, the *Daily Mail*'s naval correspondent disclosed in a report from London.

The interceptors stalk convoys through their change of course and are able to radio their rendezvous ahead to U-boat packs by a new underwater communications system. Interceptors will only attack the convoy when there is little chance of arranging a meeting with U-boat Packs, the report said.

The U-boat attacks continued. During 11 and 12 April, ONS.176 lost one merchant ship and one destroyer, and HX.232 was attacked by wolfpack *Lerche* and suffered four merchant ships sunk and one damaged. The following convoy, HX.233, routed along a southerly course passing some 400 miles north of the

Azores, was also attacked, losing one merchant ship in exchange for *U-175*, both sunk on 17 April. By 19 April, no fewer than five convoys were threatened by U-boat wolfpacks deployed across their path in the sea area north-west of Newfoundland. Four westbound convoys (ON.178, ONS.3, ONS.4 and SC.127) were being routed to the extreme north (almost as far as Greenland) in an attempt to pass around the north-west corner of the wolfpacks' line, and the fifth eastbound convoy (HX.234) was routed towards Greenland, east of Newfoundland and Labrador, in an attempt to pass to the north-west of the wolfpacks' position. ONS.4 and SC.127 were not detected, but wolfpack *Meise* was responsible for attacks on merchant ships (mostly stragglers) from three convoys (HX.234, ONS.3, ON.178) between 19 and 23 April, sinking two merchant ships and damaging one from HX.234, two from ONS.3 and one from ON.178. The USN carrier *Bogue* and her support group protected HX.235 between 27 April and 4 May. The convoy was not detected.

The next convoy to be attacked, ONS.5, had sailed from Liverpool at 10.00 on 21 April 1943 for Halifax, Nova Scotia, with a few ships heading on to New York and Boston. Unlike the eastbound convoys, not all those westbound sailed from a single assembly point but joined from individual ports. Notably, although the first escort carrier had been deployed to cover the mid-Atlantic air gap, ONS.5 had no air cover. Also importantly at the time, the German Radio Listening Service was able to intercept and read the Anglo/American Naval Cipher No. 3 used to route the convoys. The messages transmitted including the Admiralty and United States Navy Daily U-boat Situation Reports – providing valuable intelligence to the BdU.

ONS.5 sailed on oblivious to the developing threat. Visibility had fallen to about three miles and air cover was no longer available; with the airfields in Iceland 'closed down' by poor weather, reconnaissance aircraft were unable to take off, leaving the convoy without a protective umbrella. By nightfall on the 24th five U-boats had arrived in the vicinity of the convoy, but fortunately the failure of other U-boats in the area to maintain radio silence provided Western Approaches Command with some situational awareness of the scale of the threat. Following assessment of the situation, the destroyer *Oribi* was ordered to transfer from the escort of convoy SC.127 to reinforce ONS.5, and the 3rd Escort Group sailed from St John's, Newfoundland at a speed of 15 knots to rendezvous with the convoy and provide additional protection.

Dawn on 25 April broke to reveal a moderate gale from the west-north-west. In the extreme conditions the merchant ships were now struggling to keep in station, their speed being reduced to a mere 2 or 3 knots. Steering an accurate course in these conditions was by now well-nigh impossible. The storm became so bad that the convoy was to all intents and purposes 'hove to'.[10] The weather then began to improve, and visual contact with the merchant ships was regained. The escorts began to round up their charges and shepherd them back into formation

At noon on the following day, the BdU changed the German Naval Enigma Cipher used to transmit instructions to the U-boats. This disrupted the flow of intelligence and blacked out detection of the sixteen U-boats moving in to form wolfpack *Star*. There was no opportunity to warn ONS.5 to change course. It would take the Bletchley code-breakers until 5 May to break the new code, then decrypt and read the U-boat message traffic. This was a critical time during the convoy's westward journey. Fortunately, ONS.5 had been routed on a northerly course to maintain the air escort from Iceland for as long as possible. Since the more recent attacks by U-boats on convoys had taken place further to the south, it was hoped this new route would avoid the wolfpacks.

ONS.5 arrived in the wolfpack *Star*'s patrol area on 28 April and was sighted at 09.00 by *U-650*. Despite being forced to dive three times to avoid approaching aircraft, the U-boat maintained contact and by nightfall was joined by four others The contact reports transmitted by the U-boats alerted the SOE to their presence on the convoy's port bow, beam and quarter, and astern. The convoy was now surrounded. At dawn on 29 April *U-258* lying submerged ahead of the convoy route slipped inside the escort screen and under the convoy, taking up a position at periscope depth to starboard of the No. 4 column. *U-258* fired a number of torpedoes in broad daylight and reported hits on three ships, but sank only one.

April had brought some respite to the convoys, as the BdU was unable to maintain such a large presence in the Atlantic after many of the boats heavily involved in the March operations returned to base for replenishment; nevertheless, those boats still operational during the month remained active.

The USN Atlantic Fleet transferred responsibility for escort of convoys between Halifax and the United Kingdom to British and Canadian naval forces on 30 April. Although sufficient VLR aircraft had now been introduced into service, flying from Iceland, Newfoundland and Greenland, their operational effectiveness was limited by their small number and by poor weather. The first escort carriers designed to provide air cover for the convoys also now appeared, but contrary to general claims, there were in fact only two British ones – *Biter* and *Archer* – and one American (*Bogue*) available for protection of Atlantic convoys at sea during April, May and the first week of June 1943. With up to three east- and three westbound convoys at sea in the Atlantic at any one time, this number was insufficient to provide total cover across the route. In April fifteen newly modified VLR aircraft delivered to the RCAF in Newfoundland began operating in the air gap.

The months of April and May also saw the introduction of the first escort support groups, two of which included an escort carrier designed operate in the air gap by coming to the aid of any convoy besieged by a wolfpack. The first carrier, *Biter*, was deployed on 23 April with destroyers *Pathfinder*, *Obdurate* and *Opportune* of the 5th Support Group in a search for U-boats attempting attacks on ONS.4. The second carrier, *Archer*, was deployed 2 May with destroyers *Milne*, *Eclipse* and *Fury* of the Fourth Support Group for Atlantic convoy defence. Later, on 21 May, *Archer* joined HX.239 with ships of the Group to supplement defence against attacks by U-boats of *Mosel* and *Donau* wolfpacks.

By May 1943 a record number of U-boats were at sea, with over forty deployed against the North Atlantic convoys in three patrol lines off Greenland and Newfoundland. A group operated to the far west of the Bay of Biscay. Others were passing through the northern transit area,[11] and over thirty were on passage between their Biscay bases[12] and the North Atlantic, with more still in the South Atlantic. The numerous Allied convoys crossing the North Atlantic presented perfect targets.

The BdU War Log for 1 May contained a report on the initial attacks on ONS.5:

> The continuing bad weather also prevented contact being re-established on 1 May. As there was little prospect of picking the convoy up again while weather remained hazy, the boats were ordered to break off the operation at dusk on 1 May.

To sum up:

> The operations against the convoy with sixteen boats in all suffered from first to last from very hazy weather and strong S.W. wind, against which the boats had to struggle during their pursuit of the enemy. Lookout, finding and shadowing of the convoy were much hampered thereby. In all, only five boats contacted the convoy. After 29 April contact could not be re-established.
>
> The only success was scored by *U-258*, which probably sank two ships and torpedoed a third. Naval defences were not reported as very strong. No reports were received about them. There was some air activity on the first day, but only seaplanes. During the last night a boat reported continuous air patrol, probably based on Greenland. The same boat observed what was probably a new type of location gear. The Commander repeatedly noticed planes approaching at great height and carrying a light like a planet that went on and off. No location was heard at the time.
>
> Two boats had to give up the chase because of enemy counter-measures. They were bombed and depth-charged and badly damaged. No boats were lost while attacking the convoy.

On 2 May Dönitz ordered the U-boats from wolfpacks *Star* and *Specht* (with some newcomers) to form a new patrol line to the west as wolfpack *Finke* of twenty-eight U-boats, to be in place on 3 May tasked with intercepting the westbound convoy SC.128. Although sighted by *U-628* on 1 May, SC.128 had fortunately managed to avoid all the U-boats, aided by the intelligence on their movements contained in the Enigma decrypts. Long Range Patrol Aircraft were sent out to sweep the U-boat concentrations.

On 3 May Dönitz issued what was no doubt intended as a message of encouragement to all U-boat Commanders:

> In his efforts to rob the submarine of her most valuable characteristic (invisibility) the enemy is several lengths ahead of us by virtue of his radar location.
>
> I am fully aware of the difficult position that this puts you in when fighting enemy escorts and anti-submarine forces.
>
> You may rest assured that I have done and shall continue to do everything within my powers as Commander-in-Chief to change this situation as rapidly as possible.
>
> Work is being carried on both within the Navy and outside it to develop and improve your weapons and gear.
>
> I expect you to continue your determined struggle with the enemy and by pitting your ingenuity, ability and toughness against his tricks and technical developments, finally to finish him off.
>
> Commanders in the Mediterranean and Atlantic have proved that even today the enemy has weak spots everywhere and that in many cases the enemy resources are not nearly so efficient as they would appear at first sight if the boat's Commander is determined to score a success in spite of everything.
>
> I believe that I shall shortly be able to give you better weapons for this hard struggle of yours.
>
> (Signed) DÖNITZ

The main attack on ONS.5 took place between midnight on 4 May and midnight on 5 May. Twelve merchant ships were sunk. Poor weather had restricted air cover to one hour on the morning of the 5th. Dönitz directed the battle in person from U-boat headquarters, continuously exhorting his U-boat commanders to press home an attack whenever an occasion presented itself. The BdU account of the operation provides a useful summary of the encounter:

> The operation against ONS.5 was broken off at 0600 on 6 May as the thick fog made it extremely unlikely the convoy would be found again

and there was no prospect of the weather improving, with the convoy now approaching the Newfoundland Bank.

The attack on 'ON.180' [ONS.5] lasted from the evening of the 4th to the morning of the 6th over a distance of 210 miles. In all, forty-one boats were detailed to a track; of these, all the boats belonging to Group *Fink* were in an especially favourable position when contact was established at 2020 on the 4th. During the first night eight boats were able to sink thirteen ships [actually eleven] straight away, probably mainly because of the suddenness of the attack. Between picking up the convoy and darkness there were only five hours; these circumstances are always favourable, as the anti-submarine defences are not usually reinforced for action for about a day. During the day two more successful underwater attacks were made and four vessels sunk.

Visibility was good and the sea calm, and during the day a total of fifteen boats had closed in on the convoy, an exceptionally high number, and especially good sinkings were expected during the night of 5/6 May. But about two hours before darkness fell, fog suddenly came up; it grew steadily thicker and spoilt all chances of a really good bag that night. Nearly all boats lost contact again, and the convoy was sighted for the last time at 0400. If the fog had held off for six hours, many more ships would certainly have been sunk. As it was, the fog ruined everything, and no further successes were scored.

If none of these boats report later, this loss of six boats is very high and grave considering the short duration of the attack. The blame can be laid mainly on the foggy period that began at 2300 on 5 May.

The fog had robbed the U-boats of the sight of their targets, whilst the effective use of radar by the escorts in turn robbed the U-boats of their invisibility, as described in a separate BdU assessment of the same date which reported:

At present, along with enemy air activity, enemy radar location is the worst enemy of our submarines. The operation against Convoy No. 36 [ONS.5] also had to be broken off because of enemy radar. Radar location by air and naval forces not only renders the actual attack by individual boats most difficult, but also provides the enemy with a means of fixing the stations manned by the submarines and of avoiding them, and he obviously makes good use of this method. Radar location is thus robbing the submarine of her most important characteristic – the ability to remain undetected.

The enemy air force is already able to take over convoy escort duties in almost all the North Atlantic area, and it must be expected that the only remaining gaps will be closed within a reasonable length of time by land-based planes, or at any rate by using auxiliary aircraft carriers.

Air escort provided by a large number of planes operating over a fairly large area round the convoy has always forced our submarines to lag hopelessly behind the convoy and prevented them achieving any successes, especially when naval and air escorts cooperate efficiently.

Anti-aircraft armament is being strengthened as a counter-measure. But the solution can be considered satisfactory only when the boats' armament permits them to remain on the surface to fight it out with the planes, or at any rate when it is essential for boats attacking a convoy to get ahead to make an attack despite enemy air escorts.

Attacks on submerged boats with new types of location methods and apparently more powerful depth charges than previously have become more concentrated.

Finally, the increasing number of anti-submarine vessels must be mentioned as a further hindrance to submarine warfare.

The weeks between 4 April and 6 May 1943 saw one of the most intensive periods of conflict during the Battle of the Atlantic, with nine convoys attacked by U-boats and thirty-one merchant ships sunk.

On 9 May, the Convoy Commodore of ONS.5, Captain K. J. Brook on board the Norwegian merchant ship *Rena*, received a telegram (addressed through HMS *Tay* as SOE) from Winston Churchill:

> My compliments to you and your unceasing fight against U-boats. Please pass to Commodore of convoy my admiration for the steadfastness of his ships.

This operation against ONS.5 cost Dönitz seven U-boats; six were sunk by the convoy escorts, and the seventh, previously damaged by a Catalina on 5 May, sank on the way back to base (probably on 7 May). Two more were sunk by long-range patrol aircraft, making a total of nine. A further seven were forced to terminate their patrols due to severe battle damage, whilst eight others received lesser degrees of damage. The human cost to the U-boat arm was 364 trained officers and men – a serious disaster for the Kriegsmarine. Several prominent and experienced U-boat commanders were amongst those lost. The declining availability of trained U-boat personnel would now become a real problem to those responsible for supplying enough trained sailors to keep sufficient U-boats combat-ready.

The next convoy attacked, HX.237, which departed New York on 1 May, also ran into thick fog for several days, resulting in ten ships straggling on

7 May. U-boats were in contact from 9 to 12 May, and three stragglers were sunk – one on 11 May and two the following day. Aircraft from *Biter* sank a U-boat on 12 May, and the escort and a Sunderland aircraft sank another the following day. The BdU account of the operation read:

> The convoy was attacked from the evening of 11 May to 13 May. The weather was fairly calm and good the whole time, with only occasional poor visibility in showers and rain squalls.
>
> Seven boats had been detailed to attack, also the boats coming out from port that were at a favourable distance from the convoy. Because of the small number of boats attacking, it was only possible to maintain contact for a few hours at a stretch, leaving long intervals completely without contact with the convoy.
>
> Right from the first day, carrier-borne planes were sighted with the convoy, and later on the carrier itself was seen once. These planes and other land-based escorts made the operation very difficult, and on the last day it had to be given up because this air activity was too powerful. Of the boats directed to attack, five were bombed singly; of these, *U-456* was probably sunk by a bomb which hit her stern. *U-89* and *U-753* have also not reported and must be presumed lost.
>
> On 13 May the operation against the 'HX' convoy was broken off.
>
> To sum up, it may be remarked that greater success was not expected in the case of this convoy, as with so few boats operating the loss of three boats when attacking the convoy is very high but, considering the enemy's ability to concentrate his entire defences on these few boats, not surprising.
>
> *U-456* was fatally damaged by the aircraft attack, the first instance of a U-boat being sunk by FIDO.[13]

The attacks continued; the next target was convoy SC.129, attacked on 11 May by *U-402* and losing two merchant ships sunk.

The BdU's final summary of the overall operation dated 14 May read:

> The operation against the 'SC' convoy en route to England was spread over three days from 11 to 14 May. In all, twenty-five boats were directed against the convoy.
>
> During the operation the weather was not really unfavourable. Moderate sea force, during the day mainly good visibility, at night often changeable visibility and moon, so conditions were less favourable for attacks at night than during the day. Because of the not very rough weather, conditions must have been good for the enemy's surface location, and this assumption is borne out by the frequent driving off of the submarines.

Only four boats were attacking the convoy during the first night from 11 to 12 May, but during the day on 12 May twelve boats contacted the convoy. But all these boats lost contact again before dark, and after 0100 on 13 May the convoy was lost and was only sighted again for a short time on 14 May.

The reason for this failure is not clearly explained by the radio messages from the boats.

During the period when the large number of boats had contact, there was still no air escort with the convoy. Planes were first reported during the evening of 14 May, after contact had been lost. As a carrier also joined the convoy later, the powerful air escort ruled out further successful operations.

The most likely reason for the failure lies in the superior numbers of the enemy escort forces combined with good conditions for location. Eleven of the shadowing boats were forced away and picked up by escort vessels during daylight on 12 May.

This represents a very high percentage and shows that the enemy must have picked up all the boats round the convoy with astonishing accuracy. As he could not possibly have sighted them, he must have used location gear. Since such a rapid detection of the boats has not previously occurred on such a scale, it is quite likely that the enemy is working with a new type of efficient location gear. It cannot have been merely by chance that the boats were forced to sheer off, as nine boats were depth-charged after being picked up, two of them with very heavy charges, so that they had to turn back.

After the boats had been forced away during the evening of the 12th, the visibility worsened, and although many boats were in the vicinity the convoy was not picked up again during the night.

U-402 scored the only success on the convoy by sinking two ships in the first night. *U-186* was lost in attacking the convoy, probably while making an under-water attack during the day.

The BdU was puzzled as to how U-boat dispositions were being detected, the 16 May Diary entry noting:

The HX convoy did not pass on its known route, according to a special intercept report, but bypassed the patrol line to the south. It can be seen from the submarine situation of 13 May issued by the enemy that the patrol line was intercepted by the enemy, and that, as a result, the course of the convoys was changed.

For the present, it remains a mystery how our submarine dispositions are so clearly intercepted by the enemy. Betrayal, breaking into codes, or far superior location methods must provide the enemy with the data. Location from planes is likely to be the means by which the enemy discovers our patrol lines.

Both groups were transferred to the south-east on the assumption that the following SC convoy will pass on the same route as the HX convoy.

Convoy ON.184, which set out from Liverpool on 15 May 1943 for New York, suffered no merchant ship losses, but on 22 March U-596 was scuttled east of Newfoundland after being badly damaged by depth charges from two Avenger aircraft from the Bogue.

In the early hours of 17 May one merchant ship from ONS.7 was sunk south of Cape Farewell. The same day, a press report appeared quoting the following article, which had been seen in the Swedish newspaper Dagens Nyheter:

According to Dagens Nyheter, British naval circles are very satisfied with the development of the Battle of the Atlantic. The decrease in ships lost is in the first place attributable to the increased employment of aircraft carriers as convoy escorts. Opinion is still divided on the use of helicopters, as they cannot carry bombs.

Between 18 and 20 May SC.130 would face opposition from three wolfpacks of twenty-five U-boats deployed in three patrol lines across its route. These had been deployed by the BdU on 15 May in response to intelligence from B-Dienst which reported a westbound convoy (ONS.7), and two eastbound convoys (HX.238 and SC.130), approaching the mid-Atlantic air gap. Although the escort carrier Archer was at sea with ON.182, convoy SC.130 had no air cover. ONS.7 had already come under attack on 13 May and, warned by this, intelligence from HF/DF readings and Enigma decrypts, the Admiralty ordered HX.238 to change course and the escort of SC.130 to be reinforced by the First Escort Group transferred from ONS.5. All attempts by U-boats to attack the convoy between 18 and 20 May were unsuccessful. The BdU concluded on 19 May that HX.238 had passed to the south of the U-boat patrol line. No merchant ships were attacked, but four U-boats were sunk, two by the escorts and two by RAF Liberators. At midday on 20 May BdU called off the operation, and the U-boats withdrew.

At the time, Churchill was in Washington for the TRIDENT Conference held between 12 and 25 May to discuss and agree strategy for the future conduct of the war. On 19 May he delivered a lengthy speech in Washington to a Joint Session of the US Congress on the progress of the war. He was warmly received, and details of the speech were widely reported in the press. The passage relating to the war at sea read:

RECORD U-BOAT KILLINGS

We took the Atlantic as our main border. Although Britain had sustained double the American losses of merchant tonnage, the prodigious output of ships in the United States yards now far surpassed the losses of both Allies, and if the efforts were not relaxed there was every reason to count on a ceaseless, progressive expansion of Allied shipping. U-boat killings this year greatly exceeded all previous experience. The last three months yielded record results. The U-boat danger was still the greatest, but he had sober confidence that it would not only be met and contained but would be overcome.

The BdU in the 'Review of First Quarter of 1943 – January to March 1943' dated 21 May 1943 attributed the relatively scant U-boat successes in the first quarter of 1943 to various causes, including bad weather, the youth of commanding officers (the youngest had joined the Navy after 1 September 1939), the strength of enemy defences – especially on North Atlantic routes – and above all, the ability of the enemy convoys to evade U-boat groups.

By mid-May the BdU had suffered a series of setbacks in operations against the Atlantic convoys and on the 21st, in a message intercepted and decoded at Bletchley Park, sent the following signal to all U-boats:

> If there is anyone who thinks that combating convoys is no longer possible, he is a weakling and no true U-boat captain. The Battle of the Atlantic is getting harder, but it is the determining element in the waging of the war.

The BdU made determined but ultimately unsuccessful attempts to intercept and attack the next eastbound convoy, HX.239, between 19 and 23 May. On 22 May Avenger aircraft from the *Bogue* attacked *U-569* which, badly damaged by depth charges, was scuttled by her crew, twenty-five of whom were rescued. In a second attack on 23 May a Swordfish from *Archer* sank *U-752* with rockets; there were seventeen survivors. The next day saw the first anti-submarine escort by a Liberator Mark V, when Liberator V 'S' FL984 took off from Aldergrove at 04.45 to escort HX.239, returning at 19.59.

The final BdU analysis dated 23 May on the outcome of the operation against HX.239 concluded:

> The boats were continually forced to submerge by very strong land-based aircraft, so that approach, quite apart from attack, was not possible.
> Since the boats were unlikely to achieve any success with the strong air and naval escort, and also damage was continually reported through

aircraft bombs, the operation was broken off towards 11.00, and the boats were ordered to withdraw to the west.

The operation has, therefore, been concluded. No successes were achieved.

The operation was very much affected at the beginning by the uncertainty of the boats' reports on 22 May. The boats were forced continually to remain submerged by numerous carrier-borne aircraft in the area of the patrol from dawn onwards, so that the first report regarding the S.W.-bound convoy was not received until 1933, and no report at all was received regarding the expected N.E.-bound convoy. It must be assumed that this convoy passed the patrol line in the area of position *U-231*, and that this boat was attacked and sunk by carrier-borne aircraft or escort forces (she has not reported up to now). In this way there was no report on 22 May regarding the convoy, and therefore no action with any prospect of success in the first night, in view of the escort at the time.

On 23 May, the number of various aircraft sightings showed that carrier-borne and land-based aircraft were being used extensively, so that in spite of the knowledge of the convoy's position, the operation had to be broken off.

The report noted two U-boats were sunk and two damaged, all by enemy aircraft. The operation against the convoy showed again clearly that it is not possible at present to attack, with available weapons, a convoy escorted by strong air cover. The case of *U-752*, however, proves that the boats will be able to ward off attacks of carrier aircraft after installation of the 2cm quadruples [20mm anti-aircraft guns].

The attack on HX.239 represented the last major convoy battle of May 1943. Dönitz acknowledged the failure of his wolfpack strategy in a series of messages to all U-boat commanders. In the first, sent on 23 May, he explained:

1. Our heavy submarine losses in the last month are to be traced back predominantly to the present superiority of enemy location instruments and the surprise from the air which is possible because of that. More than half of all losses have occurred through this surprise, and indeed on advances and returns as well as in the operational area in attack dispositions. The losses in battle against the convoys themselves were in comparison slight except for one case, in which particularly unfavourable conditions prevailed. A part of these losses, too, resulted from aircraft.
2. The momentary situation as concerns enemy aircraft and enemy radar must be bridged over by special precautionary measures en route and in the waiting disposition, meanwhile making the best of other

disadvantages. Orders for this have been issued. In that connection I will bring about further results in the choice of the attack areas.

3. My whole energy is engaged in the improvement of our own *Ortung* [location finding], defence against *Ortung*, and anti-aircraft arms. This task is being worked on the maximum application at all our stations. Practical results will appear in a very short time. The time until then must be passed with cunning and caution on cruise and while waiting, but with your old inexorable severity in the battle itself. (1753/1842/2032/23 May 1943)

The BdU War Log entry for 23 May gave an indication of what was to follow:

The serious submarine losses this month, which have so far amounted to 30–40 boats, make temporary changes in the operational methods hitherto adopted in submarine warfare necessary.

The Diary for the following day contains the following general entry:

In the last few days circumstances have arisen which give a particularly strong indication of the present crisis in U-boat warfare and force us to decisive measures. These circumstances are:

a) The further heavy losses which have occurred or been confirmed.
b) The failure against convoy SC.130 (Group *Donau*) as well as the conditions in operations against HX 239 (Group *Mosel*).

Re a): After fourteen boats had been lost in the Atlantic in February, thirteen in March and twelve in April, the extent of the losses in the Atlantic in May has already reached the figure of thirty-one boats lost up to the 22nd, and two further ones have probably been lost in the operation against HX 239.

Losses, even heavy losses, must be borne when they are accompanied by corresponding sinkings. But in May in the Atlantic the sinking of about 10,000 GRT had to be paid for by loss of each boat, while not long ago each loss only occurred per the sinking of about 100,000 GRT. The losses in May have, therefore, reached an impossible height.

From the thirty-one boats lost up to 22 May in the Atlantic, therefore, nineteen, i.e. 60 per cent, were lost while proceeding and at waiting positions in the operational area. Only twelve boats, i.e. about 40 per cent, were probably lost while directly attacking the convoy, only four five of these in the unusually unfavourable visibility which led to the breaking off of attack on Convoy No. 36.

When the losses are analysed as to whether caused by aircraft or naval forces, the result is as follows:

Twenty boats, i.e. 60 per cent, were almost certainly destroyed by aircraft, and six further ones possibly by aircraft. Only eight boats, i.e. 25 per cent, were almost certainly destroyed by naval forces.

The Royal Air Force, therefore, played an important part in causing such high losses. This is to be attributed to the increased use of land-based aircraft and aircraft carriers, combined with the possibility of surprise now through the enemy radar location by day and night.

Re b): The decisive part played by the Royal Air Force has also been confirmed in the attacks on the *Donau* convoy (No. 40) [SC.130] and in operations on HX 239 (No. 42). In the case of the *Donau* convoy, aircraft prevented the boats from being able to approach for attack and only made possible a partial, temporary contact. In the case of Group *Mosel* no real contact was taken up in view of the large number of aircraft which appeared, although presumably one of the two convoys had passed the patrol line.

The excessive losses and the lack of success in operations against the latest convoys now force us to take decisive measures until the boats are equipped again with better defence and attack weapons.

The first important measure is to prevent losses while aircraft are present. More important than ever there is the old principle 'of proceeding carefully like an old bull elephant', and not only on approach and return routes, but also in areas of the North Atlantic which are endangered by aircraft and when in waiting and attack positions.

Dönitz issued a further message and an Order of the Day to all U-boat commanders the same day:

To All Boats (Message 1769)
The situation in the North Atlantic now forces a temporary shifting of operations to areas less endangered by aircraft. The following areas come into consideration: the Caribbean Sea, the area off Trinidad, the area off the Brazilian and West African coasts. It is, therefore, intended to operate primarily with VIIc boats in these areas, as far as permitted by the supply situation. If necessary, operational boats must also be sent in to supply other boats. With the boats at present in the North Atlantic, operations will be made against the traffic between the USA and Gibraltar – as far as these boats are able to do this with their fuel. The North Atlantic cannot, however, be entirely denuded of boats. It is necessary, by means of single boats, to leave the enemy in ignorance as long as possible regarding alterations in tactics. For this operation in the North Atlantic boats are

available now which cannot be sent elsewhere in view of their fuel supplies, as are boats coming from home waters for their first operations, which must be assigned to stay in the North Atlantic in spite of the difficult conditions. It is intended to attempt attacks on a convoy only under particularly favourable conditions, i.e. at the time of the new moon. The new moon period at the end of June is the first to come under consideration, since the boats at present in the North Atlantic are no longer operational enough. It will be necessary to assign several veteran boats for this as a support for the newer boats in the North Atlantic.

These decisions comprise a temporary deviation from the former principles for the conduct of U-boat warfare. This is necessary in order not to allow the U-boats to be beaten at a time when their weapons are inferior, by suffering unnecessary losses while achieving very slight success. It is, however, clearly understood that the main operational area of U-boats is, as it always was, the North Atlantic, and that operations must be resumed there with every determination as soon as the U-boats are given the necessary weapons for this. Equipment with 2cm. quadruples, which will begin as from June to an increasing degree, will be the first step in this direction, equipment with Zaunkönig torpedoes[14] [anti-destroyer] the second step, while improvement of location devices at the moment is still to be considered. It is, however, anticipated that after equipment with quadruples, i.e. from the autumn, the Battle of the North Atlantic will be completely resumed once more.

In the meantime it is essential that the morale of the men should not be affected by these temporary defensive measures, a task which requires full cooperation of the Commanding Officers, as well as the personal touch of the Commander-in-Chief of the Navy.

(Signed) DÖNITZ

The relevant extract from Order of the Day reads:

Most Secret
24 May 1943
Order of the Day
To all U-boat Officers.

EXTRACT

You alone can, at the moment, make an offensive attack against the enemy and beat him. The U-boat must, by continuous sinking of ships with war material and the necessary supplies for the British Isles, force the enemy to continual losses which must slowly but steadily sap the strength of the strongest force. The German people have long felt that our boats constitute the keenest and most decisive weapon, and that the outcome of the war depends on the success or failure of the Battle of the Atlantic.

Each one of you must be aware of his great responsibility and every Commanding Officer must be able to say that he has conducted operations with every effort and tenacity in order to attain our important goal. I know that operations for you out there at the moment are some of the hardest and most costly in losses, since the enemy's defence at the moment is superior in view of new technical methods. Believe me, I have done everything, and will continue to do so, in order to introduce means to counter this enemy advance. The time will soon come in which you will be superior to the enemy with new and stronger weapons and will be able to triumph over your worst enemies, the aircraft and the destroyer.

In the meantime we must master the situation with the measures already ordered and with a partial change in operational areas. We will, therefore, not allow ourselves to be forced onto the defensive and will not rest but, where there is an opportunity, continue to strike and fight on with still more fortitude and decision in order to make ourselves even stronger for the decisive Battle of the North Atlantic, which will be carried out shortly with improved weapons, in the area most vulnerable for the enemy.

We will then be the victors – my faith in our boats and in you convinces me of this.

Heil Hitler
Commander-in-Chief Dönitz

Following these messages, the BdU Operations Division War Log entry for 24 May noted:

The twelve boats remaining in the North Atlantic are being set up in offensive areas south-east of Greenland and are to feign a strong group of submarines by making corresponding radio traffic.

At a Joint Press Conference in Washington with President Roosevelt on 25 May Churchill, asked if he had anything to say about the 'submarine side of the situation', replied:

I am very much encouraged by all that has happened there since the turn of the year. Really, it has been very encouraging. The output from the United States' shipyards is prodigious and has fulfilled all hopes, hopes which, when the plans were first made and published, seemed to be excessive. But they have been made good. The movement of supplies across the ocean has been on an increasing scale. The surplus of new building over sinkings over the last six months has been substantial, especially in the later months; and the killings of U-boats have improved and reached a very high pitch – never better than in the last month. That is due, of course, to the decreasing numbers of U-boats, but it is also due to the improved methods, and some wonderful things that have been thought of on both sides of the Atlantic. And, of course, we interchange everything immediately. Anything we have we share and bring into action. A lot of clever people are thinking a lot about these things.

On 31 May Dönitz informed Hitler he had withdrawn his U-boats from the North Atlantic to the area west of the Azores in the hope of encountering less air reconnaissance. He intended, however, to resume attacks on convoys in the North Atlantic at the time of the new moon, provided the submarines had additional weapons at their disposal by that time. In addressing the future prospects of submarine warfare, Dönitz informed Hitler that efforts were being frustrated by a technical device (radar) against which counter-measures would be found. It was impossible, however, to forecast to what extent submarine warfare would again, become effective. The enemy's anti-submarine defence on water and from the air would be improved, he said, and that would entail many uncertainties and unknown factors. In 1940 a submarine was able to sink an average of 1,000 tons per day at sea; toward the end of 1942 this had fallen to approximately 200 tons. This showed clearly the growing effectiveness of anti-submarine defence and the diminishing effectiveness of submarines. Nevertheless, he was convinced submarine warfare must be carried on, even if great successes were no longer possible.

Hitler then interrupted Dönitz, remarking:

> There can be no talk of a let-up in submarine warfare. The Atlantic is my first line of defence in the West, and even if I have to fight a defensive battle there, that is preferable to waiting to defend myself on the coast of Europe. The enemy forces tied up by our submarine warfare are tremendous, even though the actual losses inflicted by us are no longer great. I cannot afford to release these forces by discontinuing submarine warfare.

Dönitz then called for a sustained effort to increase submarine production, from thirty to forty U-boats per month, to which Hitler agreed.

Dönitz in his post-war comments on these developments recalled:

> From this new situation [in May 1943] it was evident that the enemy's aircraft and destroyers must now have been fitted with new radar. The U-boat losses, which previously had been 13 per cent of all the boats at sea, rose rapidly to 30 to 50 per cent. In 1943 alone, forty-three U-boats were lost. These losses were suffered not only in convoy attacks, but everywhere

at sea. There was no part of the Atlantic where the boats were safe from being located day and night by aircraft. All the U-boat entrance and exit channels in the Bay of Biscay were, in particular, most carefully watched. Losses here were especially high.

Under these circumstances, the previous surface war on convoys could not be continued because, in the meantime, the favourable conditions in the American sphere of activity had also changed and U-boat successes had diminished considerably in that theatre. The enemy air force with its modern methods of searching had produced this change in U-boat warfare.

Many published sources retrospectively claim Dönitz called off operations in the North Atlantic on 23 or 24 May (dates vary), saying, 'We had lost the Battle of the Atlantic.' This statement was not made by Dönitz at the time, nor is it to be found in contemporary BdU War Logs, but was in fact written much later, appearing on page 341 of his Memoirs published in 1954, in which he wrote:

By 22 May we had already lost thirty-one U-boats since the first of the month, a frightful total which came as a hard and unexpected blow; for notwithstanding the more powerful enemy anti-submarine forces in operation in this fourth year of the war an increase in U-boat losses had not until this time been perceptible.[15]

In the submarine war there had been plenty of setbacks and crises. Such things are unavoidable in any form of warfare. But we had always overcome them because the fighting efficiency of the U-boat arm had remained steady. Now, however, the situation had changed by radar, and particularly radar location by aircraft. Wolfpack operations in the North Atlantic, the main theatre of operations and at the same time the main theatre where air cover was strongest, were no longer possible. They could only be resumed if we succeeded in radically increasing the fighting power of the U-boats.

This was the logical conclusion to which I came, and I accordingly withdrew the boats from the North Atlantic. On 24 May, I ordered them to proceed, using the utmost caution, to the area to the south-west of the Azores.

We had lost the Battle of the Atlantic.

Roskill (*The War at Sea 1939–45*, Vol II, p.377) concludes:

By the 22nd of May, when the Germans made up their minds that they must accept defeat and withdraw the survivors from the field of battle, they had already lost thirty-three U-boats; and the toll taken during the whole month was forty-one. Donitz declared that the withdrawal was only temporary 'to avoid unnecessary losses in a period when our weapons are shown to be at a disadvantage' and that 'the battle in the North Atlantic – the decisive area – will be resumed'; and it is true that six months later he did renew the campaign on the convoy routes. But, as will be told in our final volume, the battle never again reached the same pitch of intensity, nor hung so delicately in the balance, as during the spring of 1943. It is therefore fair to claim that the victory here recounted marked one of the decisive stages of the war; for the enemy then made his greatest effort against our Atlantic life-line – and he failed. After forty-five months of unceasing battle, of a more exacting and arduous nature than posterity may easily realise, our convoy escorts and aircraft had won the triumph they had so richly merited.

Several other convoys were threatened in the first half of the month after ONS.5, but no serious losses were suffered, and the toll of U-boats losses mounted steadily. After the attack on ONS.7 on 17 May, no ship was lost in the remaining days of the month. During the whole month four out of fifteen Atlantic convoys (including ONS.5) containing a total 622 merchant ships (heavily protected by a large number of British, Canadian and US convoy escorts) lost eighteen merchant ships, or just 3 per cent of the total. ONS.5 accounted for two thirds of the losses. Twenty-three of the seventy U-boats at sea at the time were sunk. Excluding the losses against ONS.5, sixteen U-boats were lost in exchange for just six merchant ships.

Although Dönitz recognized the previous U-boat surface war on convoys in Atlantic and Pan-American waters could not be sustained, he regarded the losses as merely a temporary setback, soon to be avenged by the introduction of technical advances and improved weapons. He now moved to augment the U-boats' anti-aircraft capability to counter the air threat and introduced the new acoustic homing torpedo for use against the convoy escorts. Whilst these new techniques were finalized, U-boats would remain relatively inactive in the North Atlantic and not return in strength until September 1943.

Dönitz originally intended to resume convoy operations in the North Atlantic on about 2 July, as the BdU War Log for 2 June explains:

It had been intended when the main operations area was transferred from the North Atlantic to resume convoy operations there in the new moon period about 2 July, when it was thought the situation would be more favourable, insofar as more boats with increased flak armament would be available, and some boats would be equipped with the radar decoy device 'Aphrodite'.

It was now evident the next new moon period was the least favourable of the whole year. There were only about three hours of complete darkness at 55°N and no darkness at all at 60°N. It was in the latter area that the operation would probably take place, so in actual fact no darkness could be expected. This meant the advantages of using 'Aphrodite' would to a large extent be lost, as the device was particularly effective in the dark; and also there would never be any time during which there was no air activity and thus no chance for boats to get ahead unhindered. These circumstances were so unfavourable that it was not planned to undertake the first convoy operation in the North Atlantic until the next new moon period at the beginning of August.

The First Lord of the Admiralty, asked in the House of Commons on Wednesday, 2 June[16] whether he had any statement to make on recent progress in anti-U-boat warfare, replied:

Early in March I told the House that the shipping losses in December, January and February had been much lower than a year before. For a variety of reasons March was a poor month, though not the worst of the war. Indeed, owing to the high output of new tonnage achieved in the United States, there was a substantial net gain in that month. In April and May losses have been reduced again to the level of the three months December to February, and even below. In each of the first five months of this year there has been a substantial reduction on the figures of the corresponding period of last year, and a saving of more than one-third of the losses over the whole of the five months. With the American merchant ship programme nearing its peak, this improved level of losses has resulted in large increases to the tonnage available to the United Nations.

This improved situation in the Battle of the Atlantic reflects the growing size of our escort forces – both ships and aircraft – and the growing deadliness of our new weapons and devices. The increased escorts available make possible not only a higher scale of protection but also a higher general standard of training, and this in turn enables our ships and the aircraft of Coastal Command and the United States Air Forces to reap, by the harmony and co-operation in which they work, a higher dividend from their constantly improving tactics. The escort carriers, of which several are now in service, have already proved their worth. By these means the curve of U-boat destruction has been kept steadily rising. During the last 12 months the number of kills exceeds that of the whole of the previous period of the war, and in the last six months the rate of destruction has been 25 per cent above that of the previous six months. Large numbers have been damaged in addition. In the last two months the number of U-boats in the Atlantic Battle appears to have decreased. This has no doubt been due to more than one cause, but principally to the rising rate of 'kills' at sea. From the provisional assessments it looks as if the number of U-boats destroyed in May will exceed the number which the enemy may probably have brought into service. Certainly May is the best month of the war for kills so far. While the changed situation has thus been primarily due to the increased rate of destruction of U-boats at sea, there can be no doubt that the number of U-boats operating has also been affected by the bombing of the U-boat building yards and of the operational bases in the Bay of Biscay by both American and RAF bombers. As time goes on, the bombing of the building yards and component factories should have an ever-increasing effect.

We must no doubt still be prepared to encounter setbacks and periods of heavy loss. The enemy are bound to make great efforts to alter the present situation. Nevertheless, the report I have just made discloses a number of favourable tendencies, and I can give the unqualified assurance that the enemy are quite wrong in asserting, as they have done, that the low rate of sinkings in April was due to the small amount of shipping at sea. In that month our imports were the highest since the beginning of 1942.

Details of U-boat losses during May appeared in press reports of 5 June quoting a statement by the First Lord of the Admiralty:

Sinkings of U-boats in May are estimated at twenty at least, judging by a statement in the House of Commons by the First Lord of the Admiralty (Mr. A. V. Alexander).

English and American official announcements totalled eight certainties, four probables and two possibles, but these obviously were incomplete.

German U-boat production was at its peak in April and was reckoned between fifteen and twenty.

Mr Alexander's statement on U-boat sinkings is hailed as one of the most solid and hopeful pronouncements so far made, especially as it concerns what many regard as the greatest of all menaces.

The same day, newspapers carried accounts of an admission by the German Admiralty that the Allies had developed a new means of detecting U-boats. A typical article read:

NEW SUBMARINE FINDER UPSETS
U-BOAT CAMPAIGN

LONDON, 4 June 4

According to the Exchange Telegraph Agency correspondent in Berne, the German Admiralty admits the Allied navies' success against U-boats and also a considerable reduction in British ship losses are due to the greatly improved defence methods.

Captain Rudolf Khrone, who is a member of Admiral Dönitz's staff, in an article published in the *Völkischer Beobachter*, says: 'The Allies possess a new submarine finder, enabling the detection of submarines at long distances, thus forcing U-boats to operate with great caution. The Allies have succeeded temporarily in disturbing our strategic and tactical plans for the U-boat campaign, but it is hoped that German industry will soon find new weapons against the increased Allied defence strength and new tactics.'

Until the summer of 1943 it had been the practice for detailed information on merchant shipping sunk by U-boats, particularly in the Atlantic, to be published regularly in the national and international press. The potential security implications of this led President Roosevelt to suggest to Churchill[17] that less specific information should be released. Roosevelt had become concerned at the number of statements being made from time to time by officials and in the press on both sides of the Atlantic about the anti-U-boat war and the weapons, methods or tactics methods being used in successful anti-submarine warfare. He judged that the enemy, by piecing together portions of these statements, might glean more information about the Atlantic campaign from these than was desirable. It was therefore agreed that a monthly statement approved by the President and the Prime Minister would be issued on the 10th of each month; and that apart from any specially authorized announcements or statements by the President or Prime Minister or duly censored accounts of particular incidents and actions, this monthly statement would be the only one made on behalf of the British and American governments. All Government departments on both sides of the Atlantic were instructed to comply. It was hoped the press would, so far as possible, cooperate in keeping technical discussions of U-boat warfare within the limits of the official announcements and generally leave Germany in the dark as to what they enemy described as this most important aspect of their successful warfare at sea.

Churchill informed the War Cabinet on 7 June[18] that he had received a telegram from President Roosevelt suggesting they issue a joint statement each month on the progress of the war against the U-boats which, without mentioning any figures, would provide a broad description of the position. The First Lord of the Admiralty said he was sending the Prime Minister a note giving the Admiralty's view on the President's proposal which, he thought, contained certain risks. The War Cabinet took note of this suggestion, which would be discussed by the Prime Minister and the First Lord of the Admiralty.

The following day, in his Statement on the War Situation[19] in the House of Commons on 8 June, Churchill spoke again on the progress of the anti-U-boat war:

> In the summer of last year, as Minister of Defence, I set on foot a policy of increasing our bomber effort, which, of course, entails certain sacrifices in other directions. All that is now coming into hand.
>
> At the same time we took the measures which have thrown the very long-range air power – V. L. R. as it is called – effectively into the anti-U-boat struggle. All this is now being brought to bear.
>
> The month of May has from every point of view been the best month we have ever had in the anti-U-boat war since the United States was attacked by Japan, Germany, and Italy. At that time we gained much greater combined resources, but we exposed much larger targets. We made at that time a budget of sinkings and buildings on which we knew we could survive indefinitely.
>
> Sinkings have been greatly less than we apprehended, and buildings have more than made good the prodigious programmes undertaken by the American nation.
>
> The month of May has been one of the very best for imports carried safely into this island since the end of 1941. Our combined new building has exceeded our losses by more than three to one. This first week in June could not possibly be taken as a criterion, but as a matter of fact it is the best ever for many, many months past.
>
> During the last few months the enemy has made very heavy attacks on our convoys. This has given us the opportunity to hit him hard in open battle.
>
> There are so many U-boats employed now that it is almost impossible not to run into one or another of these great fields or screens of U-boats which are spread out. Therefore you have to fight your way through, but there is no reason why we should regret that. On the contrary, it is around convoys that U-boats can best be destroyed.
>
> New weapons and new methods and close coordination of effort between surface and air escorts have enabled us to inflict casualties which

have surpassed all previous records. The First Lord of the Admiralty made a statement of very reassuring character upon this subject the other day, and I can only repeat that in May, for the first time, our killings of U-boats substantially outnumbered the U-boat output. That may be a fateful milestone.

The Germans seem to be staking their hopes upon the U-boat war, we may judge by appeals made to them. They are encouraged to bear the evils – the terror, as they call it, perhaps not an ill-chosen word – of the air bombardment by the hope that on the sea the U-boats are taking their revenge.

If it should be made clear that this hope has failed them, they may be seriously disappointed, and they are a people who when seriously disappointed do not always find resources to confront approaching disaster once their reason tells them it is inevitable.

But again I say – I make the observation in passing – do not let us build on such deductions. It would be foolish to assume that good results of a single month are a guarantee of a continuing process. We may have setbacks, though I have always looked forward to this summer as being a period which would be favourable to us.

Moreover, of course, the enemy may decline battle, or he may look only for the most tempting opportunities. In this case we shall have fewer killings but more imports, and the freer movement of troops and munitions will be possible to all the various theatres.

I must say I feel confident that the U-boat war will not stand between the United Nations and their final victory, while all the time the air war will grow in weight and severity. I might well speak with more emphasis upon this point, but it is prudent to forbear.

The press were prone to paraphrase Churchill's speeches, as the following typical example from 10 June illustrates:

WAR ON 'WOLF PACKS'

There could be no more important aspect in the progress of the war than the favourable turn now taken in the fight against the enemy submarine campaign. In his speech to the House of Commons, Mr Churchill observed that the month of May was the best for the Allies since the Axis U-boat attack in the Atlantic. 'In May for the first time our killings of U-boats substantially outnumbered the U-boat output', he said, and he added that the first week in June was even better than the May record.

Ships spell victory in a global war. Every successful voyage is an individual victory over the enemy, and every convoy safely delivered is a strategic triumph. Lack of shipping means that offensives cannot be launched at the most advantageous times, for the highways of the ocean must be available to the Allies, and ships to sail them must be afloat. It may be said truly that whilst Hitler can never win this war, he will never lose it, finally and irrevocably, unless the Allies destroy the submarine wolf packs ranged against our marine services. Any set of circumstances that could bring about a conclusion of the war before the U-boat campaign was completely crushed would not be in the best interests of the subsequent peace.

Earlier this year, Goebbels boasted that Germany would have 1,000 submarines in commission before the end of 1943. 'With our U-boat warfare we have seized Britain by the throat,' he said. 'I spoke with the knowledge', [said Churchill], 'that British ship sinkings had become so severe by the close of 1942, and submarines were being produced so rapidly, that some of our Allied naval strategists feared a crisis similar to that of the dark days of April-May 1917.'

Instead, there has been a marked change in the picture. British Naval warriors gradually formulated new plans to combat the U-boat menace, and although the world has not yet learned the details of the cooperative system now being employed, the results speak for themselves. It is known, of course, that the steel lanes across the Atlantic – lanes of steel fighter craft and escort vessels that are linked in parallel chains across the ocean, and through which supply liners pass – are now greatly reinforced. Gaps in the steel 'fences' over the ocean have been filled by small aircraft carriers.

This system is breaking up Admiral Dönitz's 'wolf pack' methods, which were such a terror to Allied shipping. It was shown by Dönitz that whereas only the most skilful and daring of U-boat commanders could operate singly with success, a method of hunting in packs with resolute leadership could facilitate attacks on the largest of convoys and effect the greatest damage. The danger to the Germans was that the whole pack might be destroyed if the action went against them. And it is at this point that British strategy, in the counter-offensive against packs, changed the fortunes of submarine warfare. Whole packs were destroyed and are being destroyed. Combined with this improvement in the Allied fortunes of war at sea, there are the devastating RAF raids on U-boat nests, supply bases and conditioning factories on European coasts. These attacks are especially important, because the U-boat campaign has been the No. 1 item in German propaganda; it has been used to bolster up morale and as the talisman of Axis strategy. The breakdown of the U-boat campaign will mean much towards the complete breakdown of the Axis.

The decision by Dönitz to withdraw the U-boats from the Atlantic pending update of equipment and tactics was disclosed in press reports of 24 June:

NAZIS TO REVISE U-BOAT TACTICS

From Our Own Correspondent, STOCKHOLM, Wednesday
Admiral Dönitz, C-in-C, German Navy, is reported to have withdrawn two-thirds of his submarine fleet from action and to be considering a fundamental revision of U-boat tactical methods and equipment to meet the successful Allied counter moves. The principal modification is likely to be a reduction in the number of submarines in each pack as it has been discovered that large groups of submarines are too vulnerable to depth-charge attacks once they are found.

The planned return of U-boats to the Atlantic was further delayed when on 30 June the BdU announced, following the loss of *U-194* and *U-200* (both sunk on 24 June south of Iceland by RAF Liberator aircraft) and previous experience, that Dönitz had ordered, with immediate effect, no U-boat was to put out to sea without quadruple-mounted anti-aircraft guns. A temporary postponement of operational orders for three to four weeks and a hold-up in German shipyards had to be taken into account.

In his speech the same day at a Guildhall lunch Churchill provided a dramatic account of the convoy attacks of the previous month:

There was another, a no less notable battle, which was fought in May in the Atlantic against U-boats. In May the German Admiralty made extreme exertions to prevent the movement to Great Britain of the enormous convoys of food and materials which are continuously received from the United States and which we must bring in safely if our war-making capacity is to be maintained. Long lines of U-boats were spread to meet these convoys and fifteen or twenty U-boats were concentrated in each attack.

To meet this, the British and American and Canadian forces of the sea and air hurled their strength at the U-boats. The fighting took place mainly around the convoys and also over a wide expanse of ocean. It ended in the total defeat of the U-boat attack. More than thirty U-boats were certainly destroyed in the month of May, floundering in many cases with their crews in the dark depths of the sea. Staggered by these deadly losses, the U-boats have recoiled to lick their wounds and mourn their dead.

Now as a result of the May victory and massacre of U-boats we have had in June the best month we have ever known in the whole forty-six of the war. The prodigious shipbuilding exertions of the United States and the considerable contribution of Britain and also Canada have produced an output of new ships which is somewhere between seven and ten times as much as our losses from enemy action in the month of June.

Since the middle of May scarcely a single merchant ship has been sunk in the whole of the North Atlantic. In June, also, although the convoys are not being seriously attacked at the present time, U-boat losses have been most solid and encouraging.

I give these facts purposely in a form which conveys the truth without giving precise or detailed information to circles wider than those with which we ourselves are concerned. There are two conclusions to be drawn from them. The first is that we must not assume that this great improvement will be maintained or that bad patches do not lie ahead. The second is that, although encouraged by the growing success of our methods, we must redouble our efforts and ingenuity.

The disasters of the U-boats in May and June have a bearing on another phase of our offensive war. These two months have seen the heaviest discharge of bombs on the munitions and industrial war centres of Germany. Three years ago Hitler boasted he would rub out the cities of Britain. Certainly in the nine months before he abandoned his attack, we suffered very heavy damage to our buildings and grievous hindrance to our life and work. More than 40,000 of our people were killed and 120,000 wounded. But now those who sowed the wind harvest the whirlwind.

No ships were lost from North Atlantic convoys during the month.

Chapter 10

Phase Ten: July to August 1943

The news of the Battle of the Atlantic was dominated in the early days of July 1943 by press reports on the progress of anti-U-boat warfare. The first of these, published on 2 July and headlined, 'Churchill's Statement on the Destruction of U-boats', referred to his speech at the Guildhall on 30 June. This was followed three days later by his announcement to the War Cabinet[1] of the arrangement made with President Roosevelt for the issue of a joint statement by them each month on the progress of the war against the U-boats. The Press carried further reports, this time on new methods of U-boat attack, on Tuesday 6 July. A typical article read:

U-BOAT ATTACKS
Reported New Methods

LONDON, 5 July

A Stockholm message received from Berlin says that the new tactical training of U-boat crews recently mentioned by the naval correspondent of the Essen *Nationalzeitung* consists of 'well organized and strategically regular attacks by entire U-boat flotillas'. These attacks are expected to upset all Allied counter-strokes which hitherto to a certain extent prevented a greet loss of tonnage. The naval correspondent of the Essen *Nationalzeitung* admitted that the Allies had found a 'counter-measure', but claimed that sinkings would rise again after a period 'in which U-boats had been withdrawn for technical revision and the tactical training of crews'.

There was now, however, an absence of U-boats in the Atlantic. Dönitz informed Hitler on 8 July that he had transferred U-boats from the North Atlantic, after it had to be abandoned as a result of the lost battle in May, to new areas of operations where anti-submarine measures were not yet so strong and efficient. As a result, there had been few sinkings during June; but July, he told Hitler, had begun to show some improvement. It was now evident the enemy was directing his main efforts against the exit lanes of the U-boats, i.e. the Strait of

Shetland and Bay of Biscay, where losses were still very high. Most were caused by the enemy's air force, but lately also by sub-chaser groups and naval forces cooperating with the air force for which Dönitz had no defence as yet. For the time being, the departure of submarines from home ports had been suspended until all U-boats were equipped with quadruple and twin AA mounts. Dönitz told Hitler he expected by the end of July to have an efficient warning device against enemy radar location – although there was no indication as yet that the enemy was using a new radar system. After these defensive improvements against air attack had been made, and the long nights again gave the U-boats an advantage, the northern route could be used once more. Of equal importance to these measures was the development of the anti-destroyer torpedo to combat enemy surface vessels. Until this was ready for use, Dönitz did not intend to resume attacks on convoys in the North Atlantic.

The draft of the first monthly Joint Statements by Churchill and Roosevelt read:

1. In June the losses of Allied and neutral ships from submarine attack were the lowest since the USA entered the war. The losses from all forms of enemy action were the second lowest since the war between Britain and Germany began.
2. The number of targets offered to the anti-submarine vessels and aircraft of the United Nations was not as great in June as previously, but the sinkings of Axis submarines were substantial and satisfactory.
3. The heavy toll taken of U-boats in May showed its effect in June in that the main trans-Atlantic convoys were practically unmolested, and the U-boat attacks on our shipping were in widely separated areas. However every opportunity was taken of attacking U-boats leaving and returning to their bases in western France.
4. New weapons and devices have achieved a good measure of success and are continually being improved.
5. The merchant shipping tonnage of the United Nations has shown a large net increase every month this year. Anti-submarine vessels and aircraft are coming into service in considerable numbers.

Roosevelt approved the draft statement except for the reference to new weapons and devices in paragraph 4, as he had been advised that all public reference to new weapons should be avoided. The agreement was then briefed to the War Cabinet on 9 July, the Minutes of which read:

The Prime Minster reported[2] the draft of the first monthly statement on the progress of the anti-U-boat war had been communicated to President

Roosevelt, who had accepted the draft subject to the omission of certain references to new methods and weapons. The statement would be published in the Press on the following day. The Minister of Information had been asked to inform the Press that these statements 'would in future be issued at monthly intervals; and to ask them to refrain, as far as possible, from publishing other articles or statements about the progress of the anti-U-boat war or the weapons and methods used.'

Now that this authoritative statement was to be made each month, it was more than ever important that other statements and comments about the progress of the anti-U-boat war should not be made. The War Cabinet endorsed the Prime Minister's views, and invited the Secretary to the War Cabinet to see that their wishes in this matter were brought to the notice of all concerned.

The first of these Statements was then published on 10 July 1943, and they would continue to be published monthly until June 1945. The same day, press reports appeared quoting Dönitz's admission of setbacks in the U-boat campaign. A typical article read:

NAZIS ADMIT U-BOAT SETBACK

German Navy spokesman, Admiral Dönitz, admitted in a broadcast to the German people that the Allies had gained the upper hand in the war against U-boats.

The use of aircraft carriers and other new weapons by the Allies had caused a serious setback to Germany's U-boat campaign, he said.

The situation was so serious for the U-boats, he added, that hunting in pack formation had been abandoned.

Further reports appeared the following day, Saturday, 10 July 1943:

NEW U-BOAT DRIVE PROMISED

LONDON, Friday
A Stockholm message stated that the German Admiralty had announced that the U-boat lull will end soon as they were being refitted with new weapons. Operations will resume about the middle of July.

The BdU War Log's resumé for 11 July of 'the U-boat Situation in the North Atlantic since 24 May' explained the delay in resuming Atlantic operations:

When convoy operation *Donau*[3] failed, all the boats still well off for fuel were ordered to proceed to the central Atlantic. It had been intended that the remaining boats in the North Atlantic occupy varying attack areas and deceive the enemy as to the number of boats actually in the area by heavy dummy radio traffic. Altogether thirteen boats remained in the northern operations area, and during the first few weeks it was actually possible to keep the enemy in the dark as to the number of boats there, as English U-boat situation reports have shown – [the enemy] continued to believe that there were two or three large groups of U-boats.

It was intended to keep the number of U-boats remaining in the operations at approximately the same level by relieving them with boats sailing from home ports. Within a short time, however, several boats had to return owing to fuel consumption and damage and two, *U-202* [2 June] and *U-304* [28 May], were lost. The number of boats coming from home ports was not sufficient. After it became known on 24 June that *U-194* and *U-200* had been lost, the sailing of all boats without quadruple flak from home ports was cancelled. This meant a postponement of approximately four weeks for all sailing dates. Four boats on their way to the Atlantic were diverted to Norway.

This led to the North Atlantic being practically devoid of U-boats except for one, *U-667*, still in the northern operations area. It was presumed the enemy was no longer deceived about the actual state of affairs. As far as could be gathered from the press, the enemy believed the use of more auxiliary carriers had succeeded in chasing the U-boats off the North Atlantic convoy routes. At present, chances of attacking were so slight owing to the strength of the escort forces, and chances of finding the convoys so remote with so few U-boats, that there was little purpose in sending boats from Western France to fill this gap in the northern operations area. In practice, boats would have to operate in the North Atlantic with very small prospects of success.

The plan to resume convoy operations in the North Atlantic at the end of July with stronger forces had been abandoned; neither the Zaunkönig [torpedo] nor the improved radar interception gear necessary to prevent surprise attacks by aircraft would be available in time. If it was possible to equip boats leaving Western France by the middle of August with these, action against convoys on the England–America route would be resumed during the new moon period at the end of August.

This lack of U-boat activity in the North Atlantic translated into lower sinkings of merchant ships, as reported on 11 July:

LOWER U-BOAT SINKINGS

LONDON, July 11

Losses of Allied and neutral merchant ships by U-boat attacks in the Atlantic last month were the lowest since the United States entered the war, the main trans-Atlantic convoys being practically unmolested.

It is officially announced also that losses from all forms of enemy action during June were the lowest recorded since the outbreak of the war between Britain and Germany.

'The targets offered to anti-submarine vessels and aircraft of the United Nations,' the statement continued, 'were not so numerous during June as previously, but the sinkings of Axis submarines were substantial and satisfactory.'

'The heavy toll taken of U-boats during May showed its effect in June, when the main trans-Atlantic convoys were practically unmolested. U-boat attacks against our shipping occurred in widely separated areas. However, every opportunity was taken to attack the U-boats leaving and returning; to their bases on the west coast of France.

'The merchant shipping tonnage of the United Nations has shown a large increase every month this year, while anti-submarine vessels and aircraft have been coming into service in considerable numbers.'

The statement announced that Churchill and Roosevelt would in future issue an approved report on the shipping position once a month, and continued:

'The United States and British Governments are concerned at the number of statements that public persons and newspapers on both sides of the Atlantic are making about the U-boat war and the methods and the devices employed in it.

'The enemy, by piecing together these statements, may glean more Information than is desirable.

'This will be the only one made on behalf of the two Governments, apart from especially authorised announcements, statements, or censored accounts of particular incidents and actions.

'It is hoped that the press, as far as possible, will co-operate In keeping technical discussions about U-boat warfare within the limit of official announcements, and so leave the enemy In his present state of doubt and anxiety upon this most important aspect of our successful warfare at sea.'

By 17 July Dönitz felt able to report to Hitler that work on the anti-destroyer torpedo had reached the point where it would be possible to equip submarines at the beginning of August – two to three months earlier than expected – to enable attacks in the North Atlantic to resume by the end of August.

In the meantime, the deployment of auxiliary aircraft carriers to escort Atlantic convoys earlier in the year began to filter into the media, with the first press reports appearing on 24 July:

WAR ON U-BOATS

Baby Aircraft Carriers

Effective partial lifting of the veil of official secrecy about the war on U-boats in the Atlantic revealed that an effective new weapon was small aircraft carriers known as 'Baby Bs'. These had proved to be able to put up air cover which kept U-boat 'wolf packs' 18 miles or more away from convoys. So heavy were the blows aimed at U-boats that numbers of prisoners, comprising destroyed U-boat crews, mounted steadily. Helicopters, fighters and light bombers were now sea-based aircraft operating in the Battle of Atlantic. Many convoys were getting across without any damage or losses at all, and it was reported that U-boat crews were losing their morale.

In a speech to the Commons on 27 July during the debate on 'Italy and the War', Churchill exclaimed, 'German hopes of U-boat warfare turning the tide of war are sinking as fast as the U-boats themselves.'

No Atlantic convoys were attacked during July, but attacks on unescorted tankers and freighters continued. The Joint Statement for the month read:

During the month of July very poor results were obtained by the U-boats from their widespread effort against the shipping of the Allies. The steady flow of trans-Atlantic supplies on the greatest scale has continued unmolested, and such sinkings as have taken place in distant areas have had but an insignificant effect on the conduct of the war by the Allies. In fact, July is probably our most successful month, because the imports have been high, shipping losses moderate, and U-boat sinkings heavy.

Our offensive operations against Axis submarines continue to progress most favourably in all areas, and during May, June and July we have sunk at sea a total of over 90 U-boats, which represents an average loss of nearly one U-boat a day over the period.

The decline in the effectiveness of the U-boats is illustrated by the following figures:

In the first six months of 1943, the number of ships sunk per U-boat operating was only half that in the last six months of 1942 and only a quarter that in the first half of 1942.

The tonnage of shipping in the service of the United Nations continues to show a considerable net increase. During 1943 new ships completed by the Allies exceed all sinkings from all causes by upwards of 3,000,000 tons.

In spite of this very favourable progress in the battle against the U-boat, it must be remembered that the enemy still has large U-boat reserves, completed and under construction. It is necessary, therefore, to prepare for intensification of the battle both at sea and in the shipyards and to use our shipping with utmost economy to strengthen and speed the general offensive of the United Nations. But we can expect continued success only if we do not relax our efforts in any way.

A BdU assessment dated 5 August of the general U-boat situation noted

unusually high losses, the majority attributed to enemy air superiority, to which the inferiority of U-boat radar interception gear probably contributed. It has recently been discovered Metox sets [designed to pick up ASV, Air to Surface Vessel, radar] radiated to a far greater extent than previously known or suspected. In many instances U-boats have given themselves away to enemy aircraft by operating their radar interception gear. The uncertainty has now made it necessary to cancel the sailing of all boats until they have been fitted out with the new Hagenuk set.[4] It was also now suspected the enemy was using new weapons on which there was no further information. Radio Intelligence reports suggested a Hedgehog[5] gear was in use.

The intention to resume convoy operations during the new moon period at the beginning of September has been frustrated by the cancelling of all sailings until the new radar interception gear was delivered, and resumption of operations was postponed until the end of September. The new weapons available for these operations would be the Zaunkönig torpedo the reinforced flak armament, the new radar interception gear and new radar decoy device, Aphrodite.[6]

In a further development, U-boats were warned on 9 August in BdU Serial Order No. 33 of the possible use by the enemy of long-range reconnaissance aircraft and carriers, to give air cover not only in areas off the coast, but over the whole of the North and Central Atlantic. The danger of U-boats being depth-charged when using their radio had therefore increased.

Despite earlier forecasts, the U-boats had still not returned to the North Atlantic. On 19 August Dönitz informed Hitler that the resumption of attacks on convoys in the North Atlantic was now scheduled for the end of September; he hoped the improvement in weapons would enable a resumption of battle but recognized the struggle would no doubt continue to be a hard one.

The BdU War Log for 23 August explained that events during the month of May had shown it was not possible, owing to the excessive losses, to continue the fight in the North Atlantic. If U-boat warfare was to be continued at all until the introduction of new weapons and apparatus, deployment of all outward bound VIIc and IXc boats could only take place in the areas mentioned (the Caribbean and the Atlantic between Trinidad and West Africa). Warfare in this area had to be abandoned sooner than anticipated. Even if the success achieved appeared proportionally slight compared with the losses, it had to be stressed that U-boat deployment would lead to a strong combination of the defence forces in the entire mid-Atlantic area and thus greatly tax the strength of the enemy air forces. In this way, the operational objective – the momentary use of U-boat forces for defence purposes – would be achieved, even if the sacrifice was great. All boats arriving in this area in future were to be equipped with new Fu.M.B. (Hagenuk) and anti-aircraft armament reinforcements [quadruple and twin-mounted guns]. The use of the Hagenuk anti-radar device would complicate the location of U-boats by the enemy, lessen the danger of surprise air attacks and facilitate more mobile night operations.

Dönitz later wrote:

After the winter of 1942 had produced changes in the situation in Russia and in the Mediterranean unfavourable to us, there appeared in the spring of 1943 a similar change in the U-boat warfare which was, however, quite independent of the former and due to completely different causes.

Although in March the major attacks on convoys could still be carried out, by May it was quite clear that the enemy's air strength in the Atlantic, consisting of long-range planes and carrier-borne aircraft, had increased enormously. Of even greater consequence, however, was the fact that the U-boats could be located at a great distance by the enemy's radar, apparently on short wave, without previous warning on their own receivers. They were then heavily attacked by destroyers and aircraft carriers without even seeing the convoy, which had been diverted. If, however, in spite of this a convoy was contacted, it was discovered that the problem of finding it was no longer the only difficulty, in that U-boats could not now attack the convoy because its firepower forced them to submerge.

From this new situation it was evident that the enemy's aircraft and destroyers must now have been fitted with new radar. The U-boat losses, which previously had been 13 per cent of all the boats at sea, rose rapidly to 30 to 50 per cent. In 1943 alone, forty-three U-boats were lost. These losses were suffered not only in convoy attacks, but everywhere at sea. There was no part of the Atlantic where the boats were safe from being located day and night by aircraft. All the U-boat entrance and exit channels in the Bay of Biscay were, in particular, most carefully watched. Losses here were especially high.

Under these circumstances, the previous surface war on convoys could not be continued because, in the meantime, the favourable conditions in the American sphere of activity had also changed and U-boat successes diminished considerably in that theatre. The enemy air force with its modern methods of searching had produced this change in U-boat warfare.

As counter-measures, the ideas already started had to be followed up with all speed. These were: firstly, to produce as quickly as possible a new U-boat with as much manoeuvrability when submerged as U-boats had, up to now, possessed on the surface; and secondly, until production of these new boats, to make all possible alterations to the existing U-boats so that, in spite of the enemy's radar and superior air power, they might be as effective as possible.

Twenty-five U-boats were lost during August. No Atlantic convoys were attacked during the month. The Joint Statement read:

1. August has been another successful month in U-boat warfare. Owing perhaps to rearmament and other causes, there appear to have been fewer U-boats at sea than in recent months, and shipping losses have continued to decrease.
2. It is significant that the enemy made virtually no attempt to attack North Atlantic shipping, and opportunities for attacking the U-boats have been relatively few. Nevertheless, U-boats have been hunted relentlessly on all stations wherever they have appeared, and a heavy toll has been taken of the enemy. In fact, more U-boats have been sunk than merchant ships.
3. Surface and Air forces have both contributed to this satisfactory month's work by the efficiency of their escorts, patrols and offensive operations. Shore-based aircraft have often had to face powerful enemy. Air opposition and carrier-borne aircraft have played a most important part.
4. We are ready to attack the enemy with utmost vigour should he provide the opportunity by resuming a general attack on our shipping with the very large number of U-boats at his disposal.

Chapter 11

Phase Eleven: September to December 1943

In September 1943, after an absence of almost four months, the U-boats returned to the North Atlantic; this shows that there are no grounds for believing, as many historians have claimed, that the Battle of the Atlantic had ended in May. Dönitz now mounted his autumn offensive, and during September alone, attempts would be made to intercept five westbound and eight eastbound convoys.

At the Führer Conference on Naval Affairs held between 10 and 12 September, Dönitz was able to inform Hitler that fewer U-boats had been lost since the Hagenuk device was introduced and Metox switched off. Conditions for deploying submarines had definitely improved. Operations against convoys in the North Atlantic would begin again at the advent of the new moon in September, with an attempt made to take the enemy by surprise. Difficulties might be encountered in locating the convoys, and it would be a hard fight in spite of the new weapons (anti-aircraft guns, anti-destroyer torpedoes). Dönitz remained in no doubt that enemy defence measures would rapidly be brought back to their previous strength.

This planned resumption of the U-boat campaign in the North Atlantic was presaged in the text of an order sent by Dönitz to all U-boat commanders dated 13 September:

> After an interval lasting for months, you will once again wage submarine war in the North Atlantic, the most important theatre. You have been provided with new weapons and gear for this task. Events in Biscay have shown that in the field of radar detection the situation has changed materially in your favour. All the essentials for a successful campaign are to hand. I am sure that you will take up this challenge with the old fighting spirit of the submariner, for this struggle is decisive for our nation's future. The Führer is watching every phase of your struggle. Attack, follow up, sink!

The first deployment of the autumn offensive began on 15 September, when Zaunkönig-armed U-boats and some others from home waters were formed as wolfpack *Leuthen* to take up position 17 miles apart in a patrol line at 20.00 on 20 September, to intercept an ONS convoy (ONS.18); this was expected to arrive during the following afternoon, although there was a possibility it might arrive later, as the dead reckoning could not be relied upon absolutely, the data being scanty. As no convoys had been attacked in the North Atlantic since May 1943, it was assumed they were again using the shortest route between America and Britain. The patrol line lay on the Great Circle, beyond the range of the constant air reconnaissance over which radar watch was maintained from Britain.

The German U-boat Division files for 16 September noted:

> Dönitz was determined to resume attacks in the North Atlantic, as counter-measures against enemy defence had been found, and boats were being equipped with better devices against aircraft, anti-submarine vessels (destroyers, corvettes, etc.) and enemy location. The date of resumption of activity could not yet be given.

The *Leuthen* U-boats fuelled in mid-ocean from *U-460*, and by 16 September twenty formed a patrol line designed to intercept slow outward-bound (ONS) convoys. Dönitz's orders made the escorts the primary targets. Fortunately for the convoys, the patrol line was detected, and the same day, the Admiralty diverted the Eighth Escort Group, previously destined for the Bay of Biscay, to reinforce ONS.18. The same day, the wolfpack was ordered to operate only on westbound ONS and ON convoys – eastbound convoys if sighted were only to be attacked in favourable circumstances. The wolfpack also received a series of detailed instructions on action to be taken if attacked by aircraft, including the number of lookouts, readiness of flak guns and restrictions on numbers of personnel on the bridge – even in mid-Atlantic. Crew were to be allowed on the upper deck during daytime only in exceptional circumstances, and no '*Kraft durch Freude*'[1] exercises were permitted. U-boats were exhorted to keep moving at all times and always remain quickly manoeuvrable.

At noon on 18 September ONS.18 was in 56° north 23° west, with ON.202 about 120 miles astern. The weather had so far frustrated the air escort. That afternoon, there were indications of U-boats ahead of ONS.18, and the Admiralty diverted the convoy to the north-west. The following day, the two convoys were within about 90 miles of each other some 650 miles out in the North Atlantic. Air cover was now being provided by long-range Liberators of No. 120 Squadron from Iceland. That afternoon and evening, there were indications U-boats were in contact with both convoys. Once Western Approaches Command became aware of the deployment of the wolfpack, it was decided to send Support Group 9 comprising the destroyer *St Croix*, frigate *Itchen* and corvettes *Chambly*, *Morden* and *Sackville* north to reinforce the escort of ONS.18, and ON.202 was ordered to 'close up' with ONS.18. The wolfpack approached during the day but lost two U-boats sunk by air patrols. *Leuthen* was then ordered to operate mainly at night and only utilize favourable opportunities for attack by day. The sinking of *U-341* on 19 September south-west of Iceland by a No. 10 Squadron Liberator finally demonstrated the 'air gap' was closed.

During the night of 19/20 September the destroyer *Escapade* detected a pair of U-boats approaching the convoy, neutralized the first ASDIC contact with a quick counter-attack, then proceeded to put down and hunt the second. Despite the counter-attacks, the U-boat (*U-270*) escaped. During the action, premature explosion of a salvo from *Escapade*'s 'Hedgehog' anti-submarine mortar mounting killed three officers and sixteen ratings; two officers and eight ratings were seriously injured. The ship's bridge and forecastle were severely damaged, and *Escapade* was forced to detach and return under escort to Portsmouth, where she arrived on 25 September to undergo repairs. Several U-boats were in contact during the night, and *U-260* made an unsuccessful attack.

In the early hours of 20 September the frigate *Lagan*, investigating a nearby H/F D/F contact, was hit by an acoustic torpedo fired by *U-270*. This blew off her stern and propellers, leaving the remaining after deck badly damaged and the forward superstructure damaged by falling debris, including tinned food and depth charges. The attack left one officer and twenty-eight ratings killed or missing. The destroyer *Gatineau* arrived on the scene at 28 knots, swept around the wreck and dropped ten depth charges on one suspected contact. The badly damaged frigate was towed by the tug *Destiny* to the Mersey, arriving on 24 September. The *Lagan* was the first victim of the newly developed acoustic torpedo. *U-238* in a submerged attack from the port side of the convoy, now about 500 miles south-west of Iceland, sank two merchant ships before the air and sea escort drove off the U-boats, which temporarily lost contact. Later that morning, *U-238* sank two merchant ships.

In the evening the U-boats attacked the escort again. A few minutes before 22.00, and only a few hours after joining the escort, the Canadian destroyer *St Croix* was hit in the stern by an acoustic torpedo and disabled. Attacked again around forty-five minutes later, she sank within six minutes after being hit by a 'coup de grâce' torpedo from *U-305*. Sixty-six of her crew were lost. The *St Croix* was the second victim of the newly developed acoustic torpedo. Around ten minutes later, *U-305* missed the frigate *Itchen* with another acoustic torpedo.

The BdU War Log recorded the weather in the area of the convoy on the 20th and the night of 20/21 September as offering extremely good conditions for the operation. There were aircraft over the convoy by day and night, and two U-boats reported aircraft attacks. At 17.13 *U-338* gave the agreed short signal, 'Remaining surfaced for flak defence', an indication for all boats that air cover was too strong for them to approach without being observed. All the boats should have remained surfaced as ordered after receiving this signal, in order to take defensive action together against aircraft. Unfortunately for them, the short signal came at a time when there were still too few in the vicinity of the convoy, so the intended effect, i.e. to disperse the escort, was unsuccessful, and the small number of boats close to the convoy bore the brunt of the attacks. It was also unfortunate the boats could not be massed quickly near the convoy; great variations in fixes from the reports received made it very difficult for the boats to find the convoy.

At 00.22 on 21 September *U-952* fired an acoustic torpedo at an escort of ON.202 then heard a detonation after a run time of three minutes, followed by sinking noises. The target, the corvette *Polyanthus*, searching behind the convoy for the attacker and survivors of the *St Croix*, sank immediately after being hit. Her Commander, six officers and seventy-eight ratings were lost. The only survivor picked up by the *Itchen* died when the frigate was torpedoed two days later by *U-666* and sank.

The same day, Churchill provided a further statement to the House of Commons on the 'War Situation',[2] in which he informed the House of 'The Revolution Effected in our Position at Sea':

Our greatest danger in this war since invasion has become so much more remote is the U-boat attack upon our sea communications and upon Allied shipping all over the world. This must be measured by three tests: first, the sinkings of our own ships; second, the killings of the enemy U-boats; and third, the volume of new building. The great victory which was won by our North Atlantic convoys and their escorts in May was followed by a magnificent diminution in sinkings. The monthly statements which are issued on the authority of the President and me, and about which the Canadian Government, who contribute to the Battle of the Atlantic brave men, planes and escort vessels are also consulted, deserve close attention ... for the four months which ended on 18 September no merchant vessel was sunk by enemy action in the North Atlantic. The month of August was the lowest month we have ever had since the United States entered the war, and it was less than half the average of British and Allied sinkings in the 15 months preceding the American entry into the war. During the first fortnight in this September no Allied ships were sunk by U-boat action in any part of the world ... One convoy is being attacked at the present time. If they will come and attack the convoys, we shall be able to attack the U-boats.

The output of new building from the United States has fulfilled all that was ever hoped from it and more. We build our regular quota in this

Island, and the Canadian output, an entirely new development for Canada, is also remarkable. The credit balance of new building over losses of all kinds, including marine risks, since the beginning of the year, the net gain that is to say, exceeds 6,000,000 tons, and should the present favourable conditions hold, we shall soon have replaced all the losses suffered by the United Nations since the beginning of the war. As set forth in the letter from the President to me which I laid on the Table of the House before we rose, the massive achievement of United States' shipbuilding has been shared generously with us on those principles of the division of war-labour in accordance with the highest economy of effort, which were from the beginning of our association with the United States in this war our guide and which are now becoming increasingly our rule. The favourable position now enjoyed has enabled a larger number of faster ships to be built and projected with all the advantages attaching to speed.

We have taken full advantage of the lull in the U-boat attack to bring in the largest possible convoys and have replenished the reserves of all essential commodities, especially oil fuel, which is almost at its highest level since the outbreak of the war and have substantial margins between us and what is called the 'danger level'.

The subsequent BdU War Log record of the attacks on ONS.18 and ON.202 noted:

On the morning of the 21st there was fog in the area of the convoy which persisted the whole day and during the night of 21/22 September. On the 21st by day and in the night of 21st/22nd there was no air cover with the convoy, probably because of the fog. For this reason several boats came up close to the convoy. Also, reports regarding escort groups became fewer, and there were only reports of single destroyers.

After the great success achieved against the escort on the previous day, conditions were now good for a main attack on the ships. Unfortunately, however, this was frustrated by the weather situation – fog, visibility at times only 200m.

When the fog temporarily lifted that afternoon, ONS.18 was almost in station on the starboard beam of ON.244. Very long-range Liberator aircraft of 10 Squadron RCAF then appeared, over 800 miles from their base in Newfoundland.

From about 21.30 on 22 September until 02.30 on 23 September, U-boats operating independently or in pairs were attacking the two convoys more or less continuously from all directions. In the early hours of 22 September the frigate *Itchen*,[3] sailing ahead of ON.202, detected a surfaced U-boat a short distance ahead, turned on a small searchlight and opened fire. About fifteen seconds later, *Itchen* was struck in her forward magazine by an acoustic torpedo, blew up with a blinding flash, broke in two and sank, showering debris onto the conning tower of the U-boat and nearby ships. The *Itchen* had previously rescued survivors from the *St Croix* and *Polyanthus*. Only two survivors from the *Itchen* and one from the *St Croix* were rescued by the Polish merchantman *Wisla*. Just after midnight, *U-238* penetrated the escort screen and sank three merchant ships, while *U-952* torpedoed two more.

At daybreak on the 23rd more Liberators arrived from Newfoundland. Their reports and other indications confirmed U-boats were still in contact, with two attacks carried out in the vicinity of the convoy. By nightfall a few U-boats seemed to have worked their way ahead of the convoy, two being attacked by the escorts shortly before midnight and another soon afterwards. The fog set in again, and to quote a report, 'The enemy seems to have been easily discouraged from pressing home his attacks.'

The BdU War Log for 24 September contains a comprehensive account of the operation, although the claims made for numbers of escorts sunk were, as often, exaggerated:

For the first time in months a U-boat group was again sent in to operate against a convoy in the North Atlantic. The group consisted of nineteen boats equipped with the newest weapons and devices – the Zaunkönig torpedo, the Hagenuk wave indicator as a new radar interception device, Aphrodite radar decoys and finally, the strongest flak armament at present of one quadruple and two twins.

The convoy was intercepted on the morning of the 20th as the boats were taking up their disposition. The position of the boats was, therefore, quite favourable. In fact, the danger was overcome of the boats being discovered disposed in the patrol line. The escort with the convoy was so strong, according to reports by the boats, that it must be assumed that the enemy had provided extra defence for this first engagement.

The operation lasted from the morning of the 10th to that of the 23rd. It was directed against ON.202, the fast convoy proceeding at 9–9.5 knots from England to America. The convoy was intercepted in AL 1944 and chased up to AJ 9524.

At the beginning of the operation on the day of the 20th and in the night of the 20th/21st the weather was extremely favourable, with visibility clear and little wind, but subsequently on the morning of the 21st there was a thick fog, which persisted up to the evening of the 22nd. It cleared for five hours during the first half of the night of the 22nd/23rd but returned afterwards with poor visibility. This unfavourable weather and interruption of the operation after the first night for two days and a night were very decisive for the whole course of the operation.

After intercepting the convoy on the morning of the 20th, the boats were near it during the evening and the first night. It was at once clear that the convoy was surrounded by an unusually strong remote escort. Hardly one boat sighted the convoy itself. All came up against escort vessels before even reaching the actual convoy. The boats utilized the situation with surprising success and sank, in the first night, with certainty seven destroyers of the escort and probably two more.

The preliminary operations for attack on the ships were, therefore, complete, and it was to be expected that the ships could be attacked during the next night without any great difficulty.

The enemy must have realized the great danger to the convoy after the loss of so many escort vessels. He apparently then did all in his power, with the great advantage of two days' fog, to surround the convoy as quickly as possible with a new escort force

When on the evening of the 22nd the fog cleared for five hours the boats had again to deal primarily with escort force and did not find it any easier to deliver an attack against the ships. The sinking of five further destroyers proves this. It is significant, however, that three destroyers of the close escort were sunk, so that approach to the convoy became easier. Three boats were able to attack the mass of ships and sank five, torpedoing two further ones.

It was now certain that the main blow could be directed against the convoy. Between twelve and fifteen escort vessels in all had been eliminated, which would have made it considerably easier for the boats. Unfortunately, however, the fog again set in, and as there was no hope of the weather improving, the operation had to be broken off on the morning of the 23rd.

On the first and third day the enemy had normal air reconnaissance over the convoy. Apart from four-engined land-based aircraft, flying boats and carrier-borne aircraft were reported. The fact that the boats remained surfaced and warded off attacks with all guns led to success, even though one boat was probably lost. Contact with the convoy was, however, maintained and the boats remained in the vicinity. It is essential that as many boats as possible of a group are always up to the convoy so that convoy escort – aircraft and escort vessels – are split up as much as possible and just a few boats of the convoy do not bear the brunt of their attack. If aircraft only engage a few boats, many others can approach the convoy.

The question of the strength of naval escort has already been discussed. The interruption of the operation by fog must be considered an important factor, the enemy having gained time thereby to bring up new escorts. The enemy would hardly have been able, if the course of the operation had been normal, to supplement his escorts so quickly.

The aggressive action against the escort forces also resulted in the great advantage that the hitherto numerous depth-charge attacks were not made. Only one boat had to break off operations owing to depth-charge damage. The losses amounted to two boats, *U-338* and *U-229*, the former probably through aircraft attack; two boats were badly damaged, *U-270* by aircraft and *U-386* by depth-charges. These losses and this damage bear no relation to the losses by the enemy. The total sinkings were twelve escort vessels and three further probables; also nine merchant vessels sunk, 46,500 GRT, and two torpedoed. This was therefore a very satisfactory result, which might have been considerably better if the weather had been favourable.

Although the claims by the various U-boats were considered 'a very satisfactory' result by Dönitz, the actual losses were three escorts and six merchant ships sunk, and one escort and one merchant ship damaged. Three U-boats were sunk, with three damaged and forced to return to base.

Details of the attack appeared in the War Cabinet Weekly Resumé for 16–23 September, 'West Atlantic':

During the U-boat attacks on an outward-bound convoy in the N.W. Approaches, HMCS *St Croix* (destroyer), HMS *Polyanthus* (corvette) and HMCS *Itchen* (frigate) were sunk, and HMS *Lagan* (frigate) was torpedoed. Five officers and 76 ratings were rescued from *St Croix* but there was only one survivor from *Polyanthus*. HMS *Escapade* (destroyer) and HMCS *Gatineau* (destroyer) were damaged by the premature explosion of anti-submarine equipment. Three officers and 12 ratings were killed, and there is one rating missing in *Escapade*.

Escort Carriers

Evidence of the effect of shore-to-shore air cover for convoys is given by the Escort Carriers *Biter, Archer* and *Battler*. Not one of the great number of merchant vessels comprising eight separate convoys was lost while under their protection.

HMS *Biter*: The submarine packs concentrated on convoys covered by HMS *Biter*. In no instance was a U-boat able to break through the defence and make an attack while *Biter* was present. Fog, poor visibility and frequent rainstorms made air patrol over the Atlantic convoy HX. 237 difficult and hazardous. (12 May – three ships sunk) In spite of this, sixty-three sorties were made, and seven submarines were attacked. Air crews operated continuously for nine days, but never failed to carry out their task. Equally satisfactory results were obtained in two other convoys – SC.129 and HX.242.

At the subsequent Führer Conference on 24 September Dönitz presented Hitler with an extensive report on the successful submarine campaign in the North Atlantic. Hitler reportedly pointed with unprecedented emphasis to the importance of submarine warfare against shipping as the only bright spot at present in an otherwise dark war situation. Submarine warfare, he said, must therefore be stepped up by all available means.

ONS.18 reached Halifax on 29 September, while ON.202 arrived at New York on 1 October without further incident. This major U-boat operation was notable as marking the first battle of Dönitz autumn offensive on the North Atlantic convoys after the four-month hiatus following the withdrawal of U-boats in May, and the first use of the new T-5 acoustic homing torpedo, intended to eliminate the convoy escorts and allow the unprotected merchant ships to be attacked with conventional torpedoes.

In his later assessment of the operation, Dönitz wrote:

In September 1943 another surface attack on convoys in the old manner was tried out in the North Atlantic with these more heavily armed boats. The boats were ordered to remain on the surface when attacked by aircraft and to cooperate in fighting off the attack. They were then to attack and break up the destroyer screen with acoustic torpedoes and, in the third phase of the battle, attack the convoy now deprived of its protection. It was a bold attempt which demanded a great deal of pluck and a high standard of ability from the U-boats. The vulnerable boats had to combat the enemy's overpowering defences in the air and on the water before they could fulfil their main task of sinking the ships. This succeeded insofar as they managed to remain on the surface in spite of aerial attacks, and in the second phase of the battle to sink a number of destroyers. The third phase of the battle, the sinking of the ships, was, however, not so successful, because a smokescreen was laid in which the ships were not visible. In this action the U-boat losses were small. The success of the experiment encouraged a repetition. However, it appeared that in the first attempt the smoke had also impeded the enemy's air activities. In further attempts the air force was so powerful that, had the U-boats remained on the surface, they would in all probability have been completely destroyed.

It was, therefore, finally clear that surface warfare for U-boats had come to an end. It was now a matter of filling in time until the new type could be made ready for action. At the same time the Schnorkel was being developed for all types, to enable the boats to recharge under water. The Schnorkel was not yet ready as its use necessitated alterations to the Diesel, and extensive trials had to be made in order that its use at sea should not endanger the crew.

The joint AngloAmerican statement on submarine and anti-submarine operations for September read:

1. Until the third week in September no Allied ship was lost by German U-boat attack. Then, on 19 September, the U-boats ended the four months' lull in the North Atlantic, and a pack of at least fifteen U-boats concentrated on a westbound convoy.[4] The combat lasted four and a half days. The loss of three escort vessels has already been announced. A small number of merchant ships were sunk, but as a result of vigorous counter-attacks by the surface and air escorts a larger number of U-boats were sunk or damaged.

2. In spite of the increase in U-boat activity at the end of the month, the average merchantship losses from all causes in September and August together are the best record of the war.

3. Nevertheless, this resumption of pack tactics is evidence of the enemy's intention to spare no efforts to turn the tide of the U-boat war, and the utmost exertion and vigilance will be required before its menace is finally removed.

Wolfpack *Leuthen* was disbanded on 26 September, its twelve U-boats reconfigured as wolfpack *Rossbach* and joined by nine U-boats from home bases to attack the next eastbound convoys. The first expected convoy was diverted to the north and escaped completely, and despite further northern shifts of the line, each succeeding convoy passed unscathed.

Eye-witness accounts of the attacks on ONS.202 appeared later in a Canadian newspaper article published on 2 October:

STARK HORROR OF U-BOAT BLITZ

MONTREAL
'Ships broke in half as torpedoes ripped their hulls and injured and dying men struggled for hours in the icy, oil-thickened waters,' said a survivor of the terrific convoy battle mentioned by Mr Churchill in his recent address to the Commons.

The long-running battle occurred on the outer rim of the Arctic Circle, when an Allied convoy encountered a pack of U-boats. The Canadian destroyer *St Croix* and several Allied merchantmen were lost. At least one U-boat was sent to the bottom.

An eye-witness arriving at an east Canadian port said it was one of the starkest battles of the war.

A survivor of an American merchantman watched a U-boat being blasted from the water after being caught in the beam of a warship's searchlight. 'It was the best fireworks I ever saw,' said the captain, adding that the sub must have been hit in the magazine, as there was a tremendous blast of flame.

The sinking of the *St Croix*, of whose crew of 147 only one was rescued, is described as 'the heaviest single loss the Canadian Navy has so far suffered'.

Survivors who landed at another port stated that at least six Allied vessels were sunk, including three war vessels, with heavy loss of life.

At least two U-boats were sunk, and six others damaged.

'The U-boat pack followed two Canada-bound convoys like a pack of wolves,' said one Norwegian survivor. 'They kept after us for ten days. I believe that they used new and more deadly torpedoes, sinking one ship in one minute and another in four minutes.'

The British frigate *Itchen*, whose loss was announced from London, had picked up five officers and seventy-six men from the *St Croix*, and then rushed to attack a U-boat. Twenty minutes later, she sent out an SOS that her bows had been blown off. A stoker was the only final survivor of the *St Croix*.

Among the officers lost in that ship was Surgeon-Lieut. William King, nephew of Mr Mackenzie King, Canada's Prime Minister. This U-boat chase marked the re-opening of the U-boat campaign after a four months' spell.

Wolfpack *Rossbach*, deployed between 26 September and 6 October to intercept the next westbound convoys (ON.204 and ONS.19), was located by aircraft, and the convoys were safely diverted to the north of the patrol line. An eastbound convoy (HX.258) passing through the danger area was given strong air escort until 2 October, when the aircraft were transferred to search the location where the *Rossbach* U-boats had been sighted earlier. On 4 and 5 October they sank three U-boats and damaged a fourth. *Rossbach*, now comprising fourteen boats,[5] was redeployed on 6 October to intercept expected westbound convoys HX.259 and SC.143. Western Approaches Command, alerted to *Rossbach*'s position by intelligence decrypts and deciding to engage the wolfpack, diverted HX.259 to the south and sailed SC.143 towards *Rossbach* as bait.

Dönitz was once again talking up his ambitions to intensify the war against merchant shipping, as illustrated in a speech of 8 October:

THREAT OF INTENSIFIED U-BOAT WARFARE

LONDON, 8 October

In a speech at Berlin today Admiral Dönitz, the Commander-in-Chief of the German Navy, declared that U-boats with new weapons and devices would start the greatest naval war that had so far been witnessed. 'It is my firm and fanatical intention to carry on the war against enemy tonnage to the highest level of perfection with all the means at my disposal,' added Dönitz.

The BdU War Log later commented on the *Rossbach* operation:

Wolfpack *Rossbach* was deployed in a patrol line between 26 September and 6 October to act against ON.204 and ONS.19, but met with no success, because the convoys managed to evade the boats, even though the patrol lines were moved north several times. On the other hand, there were several losses (probably three boats) due to enemy aircraft. *Rossbach* was then deployed between 7 and 9 October against HX.259 and SC.143. The wolfpack picked up several groups of submarine chasers in the vicinity of the convoy, but not the convoy itself. The boats contacted these submarine chasers while they were on their way south to their new dispositions and not in the positions intended. The convoy itself was only picked up later by our air reconnaissance. Three destroyers were sunk, but two boats were lost to enemy air attack.

Both operations clearly showed the effectiveness of the enemy air force, which discovered the extent and position of the patrol lines and played a decisive part in the action against the U-boats.

The focus of the second battle of Dönitz's autumn offensive targeted convoy SC.143, first attacked in the morning of 8 October when the Polish destroyer *Orkan* was hit by an acoustic torpedo and sank within five minutes. During the day the convoy's air cover was able to mount several successful anti-submarine attacks and sank three U-boats; two others were damaged in air attacks and forced to return to base. That night, an aircraft equipped with a Leigh Light (a powerful carbon arc searchlight) remained with the convoy after dark. This was later described as another positive development in anti-U-boat warfare, but only one aircraft was available, and after it returned to base one merchant ship was sunk. The *Orkan* was the only escort ship sunk, for the loss of three U-boats. SC.143 was the only Atlantic convoy attacked during October.

Reports of Churchill's 21 September speech appeared in US newspapers on 8 October. A typical article read:

U-BOAT WARFARE

Mr Churchill in most of his statements since the tide of war began to turn against the enemy has been careful to emphasise that Allied setbacks must be expected; and the U-boat attack on an Allied convoy to which he referred in his House of Commons speech of September 21 as 'at present in progress' was one of them, according to latest reports from Canadian sources.

The British Prime Minister, after reviewing the nearly six months of the present year during which the Allies had been definitely on top of the enemy submarines in the. Atlantic, said that during the first fortnight of September no Allied ship had been sunk by a U-boat anywhere in the world; but he promptly warned that such immunity could not be expected to continue, adding that a new herd of U-boats, doubtless with the latest equipment, had been entering the Atlantic during the last week and were already in action.

The Canadian account certainly indicates that the six months of comparative inactivity, which German reports said was spent in re-equipment and training in new tactics, have enabled the U-boat packs to recover some of their lost punch. The ten days which the German pack spent trailing two westbound convoys, which subsequently merged into one, ended in a three-day running battle in which, according to the official account, we lost a destroyer, a corvette, a frigate and five merchantmen, with heavy loss of life, while at least two U-boats were sunk and six possibly damaged. It is not quite clear if all these Allied losses occurred during the closing, battle, but if so, as four merchant ships had been sunk and two escorts crippled during the earlier stage of the operation, that would take the total Allied losses to three warships sunk and two damaged, and nine cargo craft sunk. That would make the expedition quite sufficiently expensive from an Allied point of view; but as a total of 70 merchantmen were involved and they were in charge of at least 20 escort vessels, the great bulk of the cargo craft – over 87 per cent – got through. There is no doubt, owing to the relative shipbuilding positions of the opposing sides, that the

Allies can afford their losses much better than the Germans can afford to lose the two submarines certainly sunk.

The whole operation, indeed, is very far from representing a crushing success for the most up-to-date of U-boat packs, including new devices and employing new tactics for the first time, and thus having all the advantages of surprise. The innovations used by the enemy included at least one submarine anti-aircraft vessel mounting ten guns, and an extra powerful torpedo, stated to combine magnetic guidance with acoustic detonation, which is fired at a ship from the rear and explodes within the radius of propeller vibration, blowing off the victim's propeller and crippling, if not sinking her.

In his speech on 21 September, while the convoy battle was in progress, Mr Churchill declared that whatever the U-boat designers produced, the Allies had not been idle, and he looked forward to the issue with sober confidence. That attitude seems to be soundly based. Doubtless some amendment will be necessary in Allied anti-U-boat measures; but the enemy appears to have produced nothing revolutionary either in equipment or tactics, and only completely revolutionary success by the U-boats could be of any ultimate use whatever to Hitler at this stage, for the six months' lag in U-boat sinkings permitted the Allies to establish a lead of over 6,000,000 tons of new building over destruction, and this, plus their amazing building rate, placed them in a position which only sweeping U-boat successes could possibly menace.

In an early indication of the return of the U-boats to the Atlantic in the autumn offensive, reports appeared in the press on 9 October of a speech made by Dönitz in which he boasted of the dangers to come:

GERMAN ADMIRAL'S THREAT

LONDON, Friday
Admiral Dönitz, C-in-C of the German Navy, in a speech at Berlin, declared that U-boats with new weapons and devices would bring about a naval war greater than anything so far witnessed.

The same day Dönitz, who had ordered, 'Smash the destroyers, sink the ships. Make up for your long wait', instructed the attack on SC.143 to be broken off, and the *Rossbach* wolfpack, now reduced to just six boats, disbanded. SC.143 continued its passage and arrived without further loss at Liverpool on 12 October. Six U-boats had been sunk – all by aircraft – and six seriously damaged and forced to return to port. A further three, although damaged, were able to remain on patrol. In total, fifteen U-boats out of the original twenty-six were lost or damaged, at the cost of one merchant ship and one escort sunk.

An interesting article published on 11 October suggested an increasing lack of enthusiasm among U-boat crews:

NEW PHASE IN U-BOAT WAR

A new phase of the Battle of the Atlantic has opened with a different German conception of the power of submarines.

U-boats formerly made up an invisible fighting arm but have been changed into craft that sometimes go into action on the surface. This is a clear indication to U-boat crews, many of whom are new to the submarine service, that they cannot hope for safety by submerging. And this is at a time when, as a result of heavy losses; the U-boat crews' feelings have to be studied to a greater degree than ever before.

'Reduced enthusiasm'

A leading naval commentator, A. J. McWhinnie, in an exclusive survey by arrangement with the British Ministry of Information, says:

'The battering inflicted on U-boats in the past year is having its effect. There have been signs of reduced enthusiasm for U-boat service, and Goebbels has been concentrating for months on methods of bolstering U-boat crews' morale by using a film star publicity technique to give the U-boat men the feeling that they are heroes everyone. Even before the recent lull of four months in which not a single Allied freighter was sunk in the North Atlantic by U-boats, all operational submarines returning from patrol were met by staged 'reception committees' consisting of brass bands, clicking cameras, eloquent admirals and pretty flower-throwing girls.'

Despite the losses suffered by *Rossbach* and the poor performance in the encounter with SC.143, Dönitz continued to believe the new weapons and tactics recently introduced could still deliver the U-boats an operational edge, and so reorganized those U-boats still in the North Atlantic as wolfpack *Schlieffen* (14–18 October) in his third autumn offensive. *Schlieffen* was made up of eighteen U-boats from the *Rossbach* wolfpack reinforced by fresh boats newly arrived from bases in France and Germany and was ordered to take up a patrol line to intercept anticipated westbound convoys ONS.20 and ON.206 When Ultra decrypts revealed the position of *Schlieffen*, Western Approaches Command ordered the two convoys and their escorts to combine and sent Escort Group B7 as reinforcement.

Late in the evening of 15 October, ON.206 and ONS.20 transiting south of Iceland were sighted and reported by one of three U-boats en route from Germany to reinforce the *Schlieffen* wolfpack. One hour later, *U-844* sighted what was believed to be ONS.20 and called for the pack to converge on its position. *U-844* had in fact sighted ON.206. *U-844* was directed to shadow the convoy, and the wolfpack (already formed in a patrol line 120 miles away to intercept ONS.20) was ordered to converge on *U-844*'s position and a new patrol line repositioned into the path of ON.206 in expectation it would be reached at 24.00 on 16 October. By that evening a number of the U-boats were in position and commenced an attack which would become one of the most calamitous of the entire U-boat campaign.

During the night of 15/16 October the U-boats attacked but were repulsed. On 16 October *U-844* and other two U-boats en route from Germany, travelling on the surface in full daylight as their only means of reaching their target area in time, were spotted by a patrolling aircraft, which called in an air attack from several different squadrons. In the fierce battle which ensued, two RAF Liberators were shot down and all three U-boats sunk. Although placed directly across the routes of two convoys, and having gained good contact with one, the wolfpack managed to sink only one merchant ship. Two more U-boats were sunk the following day one by a frigate and one by depth charges from two RAF Liberator aircraft, and another was seriously damaged and forced to return to base.

During the night of 17/18 October another U-boat was sunk. The convoys then made a drastic alteration in course to shake off any pursuers; this was successful in that BdU received conflicting sighting reports from two U-boats and sent the wolfpack off in the wrong direction, unable to regain contact and having lost six U-boats – four sunk by aircraft – in exchange for a single merchant ship. In view of the losses sustained, BdU ordered the wolfpack to retire.

Dönitz recognized the decision by U-boat Operations Control to order the boats to fight the escort aircraft on the surface during the day had directly led to the loss of six boats. The operation had been a complete failure. A U-boat with 20mm flak guns could not stand up to a heavily armoured large bomber or flying boat. Convoy action by day would no longer be possible in future with the present flak armament of eight 20mm guns if there was strong enemy air escort.

On 19 October the U-boats were informed of the position where HX.261 was to be expected at noon the following day. The convoy was not found (the

War Log reads: 'Cipher compromise presumed'). The *Schlieffen* wolfpack was then disbanded on 22 October, a number of its U-boats forming the nucleus of a new wolfpack *Siegfried*. *Schlieffen* would be the last of the old-style wolf packs to operate in the mid-Atlantic.

Dönitz accepted the outcome as a setback but remained confident the U-boats' new weapons and tactics would achieve success. It was in reality a major defeat, and signalled the Germans had for the present lost the tactical and technical initiative in the Battle of the Atlantic. The outcome also emphasised the value of VLR aircraft in convoy protection, with four out of six U-boats sunk by aircraft, albeit at the cost of four aircraft lost and two seriously damaged.

Dönitz sent the *Siegfried* boats the following message on 23 October:

> The convoy battle of Group *Leuthen* was a complete success. The battle of Group *Schlieffen* was a setback. The next operation must again lead to success. By tight positioning, the fast and simultaneous strike of many boats is made possible; conditions are established for this. I am sure that there will be enough of you.

The BdU War Log for 20 February 1944 explains the failure of the *Schlieffen* operation:

> The wolfpack was formed to pick up ON.206 and/or ONS.20. On the basis of a Radio Intelligence report, the patrol line was moved north. ON.206 was picked up further east by a boat coming home to join the group. She lost contact owing to strong forces of escorting aircraft and could not find the convoy again. Operations Control ordered the boats to fight the escort aircraft surfaced by day (the aim being to continue shadowing by day and to get ahead). This led to the loss of six boats. The operation was a complete failure, only one steamer being sunk and one torpedoed.
>
> Lessons learnt from this operation were: a U-boat with 20mm flak guns could not stand up to the heavily armoured large bomber or flying boat, and convoy action by day would no longer be possible in future with the present flak armament of eight 20mm guns if there was strong enemy air escort.
>
> These facts were not realized to the full at the end of the *Schlieffen* operation, because the positive results of the Zaunkönig convoy outweighed the negative results of later operations.

The remaining boats of wolfpack *Schlieffen* and some fresh boats arriving from Western France were formed into a new wolfpack, *Siegfried*, deployed on 22 October to intercept eastbound convoy HX.262 in mid-Atlantic on 24 October, while the U-boats were returning towards their refuelling group and home bases in France. *Siegfried* consisted of nineteen boats – nine from *Schlieffen*, plus ten from bases in France and Germany, supported by a refuelling group of three U-boat tankers escorted by a flak boat. A further four boats joined on 25 October. When Western Approaches Command became aware of *Siegfried*'s position, several HX and SC convoys in the area were diverted, and the westbound ON.207 was left to continue on course as bait.

On 23 October *U-274*, attempting to contact ON.207, was sighted and attacked by a Liberator of No. 224 Squadron RAF. The escorts *Vidette* and *Duncan* of Escort group B7 also attacked with depth charges, and *U-274* was destroyed, with no survivors. On 26 October *U-91* was attacked by a Liberator of No. 10 Squadron RCAF but escaped with little damage. Later in the day, another Liberator of 10 Squadron attacked and sank *U-420*. The next day, *U-413* managed to fix the general position of ON.207 through use of intermediate-wavelength D/F to listen to the escorts, but the other U-boats did not arrive in time to enable a 25/26 October interception, and the convoy, passed undetected to the south of the German patrol line. During the time ON.207 was in *Siegfried*'s patrol area, none of its boats were able to launch an attack, and none of ON.207's ships were harmed by enemy action. ON.207 continued to its destination, arriving at New York on 4 November 1943.

ON.208 departed Liverpool on 24 October. On the 29th, Escort Group B7 detached from ON.207 to join ON.208, and following several days behind detected *U-282* shadowing the convoy. *U-282* was attacked with depth charges and Hedgehog and sunk, again with no survivors. While this action was taking place, *Siegfried*'s refuelling group was also under attack, from the USN escort carriers *Block Island* and *Card*. On the night of 25/26 October they attacked the U-tanker *U-488*, though she escaped without damage. On 28 October they attacked two U-boats; *U-220* was destroyed, and *U-256* damaged and forced to return to base. On 31 October two more boats were attacked: *U-91*, which escaped again, and *U-584*, which was sunk. Later that day, the USS *Borie* sank *U-405* in a 72-minute duel but was herself fatally damaged, sinking later that day. The operation against HX.262 was discontinued on 26 October.

Following the failure of the operation against ON.207, BdU re-configured *Siegfried* on 27 October into three sections – *Siegfried 1* of six boats, *Siegfried 2* of eight and *Siegfried 3* of six – intended to cover a wider sea area. These were deployed from 28 October in shorter patrol lines east of Newfoundland in the expectation of intercepting SC.145. As the convoy approached, one U-boat transmitted several radio messages on the flank in an attempt to divert the convoy straight into the main U-boat formation. Two U-boats drove off Fairey Swordfish anti-submarine aircraft from the carrier *Fencer* with anti-aircraft fire, but the convoy bypassed the U-boat patrol line without being detected. During the time ON.207 was in *Siegfried*'s patrol area, none of its U-boats were able to launch an attack on the ships in the convoy. *Siegfried* was disbanded on 30 October after failing to contact SC.145. ON.207 continued to its destination, arriving at New York on 4 November 1943. An attempted attack on ON.208 on 29 October resulted in the sinking of *U-282* on her first patrol. In less than two weeks, in attacks on just four convoys, nine U-boats had been sunk by the highly efficient inter-service air and sea escorts.

For the next planned offensive, on 30 October Dönitz established the *Körner* wolfpack of eleven U-boats and the *Jahn* wolfpack of nine in the area to the east of Newfoundland, for joint attacks on SC.145, ON.208, HX.263 and ONS.21. For the first operation the wolfpacks were deployed in a patrol line to intercept ONS.21 and ON.208, but their presence was detected, and the convoys passed to north. The following afternoon, their assigned target was HX.263, but again they failed to make contact, the convoy passing to the south. Dönitz, commenting later on the outcome of the October convoy battles, remarked that fog had given the convoys a great deal of protection, while his U-boats never again succeeded in pressing home an attack in the teeth of hostile air cover. Four westbound and six eastbound convoys had been at sea during the month, of which only two – SC.143 and ONS.20 – were attacked, losing one escort and two merchant ships.

Roosevelt cabled Churchill on 1 November:

To the Former Naval Person from the President. Number 405

Our Office of War Information and Navy Department recommend the following statement, with which I agree:

1. During the months of August, September and October approximately 60 U-boats were destroyed. This brings to more than 150 the number of U-boats destroyed during the last six months. The record of the last three months is particularly gratifying because during most of this period fewer U-boats were operating. Fewer targets were presented for our air and sea forces.

2. During August, September, and October more U-boats were destroyed than Allied merchant ships were sunk by U-boat action. The ratio of U-boat to merchant ship attrition during October was more satisfactory than in any previous month. In fact our tonnage losses from all causes in October were the lowest of any month of the war.

After analysis of the outcome of the attacks on ONS.18 and ON.202, the BdU concluded on 1 November:

The attempt to force attacks on convoys with all boats remaining surfaced at the same time will have to be abandoned until the boats are equipped with 37mm flak, despite the good experiences with the *Leuthen* convoy.

The BdU War Log then complained:

No enemy movement took place within Groups *Körner* and *Jahn*. HX 263, which had been very carefully awaited, must have already passed the area. 2 November: As the expected HX and both the ON convoys must have already passed the dispositions of Groups *Körner* and *Jahn*, both groups were liquidated, and the boats placed into five small patrol lines.

The War Log for the following day contained an account for the 'period since resuming the operations in the North Atlantic against the *Leuthen* convoy' (ONS.18/ON.202):

The operations against the *Leuthen* convoy were a complete success, with regard to destroyer combat and tactics against the enemy air force (submarines remained on the surface). The air escort attached to this convoy was stronger than at first estimated. That would emphasize still further the success resulting from the boats remaining on the surface. It must be admitted, however, that the thick fog in this operation hindered greater success against the main target, the merchant ships; also, particularly thick patches sheltered the boats from air attacks, and the fact that only two boats were lost is due to the shelter provided by the fog. For while the successful results in combating destroyers was confirmed by the use of Zaunkönig during the period in question, the same does not apply to anti-aircraft combat.

Losses resulting from air attacks have again increased seriously since the *Leuthen* convoy. Since 19 September seventy-two air attacks were reported by the submarines, as a result of which seventeen submarines were most probably lost, only two of them with the *Leuthen* convoy itself. Only a fraction of these attacks took place on the outward and inward routes, on which the boats only proceeded on the surface to recharge. A good two thirds of the attacks occurred when the submarines were below the surface in patrol lines, during the operations against convoys and in the areas for refuelling. The actual losses were in the same proportion. These losses could not be sustained, however, particularly with no successes to counterbalance them, and they necessitate tactical measures as long as the flak in the boats is not improved by installing 37mm guns.

Attempts to attack convoys with every boat on the surface at once must be postponed until these improvements have been made, in spite of the good results obtained against the *Leuthen* convoy. Until then, it will also be necessary to try and operate mainly at night, and to break off contact with a convoy during the day if strong air forces come on the scene. This state of affairs also necessitates the boats remaining below the surface in patrol lines during the day and makes it necessary to take into consideration the difficulties in making locations, due to the reduced reconnaissance area and the increased difficulties of intercommunication. This precaution is also necessary because the enemy has always succeeded in discovering the submarine dispositions through their air reconnaissance, and presumably turning away from them. It is not known as yet whether, and how far, still unknown methods of location played any part in this.

U-boats are therefore now ordered to remain below the surface during the day, taking up disposition in short patrol lines and close formation within the patrol lines, and maintaining some distance between the separate patrol lines; separate reconnaissance boats to be between the enemy and these patrol lines, to take up position so that the enemy is contacted, if possible, in the evening, and attacks made during the early part of the night, to break off the operation if stronger air forces appear. A large-scale operation against a convoy can only be undertaken under particularly favourable conditions, as only a concentration of larger numbers of boats is likely to succeed against the enemy. This can only be considered when the flak guns are improved. Conditions with regard to location will only improve when our own air reconnaissance permits the boats to move quickly from one convoy to another. With our forces as weak as they are at the moment, this can only be done in the England–Gibraltar convoy area.

After it had become clear ONS.21 had evaded the *Körner* and *Jahn* wolfpacks, the U-boats were divided on 2 November into five sections as *Tirpitz I, II, III, IV* and *V*, deployed in a crescent formation of five short patrol lines with single scouting submarines opposite the gaps designed to facilitate the location of convoys. This marked the first appearance of the new type of formation, designed to attack HX.264, expected on or soon after 5 November. This tactic failed to establish contact with any of the expected convoys. It was later discovered that they had all avoided the areas in which the groups of U-boats were stationed. Following the recognition that the enemy had discovered the last dispositions of patrol lines with his radar, the *Tirpitz* wolfpacks were disbanded on 8 November.

A BdU War Log entry dated 5 November read:

Submarine losses during recent weeks, the increasing number of reports by submarines of aircraft attacks without any fixed location and the subsequent obvious detours by convoys confirm the suspicion the enemy is using new ways and hitherto unknown methods of detecting submarines. Against these, our own location and warning devices are inadequate in their present form. It is possible that, with regard to radio location, the enemy has entered new fields as yet unknown to us. It is, however, also possible the enemy was using passive location of the electric or heat radiation given out by the submarine. Perhaps other variations of active or passive location were possible. As the visible forms of this enemy superiority were similar to those observed in certain positions from May to July, it looks suspiciously as though there has been dangerous radiation on the part of the submarines. Successes achieved through the use of radar decoys made it appear the enemy used active location, although there have been no reports of this kind during the last weeks.

HX.264 passed the U-boat patrol lines undetected. Anti-submarine air patrols then proved successful in protecting SC.146 and HX.265 from attack. Two of the twenty-two U-boats deployed against the convoys were sunk on 6 November. The following day, the BdU decided the disposition of boats in long patrol lines maintained until now had not stood the test of time:

> The majority of convoys waited for had circumvented the dispositions so obviously that a systematic method of interception must be taken into consideration. In the future, various new types of dispositions are to be tried out, with anticipated success. Group *Tirpitz* is to be liquidated.

The BDU War Log for 8 November provided a retrospective analysis of the *Tirpitz* operation:

> One boat was stationed on the enemy side between each group, to act as advance observer and report any signs of increased air activity (air escort with convoys). This did not lead to any contact with any of the expected convoys; it was afterwards discovered that they all avoided the areas in which the groups of U-boats were stationed. It was now realized that the enemy had discovered the last dispositions of patrol lines with his radar, and on the 8th Group *Tirpitz* was dissolved.

German records note:

> U-boat Command terminated the operation as further surfaced operations by day had become prohibitively costly in the face of Allied air superiority. *Tirpitz* disbanded. U-boats heading for new type lines: small, scattered.

The next operation would be undertaken between 9 and 15 November by wolfpack *Eisenhart* and targeted convoys HX.264, SC.146, and HX.265. For this, Dönitz divided the wolfpack into ten sub-groups of between one and four U-boats each (three being the most common), in three patrol lines in a checkerboard pattern loosely deployed in the area to the east of Newfoundland.

In a speech delivered at the Lord Mayor's Luncheon in London, on 9 November 1943, Churchill boldly declared, 'We have broken the back of the U-boat war, which at one time seemed our greatest peril.'

Frustrated by the continued lack of success in locating convoys, Dönitz's staff commented despondently:

> The submarine operations of recent weeks and reflections on the disposition of Group *Eisenhart* have illustrated the difficulties of locating the convoys. The enemy holds all the trump cards, far-reaching air reconnaissance covering all areas and permanently using location methods against which we still have no secure method of warning, thus safeguarding the ships and their dispositions.
>
> The lack of air reconnaissance means U-boats have done their own reconnaissance, limited to very small areas. The lack of new methods of location, coupled with minimum mobility of U-boats and danger of air attacks, have made it necessary for U-boats to proceed submerged during the day.

The War Log contained a renewed plea for far-reaching air reconnaissance and speedy improvements of active and passive location gear, and noted:

> The enemy knew all our secrets and we knew none of theirs, and such knowledge would be necessary for us to achieve successful attacks on convoys.

It went on to explain the rationale for discontinuing wolfpack operations in the Western Atlantic:

> The need to avoid too high losses to strong air forces, by travelling during the day and going into action at night, resulted in such immobility among the submarines that it became necessary to alter the former methods of attacking convoys.
>
> Following *Leuthen*'s initial success [against ON.202], U-boat locations, designated patrol areas and every alteration of the patrol lines has been detected by radio interceptions. Sufficient escorts and aircraft were now available for deployment to intercept the U-boats as they attempted to locate the convoys, which were now being regularly diverted away from the danger areas. Instead of locating the convoys, the U-boats now found they had now lost their previous key advantage –invisibility from detection.

U-boat Command continued to repeat this:

> Founded assumption ... that the enemy air reconnaissance, using location methods which in part we have not yet been able to pick up, has contacted our line arrangements. (1903/13 November 1943)

In order to reduce the risk of detection, particularly by radar-equipped aircraft, U-boats were ordered to minimize all electronic transmissions. U-boats at sea on13 November received the following wireless message:

> The submarine operations of recent weeks have been ruined by the lack of convoys located. It is assumed enemy air reconnaissance locates our patrol dispositions by means of location methods we do not fully understand, and thus the enemy have circumvented us. We must reduce the difficulties in contacting the enemy by using far-reaching air reconnaissance with location gear.
>
> The use of Zaunkönig has considerably lightened the difficulties of attacking sea forces; we have deduced from their use of depth charges that the enemy has become weaker and less determined.
>
> The automatic 3.7cm gun will also help in the battle against the main adversary, the enemy air forces, and will increase the mobility of submarines during the day. It has already been installed in seven boats, and a further eight are in process of being fitted with it.
>
> All boats putting out from Western France will be fitted with this excellent weapon at the beginning of December, and all home-based boats, in the middle of that month.

The most important points established are as follows:

> The reason for the failure of the last month's attack in the Atlantic is due to the failure to locate the convoy. You have had to combat the heaviest type of air forces, with very little chance of success. Your fighting has led to a strong cooperation between the enemy air and sea forces. These forces must not be turned against Germany. You must defend your Fatherland even though the battle seems fruitless to you.

The *Eisenhart* boats were expected to intercept HX.264 on 11 November and SC.146 on 14 November. In the event, only one U-boat sighted a convoy, and an attempted attack failed. The wolfpack was detected, convoys diverted to the south and the operation ended in failure. The BdU suspected the U-boat cipher had been compromised. This realization resulted in the autumn offensive, which had been in progress since late September, being temporarily abandoned, and this particular operation terminated.

On 15 November the *Eisenhart* boats were ordered to withdraw to the east to attempt operations against convoys on the eastern side of the Atlantic in brief sorties by night with support from air reconnaissance. Faced with Allied air superiority and intelligence intercepts, the U-boats were no longer able to close up on a convoy over great distances on the surface, and only able to launch torpedoes if the convoy passed over their position.

As a result of the evasive routing of convoys, based on interception of U-boat communications, no merchant ships were lost from Atlantic convoys during November. The Joint Statement for November read:

Anti-U-boat operations in November have been notable, for the enemy has achieved little for the great effort he has exerted. The number of merchant vessels sunk by U-boats in November is less than in any other month since May 1940.

By means of aircraft operating from the Azores we have been able to improve protection of our convoys and to diminish the area in which enemy U-boats were free from attack by our forces.

The enemy has used long-range aircraft to assist in concentrating U-boats on our convoy routes, but in spite of this our escort and counter-attack has been effective.

The caution of the enemy U-boats has lessened the number of opportunities presented to our forces for striking at them. Nevertheless, the number of U-boats sunk in November has again exceeded the number of their victims.

After two weeks of U-boat inactivity in the North Atlantic, wolfpacks *Coronel 1, 2* and *3* were formed to operate between 4 and 17 December against convoys ONS.24, HX.268 and ON.214 from a position closer to the Western Approaches than any previous wolfpack, fairly well south, across an approximate great circle route. *Coronel*, initially comprised of sixteen U-boats,[6] was assembled from waiting areas south-south-east of Iceland in mid-North Atlantic and tasked to operate against ONS.24. The attempt to intercept the convoy in the Eastern Atlantic in a short night operation on 4/5 December was frustrated when air reconnaissance by two Ju.290s on 4 December, and by one Ju.290, one FW200 Condor and one BV222 on 5 December failed to locate the convoy, which passed to the north of the wolfpack. Although the wolfpack was moved several times, it had made no contact with the convoys by 8 December. The wolfpack was re-formed on 8 December as *Coronel 2*, initially with nine U-boats to operate against HX.268, which also passed to the north of the wolfpack patrol line, again without being spotted by German air reconnaissance. German records indicate an awareness that the convoy was proceeding on a northern route, but although the longitude estimate was good, the convoy again slipped past.

The U-boats of *Coronel*, now divided into three subsidiary wolfpacks, searched for ON.214 between 11 and 13 December. Aerial reconnaissance over three days by Ju.290, FW200 and BV222 aircraft again failed to locate any ships, and interception and decoding of the U-boat radio transmissions resulted in the convoy being rerouted to pass to the south of the wolfpack. *Coronel 2*, now reduced to nine boats, was reconfigured as *Coronel 3* to operate from 13 December against ON.215. The convoy was sighted on 14 December steering west, but *Coronel 3*, sent south-west on the following day to intercept, found nothing and on 16 December was withdrawn to the east.

Dönitz had complained to Hitler the previous day:

All recent operations carried out in cooperation with the Air Command, Atlantic Coast against convoys moving north–south and east–west have failed completely due to a lack of planes. The outcome of each recent operation proves the former great successes of U-boat warfare can now be equalled only if sufficient aerial reconnaissance is provided.

Three new short-lived wolfpacks, *Sylt*, *Amrum* and *Föhr*, each of six U-boats, were formed on 18 December from *Coronel* U-boats and tasked to attack various ON, HX and SC convoys. *Föhr* was instructed to cruise on the surface even during the day, a risky operation exposing the U-boats to detection and counter-attack, and the order was soon rescinded. The problem of finding the convoys was becoming increasingly insoluble.

During a conference with Hitler on 19 December Dönitz once again stressed the need for extensive long-range reconnaissance, which could not be guaranteed by the Luftwaffe's proposed construction programme. Nothing, he said, could come of the U-boat war in 1944 without reconnaissance, for the U-boat was forced by enemy air superiority to remain submerged, thereby considerably reducing its field of vision. Dönitz requested all completed Ju.290s be used for long-range reconnaissance and not as bombers. Hitler agreed, subject to discussing this with Goering.

On 22 and 23 December convoys ON.216 and ONS.25 passed between the *Amrum* and *Föhr* wolfpacks. Over a period of seventeen days, twenty U-boats had searched an area of 5° in latitude by 12° in longitude in pursuit of seven convoys, but only succeeded in locating two and sank no merchant ships.

The end of December 1943 saw the adoption of new tactics in the deployment and operation of U-boats in the Atlantic. Twenty-eight were deployed in seven small wolfpacks – *Rügen I–VII 7* – in designated positions over a wide sea area in an attempt to intercept eleven west- and eastbound convoys.[8] These wolfpacks were formed on 23 December 1943 from sixteen of the former *Amrum*, *Föhr* and *Sylt* boats to operate in the Atlantic to the west of Ireland. Others joined later, bringing the final total to twenty-eight. They were moved from time to time between their designated positions but otherwise remained stationary, a tactic which reduced fuel consumption and enabled them to remain operational for longer periods than previously. The wolfpacks were given information (never very accurate) on the expected arrival of convoys, but little central direction on the conduct of each operation. Action was left to the discretion of individual U-boat commanders, who were exhorted to

> make determined use of chances for attack, since, owing to the small number of boats, the period of fighting is bound to be short. (1252/22 December)

Radio communication now became the exception rather than the rule. The sole success came on 30 December, when *U-545* of *Rügen I* fired four torpedoes at convoy ON.217 in mid-Atlantic, heard four detonations, claimed hits on four ships and observed one ship sinking. The only ship hit, the *Empire Housman*, was damaged but did not sink. On 3 Jan 1944 the *Empire Housman*, now straggling from the convoy, would be torpedoed by *U-744* and founder two days later.

On 26 December the German Naval High Command noted:

> As a result of the completion of air bases in England, Iceland, Newfoundland, the west coast of Africa and east coast of South America and Ascension Island, and the occupation of the Azores, the enemy has been able even in heavy weather to patrol the North and Middle Atlantic almost completely and the South Atlantic to a great extent, with large land-based aircraft.
>
> Since the spring of 1943 the enemy has been using auxiliary aircraft carriers in the northern part of the North Atlantic between 25° and 40° west and particularly in the area of the America–Gibraltar convoy routes. These stay for a long time in this area and when there are U-boat attacks proceed to the aid of the endangered convoys.

During December the evasive diversion of Atlantic convoys frustrated attempts to attack ten of these, with only one merchant ship damaged.

By January 1944 there was growing speculation in the press that the corner had been turned and the Battle of the Atlantic won, as claimed by the following article in Australian newspapers dated 1 January:

> In the European summer we were cheered by the information that convoys were practically unmolested. But that did not mean that Hitler had called off his sea-bloodhounds. As explained from Berlin, new devices had been

discovered, and results were predicted of a kind that might turn the tables in the war.

It is always folly to underestimate the strength of the enemy and to despise modern techniques. Presently it was learned that the foe had evolved an acoustic torpedo which could operate so as to guide the deadly missiles to their intended victims in the night or in fogs. Some success was met with, but the results were disappointing to the enemy, and so the Luftwaffe was again commissioned to take an active hand in the game, to direct the packs, assisted by a rocket glider. The Nazis have made much use of this rocket glider device over the land, and at one stage it appeared that a deadly menace to the Flying Fortress had been evolved. But neither at sea nor over the German cities has great success crowned the work of German scientists. That is not to say that the last has been heard of some new, menacing invention. But the fact is that the counter-measures adopted by the Anglo-Americans have been more effective than the devices for destroying cargo ships. The use of more and more destroyers of smaller type, of the corvette class, the employment of more long-range or carrier-based bombers, the use of helicopters on cargo ships and warships, and, of late, for the southern route, the use of land bases for aeroplanes in the midway islands of the Azores – all these and other inventions and devices have contributed to ensure new low levels in ship losses, allowing, with the help of new and increased tonnage, for pouring of increasing streams of men and materials over the Atlantic, ensuring a mounting tempo for the aerial war over Germany, and building up supplies for the great adventure of 1944 – the opening of the long-promised Second Front.

But despite all such optimism, Dönitz and Hitler remained undeterred. A conference between them on 1 January[9] recognized the enemy had been using a centimetre-wave for radar since May 1943, corresponding with the sharply rising losses of U-boats. Dönitz called for the development of a sensitive warning apparatus for centimetre-wave, a German radar operating on the centimetre-wave and measures to make the U-boat itself difficult to locate by eliminating enemy radar echoes.

The *Rügen I–VI* patrol lines were broken up on 7 January[10] and the U-boats deployed individually. Over a period of thirty-five days, its twenty-eight U-boats had managed to sink only one merchant ship from an Atlantic convoy, for the loss of one U-boat and the expenditure of a large amount of valuable fuel. The effects of enemy radar had now led to a change in the method of disposition of U-boats. The order given on 7 January to deploy the boats singly in the area of convoy routes marked the end of the use of reconnaissance lines to pick up convoys, with the absence of Luftwaffe air reconnaissance also a factor. The BdU now accepted the effect of enemy radio location, which during the previous year had become more and more strongly defined, as inevitable:

> In future, strong enemy air reconnaissance is to be expected ahead of convoys in the whole of the North Atlantic, and, as so far, no means of making the boats immune to enemy radar has been devised, any type of [U-boat] disposition will be known to the enemy and evaded. In future, therefore, successful mass U-boat operations against convoys will only be possible, with the types of boats available and planned, if the boats can be brought up to the convoys through constant reconnaissance by our own aircraft.

In early January 1944 U-boat operations were refocused on UK/West and North African convoys, mainly to the west and south-west of Ireland. The nineteen U-boats from *Rügen I* to *VII* were then merged into wolfpack *Rügen* (7 to 29 January), to be joined by twelve other U-boats to operate against convoys TU.5 and ON.215. This operation was also a failure; no merchant ships were sunk but four U-boats were lost.[11] *Rügen* was then disbanded, and the nineteen boats, together with four from the *Borkum* wolfpack and six others, were sent to operate in the Atlantic to the west of Ireland as individual boats in a number of different concentrations.

The BdU War Log for 10 January noted:

> U-boat attacks on convoy routes in the North Atlantic have been resumed; the first one, in which a new torpedo and a new counter-measure against radar were used, was surprisingly successful. [This presumably referred back to ON.202.] The enemy, however, were using new unknown methods of location, and aircraft were the U-boats' principal enemy. Sinking figures did not reach the old totals, and enemy anti-submarine defence was strong.
>
> Air reconnaissance is now essential to a successful U-boat war, because of the enemy's increased powers of location and air cover. Boats today were practically immobilized, through being compelled to remain submerged. Recent experience has shown that German aircraft have location equipment of inadequate range, and the enemy's fighter protection of convoys has become stronger.

Chapter 12

Phase Twelve: January to May 1944

As January progressed there was only one further loss, when a straggler from ON.219 was sunk on the 16th. The BdU now publicly admitted U-boat warfare was becoming more difficult, with radar presenting a particular challenge, and appeared to be taking a more pessimistic public view of its progress. A newspaper article dated 18 January 1944 read as follows:

GERMANY'S U-BOAT WOLVES – WAR GETTING TOUGH

'U-boat warfare has become bitter and desperate, and it will be more difficult still,' Heinrich Schlicht, spokesman for the German submarine command, admitted in a weekend broadcast.

'Allied convoy escorts became stronger each month throughout last year,' he said. 'Their destroyers are now equipped with instruments robbing the U-boat of its greatest asset – invisibility.'

Wolfpacks *Stürmer* of thirteen U-boats and *Hinein* of eight were formed on 26 and 27 January 1944, the first deployed round the island of Rockall, the second a short distance to the west of southern Ireland; the closest any wolfpacks operated to the British coast. Despite the favourable position for convoy contact and the BdU's attempts to plot the convoys correctly, they evaded the wolfpacks, and after days of fruitless searches the two wolfpacks were disbanded on 3 February. Wolfpack *Rügen* was dissolved on 26 January having sunk no ships. January had proved a good month for the Atlantic convoys.

After *U-985* sank a steamer on 8 February south-east of Iceland, air attacks on the U-boats increased in the northern area of the patrol, compelling Operational Control to move the boats farther west again. This fitted in well with the plan to co-operate with G.A.F. Commander for Atlantic Area (*Fliegerführer Atlantik*) and carry out an attack off the North Channel on an ONS convoy in the period from 14 to 18 February with all available submarines and planes. The U-boats would in any case have had to be moved to the west for this operation. Between 3 and 17 February 1944 the U-boats operating to the west of Ireland were concentrated singly and in loose formation in a double operation as the *Igel I* and *Igel II* wolfpacks in an attempt to locate and attack ONS.29 and ON.223. The *Igel I* wolfpack comprised fifteen U-boats, three of which were sunk by aircraft at the cost of only one merchant ship – a straggler from convoy UR.108. The *Igel II* wolfpack, also of fifteen U-boats, lost three of its number, all sunk by the 2nd Escort Group, and sank no merchant ships.

The Joint Statement for January was published in the press on 11 February:

LOSSES BY U-BOAT LOWEST ON RECORD

Allied merchant shipping losses as the result of enemy U-boat action in January were the lowest on record, according to the joint monthly Anglo-American statement on the U-boat war, released in London and Washington yesterday.

No figures were released, but the statement said that Allied surface craft and air patrols had destroyed more enemy submarines in January than in December, although the enemy's extreme caution and respect for convoy escorts gave only limited opportunities of attack. The statement referred to exaggerated German claims of mounting Allied merchant shipping losses as being made 'merely for propaganda purposes'.

Dönitz now ordered the establishment of the *Hai I* wolfpack of sixteen U-boats to attack HX.278 and ON.224, and on 16 February HX.278 approached the U-boat patrol line from the south-west. *U-546* and *U-984* were able to beat off the night attacks of radar and Leigh Light-equipped aircraft with their 37mm anti-aircraft guns, but were unable to attack the convoy. Meanwhile, on 17 February Dönitz sent the following message of encouragement and admonition:

The coming operation is to be fought with all available forces, in order to fight a convoy battle in the old style, with the qualification that the first night must produce the main blow from all submarines, since further operation during the day is questionable because of carrier aircraft. (2236/17)

A final sentence, indicating the vital need for a successful action against a convoy, warned, 'This long-prepared action must succeed. Do your best.'

Churchill, speaking in the House of Commons on the 'War and International Situation'[1] on 22 February, referred to the U-boat war:

I think it therefore my duty to state a few facts which are perhaps not generally realized. For instance, since Jan. 1, 1943, up to the present time in the middle of February, ships of the Royal Navy and aircraft of the RAF – that is to say, forces of the mother country only – have sunk more than half the U-boats of which we have certain proof in the shape of living prisoners. And they have also destroyed 40 per cent of the very large number of other U-boats, of which either corpses or fragments provide definite evidence of destruction.

The associated *Hai II* wolfpack of three U-boats which operated between 17 and 22 February achieved no success but incurred no losses.

The BdU War Log of 20 February1944 provides an extensive assessment of the development of convoy operations since May 1943:

By May 1943 enemy sea escort and especially air escort of convoys had reached such strength that even large wolfpacks of U-boats could no longer hold out against it and reach the centre of the convoy. This and the general increase of enemy air activity in all parts of the N. Atlantic caused such great losses, while at the same time increasingly fewer successes were scored, that on 24 May the order to clear the North Atlantic had to be given. The equipment of aircraft with excellent radar sets, which had been proceeding since March 1943, was the decisive factor in the success of the enemy air force. These sets enabled the aircraft to find the U-boats quickly, and without being noticed themselves, by day or night and in any visibility conditions at very great range, and made it possible for the aircraft to choose their own time and position for attacking, which for the U-boats meant a dangerous surprise attack. Radar made the U-boat visible; it could no longer surprise, and its fighting effectiveness was thus greatly diminished.

For the time being we tried to operate U-boats still in operations area against the America–Gibraltar convoys, as these were out of reach of land-based enemy aircraft. All dispositions tried there failed, however, because the area was so large, Radio Intelligence provided no information, and we had no air reconnaissance. In no case was a convoy found. By degrees the boats were withdrawn from the area S.W. of the Azores, passing the islands to the S., into the area between the Azores and Spain. Here again there were heavy losses, especially to enemy aircraft taking off from Gibraltar, and so the fight was finally abandoned, and the convoy battle in the Atlantic was at an end for the present.

The time had now come to use all boats (including type VIIc) in the Central American coastal area, the Caribbean, the coasts of Brazil and W. Africa. At the same time, at home, work was proceeding at a feverish rate on the development of our flak guns, and 2cm quadruple and twin mountings were fitted in the boats. It was hoped that enemy aircraft would be driven off with this flak armament, or at least deterred from making their dangerous low-level attacks.

Zaunkönig as an offensive weapon against destroyers was intended to break the superiority of the enemy anti-submarine forces. The Hagenuk Wanz was intended to enable the boats to pick up enemy location transmissions in all the enemy radar bands known, and was supposed to be free of the spontaneous radiation suspected in Metox, the radar interception set used hitherto. Radar decoy device Aphrodite was developed as an effective counter-measure against enemy radar, and all boats were equipped with it.

The date for the first operation depended on when Zaunkönig, the decisive weapon, could be ready and issued to boats. This date was fixed for 29 September, allowing sufficient time for boats to pass unnoticed into the operations area in the North Atlantic.

The next wolfpack engaged in a major operation against the Atlantic convoys was *Preussen* (22 February to 22 March), deployed in an area to the west of Ireland to operate against seven convoys.[2] It comprised at one time or another a total of thirty-one U-boats, eight of which were lost, but sank no merchant ships. As a result of Ultra intelligence derived from decrypts of the U-boats' radio communications, HX.279 and ON.225 were re-routed clear of the wolfpack on 24 February. The BdU War Log for 27 February noted:

On 27 February the boats were concentrated to intercept an ON convoy which was due to arrive, according to an intercepted radio message. However, the enemy was not contacted.

The loss of nine boats in the North Atlantic during January was still tolerable. However, during February surprisingly high losses occurred, which are as yet inexplicable. Whereas there was no clue to the loss of four boats in January, in February the number had risen to nine. When the positions given in their last reports were registered, it was established the majority were probably lost somewhere in mid-Atlantic. The danger of this area has been shown by reports from submarines and confirmed by direction-finder bearings on numerous anti-submarine units and patrolling planes. Certainly, in most cases loss may be assumed to be due to sudden air attack.

Losses in February were very high. They show the merciless hardness of present-day submarine warfare. In future, even more caution must be used, since if such high losses continue, the number of submarines in the Atlantic will fall below a tolerable level.

Despite the bitterness of the struggle, the bearing of commanders and crews is, as always, above all praise. Although aware of our heavy losses, although constantly pursued and fatigued, the submariner remains undaunted. Never sparing himself, relentless against fate, filled with hatred for the enemy, trusting his arms and confident of victory, he keeps on with the unequal struggle.

The BdU War Log's 1 March summary of U-boat numbers reported:

The number of boats on 1.1.1944 was 130; by 1.3.1944 it had fallen to 109. This was due (apart from the constant departure of boats for the Mediterranean) to the high losses, whereas only a thin trickle of boats has been coming from home waters.

In a debate in the Commons on 29 February [3] the Secretary of State for Air told the House:

Hon. Members will have noticed from the accounts of operations against U-boats that the Battle of the Atlantic is not a series of single combats between the U-boat and the aircraft or the warship but is made up of prolonged engagements over thousands of miles of sea, in which the work of the surface forces is at every stage integrated with the work of aircraft.

The war against the submarine is especially a war of wits. The many units of Coastal Command, in which American squadrons are now serving alongside our own, stretching from Iceland to Gibraltar and the Azores, sweeping the whole of the. Atlantic, have a long task of vigilance, and of danger too. Most of their work – perhaps the most trying part – is taken up with long and uneventful sweeps over barren seas, but there are many occasions when they have to meet formidable opposition. They fly in low, these coastal crews, to drop their depth charges. The Germans have increased the numbers of anti-aircraft guns carried by their U-boats in order to force up the coastal crews to heights at which the accuracy of their bombing would fall off. Admiral Dönitz, the Commander-in-Chief of the German Navy, is reported to have said – though I cannot for the life of me understand how an officer who I suppose to be competent can have made such a remark – that 'an aeroplane could no more attack a submarine than a crow a mole'. The mole is turning himself into a porcupine, but he still cannot escape Coastal Command's talons.

Only one Atlantic convoy was attacked during February, HX.278 on 9 February, when one merchant ship was damaged.

The shortage of Luftwaffe aircraft for Atlantic air reconnaissance was never satisfactorily resolved, as the following extract from a February 1944 BdU report illustrates:

Typical of a number of reports is one by Kapitän zur See Mössel, Naval Liaison Officer with G.A.F. Headquarters, on air co-operation with U-boats: 'Between 13 and 18 February 1943, strong reconnaissance forces were used against a convoy west of Ireland; altogether two Ju.88s, 17 Ju.290s, three F.W.200s and two B.V.222s were employed, of which three Ju.290s were shot down, presumably by enemy carrier-borne aircraft. Unfortunately, it was not possible to inform the U-boat patrol line of the location of the convoy, as shortage of aircraft prevented reconnaissance on the day before the expected meeting between convoy and U-boats. Once again, the shortage of reconnaissance aircraft has been the cause of failure to exploit an important opportunity.'

It has been agreed between F.O. U-boats and the *Fliegerführer Atlantik* that in future each air reconnaissance is to be followed by a fourteen days' pause to rest the air units; only in this way can long-distance reconnaissance be carried out thoroughly over two to three days and over wide areas.

A BdU review of the U-boat situation during January/February reported:

After the patrol strip of Group *Rügen 1-6* was disbanded on 7 January, the boats were stationed singly. During January the boats were shifted several times and brought closer to the North Channel. At first things went well. The enemy's air and naval anti-submarine defence measures were tolerable, and our boats were able to slowly edge in the direction of the North Channel.

The first sightings showed the enemy were scattered thickly all over the whole area without any special focal point. But shortly after, the small number of sightings and Radio Intercept Intelligence led to the conclusion the enemy was partly bypassing even the widely spaced submarine positions in the north and south. Hence the submarines on the north and south wings were moved in a little to the east, forming more or less a semicircle of boats round the North Channel and covering the inward and outward courses which we assumed were followed by the enemy.

Despite this watch on the convoy routes, contacts with the enemy remained comparatively rare. The causes were as follows: the usual bad weather conditions, particularly in the northern part of the position, and the need for boats to remain submerged during the day and surfaced at night.

It must be assumed that many convoys and single ships passed through the boats' patrol area without being picked up by them because of their short reconnaissance range. (Hydrophone range by day; at night the bad weather and heavy rolling of the extremely top-heavy boats greatly reduce the visibility range).

Towards the end of January stronger anti-submarine measures, especially in the southern area of the patrol, were already making themselves felt. The first reports of locating the air attacks were received, and radar location of enemy anti-submarine units confirmed patrols had been increased.

In March 1944 the press still remained optimistic the Battle of the Atlantic had been won. A typical article was published on 4 March:

CONVOYS HOME

Atlantic Battle Has Been Won

Allied convoys, packed with invasion tools and carrying troops, cross the Atlantic with negligible losses. After days aboard a convoy bound for England (writes a Reuter correspondent from a British port) we can testify that the Battle of the Atlantic has been won. Our convoy fought off one Nazi submarine and delivered its vital cargo without losing a single ship. The submarine never had a chance. It struck at the customary hour of dusk, and as immediately the alarm was sounded, the escort vessels assumed battle positions. The submarine menace has become so much less that escort ships can now swing from one convoy to another.

Speaking in the Debate on the Navy Estimates on 7 March 1944,[4] A. V. Alexander, First Lord of the Admiralty, reported:

The ten days from 20 March 1943 onwards were, perhaps, an even more important turning point, for, in that short space of time, the trend of merchant shipping losses changed with a suddenness it is hardly possible to exaggerate.

Between December 1942 and February 1943 merchant shipping losses showed a welcome reduction, after the peak in November 1942. This reduction is partly due to the weather, that winter in the North Atlantic being one of the worst on record, hampering the U-boats and subjecting their crews to considerable strain. The escorts and our aircraft were also affected, more than the U-boats, since they suffered more severely from weather damage.

In the first twenty days of March, the losses increased to a new high level, particularly among ships in convoy. Special escort support groups were sent to the aid of threatened convoys. In the last ten days of March, the merchant shipping losses reduced by two-thirds.

Sometimes the enemy deployed as many as thirty U-boats against a convoy, and, on our side, the number of surface ships and aircraft together, acting in close co-operation, would be of the same order. When they had been fought out, the U-boats had received such a battering that they virtually abandoned the North Atlantic for several months. As a result of this success, there were periods when more U-boats were sunk than merchant ships. The total sinkings of merchant ships for 1943 were, in fact, below our most optimistic hopes at the beginning of the year, and indeed were little more than half of the working estimate that we then thought it prudent to adopt. The reduction is further exemplified by the falling proportion of ships lost in main North Atlantic and United Kingdom coastal convoys. In 1941, one ship was lost out of every 181 which sailed; in 1942, one out of every 233; in 1943, one out of every 344. The losses in these convoys during the second half of last year were less than one in 1,000.

This improvement was attributed to a number of factors. At times the enemy have ascribed it almost entirely to the improvements which have taken place in our weapons and devices. Equally, it would be right for me, speaking for the Admiralty, to give prominence to the growth and efficiency of Coastal Command of the Royal Air Force, the ability of its Commanders and their excellent co-operation with the Navy. The past twelve months have seen a global expansion of Coastal Command, and an increase in the proportion of very long-range aircraft available to provide cover for convoys hundreds of miles out to sea and even right across the North Atlantic.

This growth in the numbers of British and American air and surface escorts enabled three things lack of resources previously prevented us from doing on anything like the scale we should have wished. The introduction of special support groups reinforce the escorts of convoys actually threatened with attack.

Secondly, it has enabled us to take the offensive with other special forces against the U-boats in the areas, principally the Bay of Biscay, through which they must maintain a dense traffic on their way to and from their patrolling grounds.

Thirdly, increased resources made more training possible; and enabled the composition of the escort groups to be kept much more stable and develop the high degree of teamwork which produced the most astounding results.

He later added:

I am anxious no one should begin to think any relaxation is possible. Indeed, we must recognize that there may yet be periods when losses will mount again. The Germans have probably at least as many U-boats now as at the beginning of 1943. In the early months of last year the production of U-boats exceeded kills, and in recent months the U-boats have often sought to avoid destruction by avoiding action. The bombing of the U-boat building centres has certainly reduced output; but there is not the slightest evidence that the enemy has in any way abandoned his intention to cripple our sea communications if he possibly can. On the contrary, the Germans are still making every endeavour to improve the performance and the equipment of their U-boats. They have provided them with greatly increased anti-aircraft firepower; they have brought their new acoustic torpedo into service; and we must expect further developments still. Recently the Germans seemed to be trying to develop tactics based upon an increased use of very long-range aircraft, acting in co-operation with their U-boats. We have already reported in the Press a number of successes against these aircraft by our ship-borne fighters, to whom credit should be given. Perhaps the best indication that Admiral Dönitz aims at putting more U-boats into the fight is the fact that more and more concrete shelters are still being built by them in the operational bases. It can, therefore, be regarded as certain that he will try, and try again, to stage a comeback, and these efforts may be more sustained than that made in September last, when the U-boats sallied out once more in force on the main Atlantic routes but failed on that occasion to keep the campaign going. We must also expect that the U-boats will, as at present, seek to expand their effort in far distant waters such as the Indian Ocean.

I have spoken of the dramatic suddenness with which the statistical picture of the Battle of the Atlantic changed last March. As the House will have realized, this change was actually the result of a long planned build-up, and those officers at the Admiralty with the greatest knowledge and acutest judgment predicted a radical improvement even in the dark days a year ago.

I have dealt in some considerable detail with the so-called Battle of the Atlantic, because, situated as this country is, that battle is fundamental to its fortunes.

Convoy HX.281 passed through the U-boat patrol lines on 10 March without incident. ON.227, which turned away south to avoid the U-boat patrol lines, was escorted on 12 and 13 March by strong air formations from Cornwall and the Azores.

At the Führer Conference on 21/22 March Dönitz and Hitler agreed that, because of high losses, U-boat operations should be restricted, and the boats should only be fully employed only in case of invasion. The War Log for 22 March, commenting on current operations, noted:

> Group *Preussen* dissolved. Boats re-disposed ... in order to keep them moving and make it difficult for the enemy to find them.
>
> Losses in the Atlantic during the last months were notably heavy in one particular area where it is suspected there is constant strong patrol by aircraft and anti-submarine groups, as the majority of convoys take this route.
>
> This area is therefore being cleared for the present, and several boats are being used against the western sector of this convoy route.

By 22 March it had become all too clear to the BdU that the standard pattern of wolfpack operations using conventional boats and straight-running T5 torpedoes was no longer practical in the North Atlantic That day, Dönitz ordered the break-up of the *Preussen* wolfpack, whose surviving U-boats were then deployed over the North Atlantic in 'free manoeuvre' areas. The last wolfpack in the history of the old-style German U-boat had ended in failure.

Although he had not yet formally declared the end of the Battle of the Atlantic, Churchill apparently felt sufficiently confident to announce during his radio broadcast from London on 26 March:

> We who dwell in the British Isles must celebrate with joy and thankfulness our deliverance from the mortal U-boat peril – which deliverance lighted the year which has ended.
>
> When I look back upon the fifty-five months of this hard and obstinate war, which makes ever more exacting demands upon our life-springs of energy and contrivance, I still rate highest among the dangers we have overcome the U-boat attacks upon our shipping, without which we cannot live or even receive the help which our Dominions and our grand and generous American ally have sent us.

The ONS convoys were now suspended between 28 March and 29 September 1944 as the escort groups were diverted to cover the Normandy landings. The seven months of U-boat operations between September 1943 and March 1944 had delivered little tangible result. Although an average of sixty U-boats a month had been deployed across the North Atlantic convoy routes and off the convoy assembly and dispersal points, only nineteen merchant ships had been sunk, at a cost of fifty U-boats.

The BdU War Log entry reported the situation for 3 April 1944:

> Only one IXc boat and ten VIIc boats in North Atlantic. The limited supply of boats from home is the reason for this, caused by the setting up of readiness Group *Mitte* in Norwegian area and *Landwirt* in Western France. Of boats stationed in Atlantic in the next few days, three will be returning on account of fuel supply, and three more in the next few weeks. By the middle of April, therefore, about eight boats only will be stationed in the North Atlantic. Strength will be up again at the end of the month as Group *Mitte* will have been disposed and the supply of boats from home will be normal again. Type VIIc boats will not sail from Western France till the end of the month.

The Joint Statement for anti-U-boat operations during March was published in the US on Tuesday, 11 April:

STILL STRONG

Merchant shipping losses in March were a little higher than in February, the British Prime Minister (Mr Churchill) and President Roosevelt reported jointly yesterday.

In general, however, the war against the undersea raiders continued successfully during the months, they said, and the rate of U-boat sinkings was fully maintained.

'The enemy persevered in vain endeavours to disrupt our supplies to Russia by the northern route, and extended his activities from the Barents Sea, on the approach to Murmansk, to the Indian Ocean,' the statement said. 'Merchant shipping losses were mainly in distant seas.'

The Allied merchant fleet continued to improve in quality and quantity, it added, but U-boat strength remained considerable and called for powerful efforts by the Allies for its destruction.

On 6 April convoy SC.156 was attacked in mid-Atlantic and two merchant ships sunk.

The Minutes of the Conferences of the Commander-in-Chief, Navy and the Führer at Headquarters Berghof on 12 and 13 April 1944, commenting on the U-boat situation, took some comfort from the fact the continuing U-boat threat was still perceived by the Allies as sufficiently serious to 'tie up' large numbers of ships and aircraft:

> Submarine Warfare. With the aid of an English monthly report captured by the Japanese and giving data on Allied shipping losses and anti-submarine warfare, the Commander-in-Chief, Navy shows the great extent to which naval forces were tied up by submarine warfare as early as January 1942. His estimate for the present time is much higher. The Reichsmarschall [Goering] stresses the large number of enemy air forces tied up by submarine warfare. The Commander-in-Chief, Navy points out that Churchill admitted in his last monthly report on submarine warfare that an extraordinarily large number of forces are being tied up in this way. The Commander in Chief, Navy therefore believes submarine warfare must continue in spite of losses.

On 16 April the tanker *Pan Pennsylvania* in convoy CU.21 was torpedoed by *U-550* about 200 miles east of New York. *U-550* was then sunk by the escorts in a counter-attack. The *Pan Pennsylvania* later capsized, and her hulk was bombed and sunk by Allied aircraft two days later. One straggler from SC.157 was sunk late in the evening of 26 April. These three sinkings were the only losses from Atlantic convoys during the month. The Joint Statement for the month read:

> In April 1944, the United Nations antisubmarine activity continued at a highly satisfactory level. Again for another month, the extraordinary fact continues that the number of enemy submarines sunk exceeds the number of Allied merchant ships sunk by submarines.

U-boat losses were now so heavy that by May 1944 their North Atlantic operations had virtually ceased, and no merchant ships were lost from North Atlantic convoys. By mid-May the focus of U-boat operations had begun to shift eastwards with the impending invasion of Normandy.

The Joint Statement for May read:

> During May our shipping losses have been by far the lowest for any month of the war, and they have in fact been a fraction of the losses inflicted on enemy shipping by our warships and aircraft, although their merchant shipping is petty compared to that of the Allies.
>
> There has been a lull in the operations of the U-boats which perhaps indicates preparation for a renewed offensive. The change which had come over the scene is illustrated by the fact that in spite of the few U-boats at sea, several are now sent to the bottom for each merchant ship sunk,

whereas formerly each U-boat accounted for a considerable number of merchant ships before being destroyed.

This is to be ascribed to the vigilance and to the relentless attacks of our Anglo-American-Canadian and other anti-U-boat forces, including the scientists who support them in a brilliant manner.

Chapter 13

Phase Thirteen: June 1944–May 1945

A review published by the BdU at the beginning of June 1944 on the general course of the U-boat war between 1 March and 31 May 1944 conceded that the course of the battle had been determined by the strength of the enemy defence, especially air radar, where improvements both in quantity and quality had led to more U-boat losses and increasing lack of success. The battle of endurance alone in the operational area, without actual contact with the enemy or targets to attack, was extremely hard and on occasion had resulted in an order to limit the duration of operations for type VIIc boats to eight weeks, to lessen sea time and relieve the intense strain on the crews.

Success had come in the form of 'tying down enemy forces', as confirmed by observations, from U-boats, agents' reports and radio intercepts, of an increase in the number of operational aircraft, escort vessels, anti-submarine patrols and aircraft carriers. The review recognized the task of the U-boat crews in achieving this was especially difficult. Chances of success had become slight, while the prospects of failing to return from patrol were very great; in the last few months only 70 per cent of the boats which sailed on patrol each month had returned.

During June, U-boat operations were focussed on countering the invasion of France and on maintaining a presence in invasion-endangered areas. No Atlantic convoys were attacked during the month. The monthly Joint Statement on submarine warfare reported:

> Hitler's submarine fleet failed on all counts in June 1944. Not only were the U-boats unable to halt the United Nations' invasion of the continent [D-Day and after], but their efforts to prevent the necessary supplying of our constantly growing Allied Army in Europe were made completely ineffective by our countermeasures.
>
> The U-boats apparently concentrated to the west of the invasion during the month, relatively few of them being disposed over the Atlantic. Their sinking of United Nations' merchant vessels reached almost the lowest figure of the entire war. For every United Nations' merchant vessel sunk by German submarines, several times as many U-boats were sent to the bottom.

Thousands of Allied ships have been moved across the Channel to Normandy and coastwise to build up the military forces engaged in the liberation of Europe. No merchant vessel of this vast concourse has been sunk by U-boat, with the possible exception of one ship. In this case doubt exists as to her destruction by U-boat or mine.

This is despite attempts by a substantial force of U-boats to pass up-Channel from their bases in Norway and France. Such attempts were of course expected, and US and British Air Squadrons of coastal command, working in cooperation with the surface forces of the Allied Navies, were ready.

From the moment that the U-boats sailed from their bases they were attacked by aircraft of coastal command. Both aircraft and surface forces followed up sighting reports, hunting and attacking the U-boats with relentless determination.

The enemy were thus frustrated by the brilliant and unceasing work of coastal command and the tireless patrols of the surface forces and have suffered heavy casualties.

Operations continue.

A few U-boats still remained active in the North Atlantic and Caribbean during July. No transatlantic convoys were attacked during the month, but the sinking on 7 July of the unescorted oil tanker *Esso Harrisburg* by *U-516* about 200 miles north-west of Aruba demonstrated that U-boats remained active in the Caribbean. The Joint Statement for the month announced:

The number of German U-boats sunk during the war now exceeds 500. It is therefore understandable that the U-boats still operating are extremely cautious. Their efforts have been ineffective during July, a month which has been so important for the success of continental operations.

The number of U-boats destroyed has been substantially greater than the number of merchant ships sunk. Seventeen U-boats have been sunk while attempting to interfere with our cross-Channel traffic since the first landing of the Army of Liberation.

The U-boat fleet is still of impressive size, nevertheless the U-boats remain the hunted rather than the hunters. They have been attacked from the Arctic to the Indian Ocean, aircraft playing a great part with the surface forces. This pressure will be maintained until all chances of revival of the U-boat campaign are killed, whatever may be the new devices and methods developed by the enemy.

The Nazi claims of sinkings continue to be grossly exaggerated. For instance, their claim for June, the latest month for which complete figures are available, was an exaggeration of 1,000 per cent.

Churchill, speaking in the House of Commons debate on the 'War Situation' on 2 August 1944,[1] urged caution:

> The losses by U-boats since the beginning of 1944, compared with former years, are almost negligible ... It is always possible that there may be a return of the U-boat war. There is talk of Germany trying to make U-boats faster under the water: there are various talks, and it is never well to discount these matters.

Mixed messages were also emerging on the state of the anti-U-boat war as illustrated by a press report dated 10 August:

BRITTANY DRIVE 'CHOKES OFF'
U-BOAT MENACE

LONDON, Wednesday (AAP)

The Battle of the Atlantic virtually is finished, says a United Press correspondent at Supreme Headquarters, who quotes naval authorities. The scale of U-boat warfare in the Atlantic has been cut by over 75 pc by the Allied break-through to Brittany. Admiral Dönitz will probably be left with bases for fewer than 50 submarines, less than half of which can operate simultaneously. The submarine menace thus has been choked off at the very moment when it is of the utmost importance to the Allies to maintain an uninterrupted flow of shipping from the United States to the front.

One week later, at least one newspaper claimed the end of the U-boat war had come. The report, published under the headline 'THE HUNTED U-BOAT', claimed:

> The monthly statement of the position of the U-boat war issued under the joint authority of Mr Churchill and President Roosevelt, which was introduced early in 1943, marked the end of the vitally dangerous phase of Hitler's underwater weapon. The Allied counter-measures have gone sufficiently well ever since to justify the Leaders in continuing to take their peoples and the world into their confidence in this respect. The story has been consistently one of enemy defeat despite his utmost efforts; and more often than not it has told of U-boat losses exceeding the number of ships they destroyed. But despite the regular cheerfulness and confidence which had marked previous monthly communiqués, that covering operations for July, which was issued on August 10, was most notable of them all, for it

appears to chronicle the end of the U-boat as a serious weapon of offence in the present war.

'Although the German submarine fleet is still of impressive size,' says this latest statement, 'it has become the hunted rather than the hunter. In consequence of their heavy losses it is understandable that U-boats still operating are extremely cautious. Their efforts during July – an extremely important month for the operations of the Allies on the Continent – were ineffective, and the number of U-boats destroyed was substantially greater than the number of merchantmen they sank.'

The whole invasion operation, necessitating the concentration of a huge aggregation of shipping in narrow waters in. close proximity to U-boat bases, would seem to have afforded the enemy's submarine fleet an excellent chance to inflict heavy damage, but the results – 17 U-boats sunk while attempting to interfere with cross Channel traffic since the commencement of the invasion, and fewer than 17 Allied ships lost through their attacks – is clear proof that the Allies enjoy virtually as complete control of the sea as they do of the air. Their air dominance, of course, very greatly assists their command of the sea. The statement added that the enemy's submarines had been attacked from the Arctic Ocean to the Indian Ocean, aircraft playing a great part with surface craft. That pressure would be maintained whatever new devices or methods the enemy used, until all chance of the revival of the U-boat campaign had been killed.

The great advance in methods of U-boat detection and destruction, compared with improvements in the construction, equipment, armament and tactics of such craft, is illustrated by the fact that in the very early stages of the 1914–18 war one small U-boat sank three British battleships (fortunately old ones) – the *Crecy*, *Aboukir* and *Hogue* – in the space of a few minutes, while so late as the end of 1942, the depredations of the Axis submarine fleets were successful on such a scale as to seriously hamper the prosecution of the war by the Allies.

Now, however, the number of U-boats destroyed in the first Great War – 216 – has been completely dwarfed by the 'over 500', which is the figure officially given for the present struggle, and it may be taken that, although it is still numerous, the back of this major section of Hitler's navy has been effectively broken. Its power to do damage –relatively insignificant as it was in July – will doubtless suffer further heavy reduction as the result of the westward and southward push of the United States armies in France. All the major U-boat bases on the northern side of the Bay of Biscay should be in American hands very soon, and it is reasonable to suppose that it will not be long before these craft are deprived of sanctuary anywhere on the west coast of France, from which for three years their operations against Allied shipping in the Atlantic have been so immensely facilitated. When the occupied ports in the Channel and North Sea are also lost, the lot of the U-boat will indeed become precarious.

On 25 August the BdU ordered all U-boats in western French ports to put to sea and proceed to Norway to carry on operations from there. A signal sent to all U-boats the following day read:

The military situation has made it necessary to prepare all U-boats at bases as quickly as possible for combat operation or transfer to Norway.

The U-boat war will continue with the old spirit and new measures. (1934B/26 August 1944)

Dönitz later wrote of the situation in August:

When in August 1944 the American troops succeeded in breaking through at Avranches, France was lost to Germany. The garrisons of the harbour fortresses on the western and southern coasts of France were strengthened, their defence being ordered to deny the enemy the use of these harbours as long as possible. This was successful in the case of the western ports and the Channel Islands until the end of the war, with the exception of the fortifications at the mouth of the Gironde. On the other hand, the ports in southern France, where meanwhile a second successful [enemy] landing in the region of the Maritime Alps had been made, were lost at an early date. The U-boats were withdrawn from the French ports, the remaining naval vessels being left there to help in their defence. The personnel not needed for defence were brought back overland as part of the retreating army, and the majority reached German soil only after taking part in much hard land fighting.

The loss of France was a setback of the utmost gravity for the conduct of the war at sea. All the strategic advantages arising from the possession of the Biscay ports were lost with one blow.

The U-boats had to fall back on the Norwegian and home bases. The resulting long passage swallowed up a disproportionately great part of the boats' endurance and, as previously mentioned, had to be made submerged.

The month saw only one attack on an Atlantic convoy when at 15.55 on 30 August the American tanker *Jacksonville* in CU.36 was torpedoed and fatally damaged by *U-482* 50 miles north of Londonderry. The August Joint Statement focussed on the withdrawal of the U-boats from their French bases and consequent restriction on their operations:

Last month, due to the effectiveness of the Allied operations in France, the principal U-boat operating bases in the Bay of Biscay were neutralized. As a consequence the Germans have been forced to operate their underseas craft from Norwegian and Baltic bases, thereby stretching even thinner their difficult lines of operation. The exchange rate between merchant ships sunk and U-boats destroyed continues to be profitable to the United Nations' cause. While U-boat operations continue, they are sporadic and relatively ineffectual.

By the end of August it was evident that the U-boats had begun their final exodus from the Biscay ports and were heading for Norway, where they would be much more vulnerable to Allied air attack. The problems of repair and maintenance of a large U-boat fleet at the small and inadequately equipped Norwegian bases would also be much more difficult. The main effect, however, of the loss of the Biscay bases was the considerable increase in the length of voyages to operating areas. The 500-ton U-boats, which comprised the majority of the U-boat fleet, were thereafter restricted to operations around the British Isles, as it was extremely difficult to refuel at sea. Even the 740-ton U-boats confined most of their later operations to the nearby Atlantic, operating near Canada and Gibraltar.

Early in September 1944, following the transfer of the U-boats from the Biscay bases to Norwegian ports, the South-Western Approaches to the British Isles were opened to Allied convoys for the first time in four years, and the North Atlantic convoys were now rerouted around the south of Ireland, through St George's Channel. There was only one attack on an Atlantic convoy when on 8 September in the North-Western Approaches, north of Tory Island, Ireland, HX.305 lost the whale factory ship *Empire Heritage* and rescue ship *Pinto*.

During the debate on the 'War and International Situation'[2] in the House of Commons on 28 September Churchill, addressing the shipping situation, forecast:

> The end of the U-boat war, when it comes, will allow us to go out of convoy in the Western Hemisphere and thus at a bound add perhaps at least 25 per cent carrying capacity to our mercantile marine, and more in the case of tankers.

The BdU was not entirely discouraged by the loss of the bases in western France, the War Log for 30 September optimistically commenting:

> The loss of the West would have been of decisive importance had the submarine war to be carried on with same types of boats as before. But a very great underwater range, high submerged speed and great diving depth

will enable the new type XXI boats to break through to the Atlantic in spite of concentrated defensive patrols, and to operate with success in the North Atlantic and other very distant areas.

By the end of September the last of the U-boats had departed from the Biscay-Channel area. The September Joint Statement contained the following upbeat but cautious message:

> During September there has been a lull in U-boat activity, which is possibly seasonal. This year, as last, the enemy may hope to renew his offensive in the autumn and may rely on new types of U-boats to counter our present ascendancy. Shipping losses have been almost as low as in May 1944, the best month of the war. The rate of destruction of U-boats in proportion to shipping losses remains satisfactory.
>
> The U-boat war, however, demands unceasing attention. Only the zeal and vigour of the Allied air and surface forces have procured the comparative safety of our shipping and the enemy's scant success.

On 1 October there were 401 U-boats in commission, of which eighty-two were deployed in the Atlantic. The BdU War Log for 1 October addressed the implications losing the bases in France:

> U-boat Section of the Naval Staff noted the western area was no longer the focal point of U-boat operations. The fortresses still holding out would fall shortly for lack of supplies. At the beginning of the enemy advance, all U-boats had to be withdrawn from the western bases.
>
> The U-boat War will be carried on from bases in Norway or Germany (Hamburg, Kiel, etc.). Preparations for this are in progress. The loss of the western bases will be felt most heavily if the U-boat war has to be continued from Norway using the same types of U-boats as before, as they are so slow underwater. The ability to use the newer types would, for the most part, defeat enemy counter-measures. Besides, the range of the new Type XXI U-boats is so great that they will be able to operate in the same areas even without the use of the western bases.

On 2 October there were eight U-boats in the North Atlantic area of operations – four off the North Channel, one off the North Minch, two off Halifax and one in the St Lawrence River. Twenty-eight boats were on return passage, and four on outward passage. The BdU War Log for the day continued:

> When the boats at present in operations areas leave, the number of boats in the Atlantic will have reached the lowest figure for about three years. It is to be expected that the enemy will soon realize this, will curtail his

anti-submarine activity accordingly and will use the naval and air forces so released for offensive operations against the coasts and against our own shipping.

Every effort must be made to increase the number of boats quickly.

During October no Atlantic convoys were attacked and no merchant ships lost or damaged. This was the first month of the war during which the U-boats were unable to sink a single ship in the Atlantic.

By 31 October there were eighty-six operational U-boats in the Atlantic. During the month there had been a daily average of forty-five at sea, seven in the operations area, eighteen on outward passage and twenty-one on return. The Admiralty assessment of the average number of U-boats at sea in the Atlantic during November was somewhat lower – only twenty-four, the lowest monthly average of this period, after completion of the transfer of U-boats from the Biscay bases.

The Joint Statement for October read:

The scope of the German U-boats' activities in October 1944 was materially below that of any other month of the war; in consequence of which, the number of United Nations' merchant vessels sunk by German submarines during the month was also the lowest of any month of the entire war.

Although the number of German U-boats destroyed was less than what has come to be considered a good monthly 'bag', it compares very favourably with the number of Allied merchant vessels sunk by U-boats.

The Allies continue to supply on schedule their evergrowing armies in Europe.

Admiral Sir Max Horton, Commander-in-Chief, Western Approaches, was reported as saying in Liverpool on 15 November:

The Battle of the Atlantic is not finished yet, and I don't think the Germans have finished building submarines. We do not expect them to give in until the war is over.

There were no merchant ship losses from Atlantic convoys in November, as the Joint Statement for the month later made clear:

Shipping losses from U-boat action have again been very small, and the number of U-boats sunk in proportion has again been satisfactory.

The enemy has by no means abandoned the struggle and has introduced new devices, such as the extensible air intake and exhaust which enable U-boats to remain submerged for long periods and so penetrate into areas denied to them for the past three years.

Reports that U-boat construction has been abandoned are probably Germaninspired and are untrue. On the contrary, improved types of U-boats may at any time be thrown into the battle, and retention of our present command of the sea will undoubtedly call for unremitting vigilance and hard fighting.

In an example of continued German ingenuity and intent, *U-1230* landed two agents on the Maine coast near Bar Harbor on 29 November.

On 1 December 1944 ninety-two U-boats were assigned to Atlantic operations. The month saw the beginning of a steady increase in the number of U-boats at sea in the Atlantic as the U-boat operational fleet expanded, a development made public in press reports of 10 December:

Reliable agent reports as follows on 26 October from London:

Commander Sir Guy Domville of the Admiralty asserted that a rejuvenated German U-boat arm will have to be reckoned with soon. The U-boat fleet, through new design and rebuilding, is now armed against English defences after their recent withdrawal. According to reports, the new U-boats are capable of 15 knots submerged. It is possible then for these boats to follow and attack Allied convoys even by day. English submarine-chasers have new ASDIC, however, which can find U-boats' positions even underwater.

The only casualty from an Atlantic convoy during December occurred on the 21st, when the merchant ship *Samtucky* in convoy HX.327 was torpedoed and badly damaged by *U-806* off Nova Scotia. Between September and December 1944 only two Atlantic convoys had been attacked. The Joint Statement for December explained:

The German U-boat warfare flared into renewed activity during December 1944. This is but another index that the European war is far from over.

Increased losses in Allied merchant craft have been officially recorded, as a result of the U-boats' spurt last month.

Despite these, the United Nations regularly continue to supply their expanding armies over the world, enabling them to resist the attackers or drive back the foe. The Allies continue to sink the enemy undersea craft in widely separated parts of the Atlantic.

The announcement of the recent landing of enemy agents from a U-boat on the Maine coast is yet another indication that the menace of Germany's undersea fleet is real and continuing.

At the beginning of January 1945 there were ninety-eight U-boats in the Atlantic fleet, of which thirty-five were at sea. Early in the month, the German

Naval Staff review of the Development of the U-boat war between 1 July and 31 December 1944 noted:

> The general withdrawal of all U-boats from the Atlantic to home waters was made when the Western bases were lost. Considerable congestion resulted in dockyard repairs, and as a result few boats left home ports to go on patrol after September. The number of U-boats at sea during October and November was thus far below the average for previous years, though actual losses were also less. It was not until December that boats left home ports in large numbers for operations. The first of the U-boats formerly based at Western ports were sent on patrol from the beginning of January 1945, on completion of repairs.

The BdU War Log for 1 January also contained an assessment of the general submarine situation in the Atlantic for November and December 1944 which highlighted what were described as two outstanding factors. These were firstly the increased number of successes and openings for attack against the enemy in their transport areas, and secondly the small number of U- boats lost. The account read:

> During November and December 1944 there was an average of fourteen boats a day in the operational area which sank fourteen ships totalling 91,000 GRT and four destroyers or escort vessels.

Although eight HX and two SC Atlantic convoys were at sea in the Atlantic at some point during month, only two attacks took place during January. In the first, on 9 January, ON.277 was attacked by *U-1055* west of Cardigan Bay; one merchant ship, torpedoed and badly damaged, foundered on 13 January after a failed salvage operation. In the second, on 17 January, *U-825* fired torpedoes at HX.332 off Cardigan Bay, just after it formed two columns to enter St George's Channel, sinking a tanker and damaging a freighter. Earlier *U-1232*, before departing American waters on 14 January, had attacked coastal convoys SH.194 and BX.141 off Halifax on 4 and 14 January, sinking a total of five merchant ships. None of the seven ON and three ONS convoys were attacked.

The Anglo-American Joint Statement for January read:

> Throughout January the enemy's U-boat activity was slightly greater than in December, but losses of merchant shipping were not substantially different. The U-boats making use of their new devices penetrated further into focal areas of shipping close inshore. Results of our countermeasures have been encouraging.

The notes of the 15 February Führer Conference record that Hitler was particularly pleased by the reports of the latest submarine successes and added:

The number of submarines in operation will be increased further in the near future. Since the beginning of February, thirty-five submarines have left for the operational areas, and twenty-three more will follow before the end of the month. Hitler asked Dönitz about the use of the new submarine types, and was informed two ships of Type XXIII were already operating along the east coast of the British Isles, and the first ship of Type XXI would be ready to leave for operations along the American east coast by the end of February or the beginning of March.

Hitler received a further report from Dönitz on 24 February on 'The Situation Developing in U-boat Warfare'. After a lengthy description of the fundamental considerations governing the employment of U-boats, this included the following brief summary of the early years of U-boat operations.

The first year of the war saw the U-boats operating predominantly in both the narrower and wider sea areas off the enemy coasts, particularly around England. In addition, use was made of what at that time were remote areas for attacks against convoys; the required concentration of U-boats for attacks of this kind is only possible in a large area. This deployment was its crowning triumph, with only a few boats, but very successful convoy battles in the fall of 1940.

In the second year of the war, as expected, the increasing sea and air reconnaissance around England forced the shifting of operations of the U-boats, surfaced and then exposed to the defences, into the open sea beyond, while American waters were still closed to U-boats. It was the year of the convoy battles, as the slowly growing numbers of submarines gradually created more favourable conditions.

The first half of 1942 opened American waters to U-boat warfare. Here boats once more were able to close the traffic concentration points in the coastal area, where the enemy still had no strong defences. This opportunity was used with all determination, not because convoy battles were no longer possible, but because it was necessary to tackle the enemy where there was the greatest opportunity for finding him. The success proved this deployment was correct.

This situation continued longer than expected, until late summer 1942. Then, even here, the U-boats, still required to surface, were again forced by the enemy's considerable air and sea resources to seek remote areas.

In the second half of 1942 the emphasis was back on convoy combat in the open Atlantic. Until March 1943, despite growing difficulties due to the increasing air surveillance, it remained possible to achieve the highest success. Then the U-boats' successes came to an almost sudden and complete halt, due to the total mastery of the Atlantic by the enemy's aircraft, in connection with the development of tracking devices. This continued in 1944, with few successes for the U-boats.

The air superiority of the enemy had freed his coastal areas from attack, due to his ability to locate surfaced U-boats. A U-boat which was tied for a substantial part of its life to the surface was not a 'U-boat', but a 'submersible' that could exploit its underwater capability only temporarily. In the times during which it was forced to surface it was inferior to the enemy's sea and air power.

At the turn of U-boat war, the BdU said, in a claim intended for the foreign press: 'The aircraft can do the submarine as little as a crow to a mole.' This phrase has since been ridiculed by the enemy again and again; nevertheless, he was right.

[The phrase has also frequently been paraphrased and misquoted.]

The U-boat then was no mole; it could not live under the surface, only carry out a part of its life there. On the surface, however, it was weaker than the enemy.

These conditions have now changed fundamentally. The snorkel has almost made even the old type of submarine into a completely underwater vessel. Its weakness when surfaced is no longer relevant, since it no longer needs to come up. Weeks-long patrols are carried out with no or only a few hours on the surface. The U-boat can again fight and achieve success in the most strongly monitored areas, where for years it could not survive. It can again bring all its advantages into play, features against which the formidable naval power of the Anglo-Saxons is essentially useless, because they rule on the water and in the air above, but not under the water.

With the perfect underwater vessel, a turning point in naval warfare has arrived. The sharp weapon of the pure U-boat is at hand. It will be even sharper with the new U-boat types and their far higher underwater performance. It is important to go into combat with many of these sharp weapons.

Signed in draft: 'Dönitz'

There were no losses from Atlantic convoys during the month, but twenty-one U-boats were lost from various causes. The February Joint Statement read:

During the month of February a moderate number of Allied merchant vessels fell victim to U-boat activity. However, the antisubmarine forces were successful in destroying more enemy submarines this past month than in January.

Despite satisfactory results now being obtained in the war on undersea raiders, our forces must maintain unceasing vigilance, because any enemy with a large number of submarines always poses a potential threat..

The number of U-boats at sea in the Atlantic increased sharply in March 1945, averaging over fifty, mostly concentrated in the waters around Britain; but there were some signs of a shift of U-boat activity towards deeper waters in the Atlantic, possibly indicating that the BdU suspected some escorts had been redeployed from ocean convoys to operate in inshore waters. Following renewed U-boat activity, convoy SC.167 was attacked in St George's Channel, off Milford Haven, by *U-1302* on 2 March, and two merchant ships were sunk.

The First Lord of the Admiralty, addressing the House of Commons in the debate on the Navy Estimates[3] on 7 March, again cautioned against over-confidence:

At the beginning of 1944 the main U-boat effort was in the North Atlantic. Here the U-boats, harassed by surface forces and by shore-based and carrier-borne aircraft, achieved very little and suffered heavy losses. In the spring the U-boats began to withdraw from the North Atlantic convoy routes, probably to re-train and re-equip after their defeat, and to prepare against the threat of our landings on the Continent. With the loss or neutralisation of the Biscay ports, the U-boats were withdrawn to operate from the Norwegian bases, and are, as a result, considerably further from their old hunting ground in mid-Atlantic. The enemy has, however, managed to maintain small numbers of U-boats in widely separated areas with the object of dispersing our anti-submarine forces.

The Prime Minister and the President of the United States announced last August more than 500 German U-boats had already been sunk. The number continues to increase satisfactorily. Despite these continued and encouraging successes it must not be assumed that the war against the U-boat is over. The enemy is employing new equipment, and new types of U-boat may be used at any time. With this new equipment we may be sure they will develop new tactics. In recent months, after a long period of comparative quiet, U-boats have appeared in the coastal waters around the United Kingdom. So far, their successes have been small, but we believe the enemy has been making great efforts to renew the U-boat war on a big scale. It is highly significant that after the trouncing which the U-boats suffered in 1943, the enemy should consider it worthwhile to continue to devote so large a part of his resources to this form of warfare. It shows that he still considers it to be his best hope of averting defeat against a nation which lives by sea-borne supplies.

The update on U-boat deployments at the Führer Conference of 13 March reported:

An average of 64 of the 130 operational submarines available in February 1945 for service in the Atlantic have been at sea. Out of this number only about seventeen were in the operational zones, due to the disproportion existing between time needed to reach the operational zone and time actually spent in operation. The trip from German ports to the operational areas in the Channel and the Irish Sea took an average of twenty-four days, while the trip from ports in the Bay of Biscay to the same areas required only about four days. It became evident the loss of the Bay of Biscay has had grave consequences for the renewal of submarine warfare.

At the Führer Conference three days later, Dönitz reported the first Type XXI submarine would depart for the operational area within a few days. Six more Type XXIs would follow in April. Dönitz also intended to send one group of eight to ten boats of Type IXc – which would be ready for action at the end of March or beginning of April – to patrol the convoy route to America (these would be for wolfpack *Seewolf*). According to reports received, there were no more enemy air patrols west of 15° west.

Dönitz's policy of deploying one or two U-boats off the North American coast, particularly in the Nova Scotia/Newfoundland area, continued throughout the winter of 1944/45. In the spring the number rose sharply. From mid-March to the end of the war, eighteen U-boats were either in or headed for the coastal waters between Cape Hatteras and Halifax. U-boats repeatedly reported weak and inexperienced defence, appraised by Dönitz in March as follows:

The usual American patrol, unwatchful and relatively unpractised, consisting of destroyers, corvettes, and PC-boats. Temporarily strengthened when (U-boats are) noticed. Aircraft irregular. (1914/16 March 1945)

The level of U-boat activity in April 1945 gave no indication the end of the war was near, marked as it was by one last attempt by Dönitz to resume attacks on the Atlantic convoys in the first wolfpack operation by schnorkel-equipped U-boats.

On 2 April, six IXc (750-ton) U-boats were ordered to leave their current positions to form a reconnaissance patrol line in the area 49°30 x N–25°W and sweep west-south-west, combing the US–UK Great Circle convoy route for convoys moving in a westward direction. After completing this manoeuvre, it was intended that *U-880*, *U-518* and *U-858* operate independently in the Halifax–Gulf of Maine area, and *U-805*, *U-1235* and *U-546* in the area from New York to the south. This plan was clarified in the BdU War Log for 3 April, which contains the entry:

The next six type IXC U-boats proceeding to the North American east coast follow one after another. Interval on average 380nm. Intention: Execution of a rake of the England– America convoy route. From there, independent boat operation in American coastal waters. Detailed instructions concerning behaviour at convoy were transmitted.

A signal sent to the U-boats the same day read:

For almost 1–1½ years the enemy has experienced no surface attacks on convoys and is prepared for only underwater U-boat operations ... attack ruthlessly and with determination. (0336/3 April 1945)

As the U-boats made their way across the Atlantic, the deployment was detected by Ultra intelligence, and Operation Teardrop was mounted to intercept the wolfpack. It was rumoured that this was to be an attempt by U-boats to bombard the USA's eastern seaboard with V-2 ballistic missiles launched from towed containers. Two US Navy carrier groups were deployed in search lines north of the Azores across what was known to be the U-boats' course. Four of the six U-boats were detected and sunk before they reached the American coast. Two survived and later surrendered on 14 and 15 May.

On 18 April HX.348 became the last convoy to be attacked by a U-boat in the Battle of the Atlantic, when *U-1107* fired a spread of three torpedoes at two overlapping ships in the convoy about 70 miles west of Brest and reported hits on the American steam merchantman *Cyrus H. McCormick* and the British motor tanker *Empire Gold*. The *Empire Gold* sank on what would have been her last transatlantic voyage before the end of hostilities. She was also the last '*Empire*' ship to be lost in the Second World War. Her master, thirty-seven crew and five gunners were lost; there were only four survivors.

Although it seemed inevitable the end of the war must be near, the Atlantic convoys still continued to run and the U-boat fleet to operate. By 1 May the latter had expanded to 167 U-boats, with approximately ninety at sea. During this period over a hundred were transferred from the Baltic to the Atlantic command. Although approximately fifty were sunk, additions continued to outnumber losses. However, the end was near. On 4 May Dönitz sent a short signal transmitted on all U-boat frequencies ordering the end of attacks on Allied shipping effective 08.00 on 5 May:

ALL U-BOATS. ATTENTION ALL U-BOATS.
CEASE-FIRE AT ONCE. STOP ALL HOSTILE ACTION AGAINST ALLIED SHIPPING.
DÖNITZ

There remains a question mark over whether all U-boats received or chose to obey the signal. At 17.40 on 5 May, *U-853* torpedoed the unescorted American collier *Black Point* sailing in fog out of Long Island Sound, about 3 miles from Point Judith, Rhode Island, headed for Boston. The *Black Point* was the last American-flagged ship sunk by a U-boat in the Second World War.

At 21.58 on 5 May Dönitz sent the following final message to all U-boat crews:

> Six years of U-boat warfare lie behind us. You have fought like lions. An overwhelming superiority in material has forced us into a very narrow space. From this small basis a continuation of our battle is no longer ... U-boat men, unbroken unashamed, you are laying down your arms ... Keep your U-boat spirit, with which you have fought bravely ... Long live Germany.

Dönitz had, with remarkable determination, maintained his U-boat offensive in inshore waters to the very end of the war, with no relaxation of effort or hesitation to incur risk, until the German surrender on 8 May 1945.

Between June 1944 and May 1945 only thirty-one merchant ships of 177,000 GRT had been sunk in the North Atlantic.

Chapter 14

The Battle Ends

Commenting on the German surrender and the war at sea in the Atlantic in his radio broadcast of 13 May on 'Five Years of War', Churchill said:

But the dawn of 1941 revealed us still in jeopardy. The hostile aircraft could fly across the approaches to our island, where 46,000,000 people had to import half their daily bread and all the materials they need for peace or war, from Brest to Norway in a single flight or back again, observing all the movements of our shipping in and out of the Clyde and Mersey and directing upon our convoys the large and increasing numbers of U-boats with which the enemy bespattered the Atlantic – the survivors or successors of which are now being collected in British harbours.

My friends, we will not forget the devotion of our merchant seamen, the vast, inventive, adaptive, all-embracing and, in the end, all-controlling power of the Royal Navy, with its ever more potent new ally, the air, which have kept the life-line open. We were able to breathe; we were able to live; we were able to strike.

Only just in time did the Allied Armies blast the viper in his nest. Otherwise the autumn of 1944, to say nothing of 1945, might well have seen London as shattered as Berlin. For the same period the Germans had prepared a new U-boat fleet and novel tactics which, though we should have eventually destroyed them, might well have carried anti-U-boat warfare back to the high peak days of 1942. Therefore we must rejoice and give thanks not only for our preservation when we were all alone but for our timely deliverance from new suffering, new perils not easily to be measured.

The German surrender on 8 May frustrated Dönitz's plans to deploy the new improved U-boat fleet, as reported in the press on 24 May:

PEACE STOPPED NEW U-BOAT BLITZ

WASHINGTON, Wednesday (AAP)
Because about twelve U-boats, mostly big ocean-going types, have so far neither surrendered nor reported themselves, strong escorts are still being maintained for Atlantic shipping. A United States naval spokesman said officials have confirmed that the Germans finished the war with about 600 submarines, including 170 which were operational. He also revealed the German surrender came just in time to prevent another 'U-boat blitz'. Five U-boats have surrendered in United States ports, two in Canadian ports and thirty at British ports.

Six merchant ships of the last slow westbound ONS convoy (ONS.51) left Liverpool on 21 May to be joined by nine from Belfast Lough and four from the Clyde. ONS.51 nominally terminated at Halifax on 4 June, after various merchant ships detached to other ports in Canada and the US. The last fast eastbound convoy (HX.358) sailed from New York on 23 May to terminate in Liverpool on 6 June, and the last slow eastbound convoy (SC.177) left Halifax on 26 May to terminate in Liverpool on the same date. The last fast westbound convoy (ON.305) sailed from Southend on 26 May 1945 to terminate at Father Point in the St Lawrence River, Canada on 10 June 1945, after most of its merchant ships dispersed to other ports.

The convoy system was now wound down. All Trade Shipping convoys ceased at midnight on Tuesday, 28 May 1945. The Official Admiralty Announcement was published in the US on the morning of 29 May:

LONDON, Tuesday
Trade shipping convoys in the Atlantic and other non-combat areas ceased at midnight last night.

Announcing this, the British Admiralty says that ships already listed for trade convoys will now sail independently.

At night they will burn navigation lights at full brilliancy and need not darken other lights.

Convoy system for merchant shipping was put into operation immediately after the declaration of war and was based on the experience of unrestricted U-boat warfare of the last war.

During this war, however, owing to the danger of air attack and the 'pack' technique of U-boats, the system was much enlarged.

Small ships added greatly to the safety of convoys.

IN NORTH ATLANTIC

Corvettes were built specially for escort work, and miniature aircraft carriers took over air control when convoys were beyond reach of land-based aircraft.

Across the North Atlantic, British, American and Canadian navies divided the work of protection.

Three months after the war began, Mr Churchill, who was then First Lord of the Admiralty, stated that 2,000 British ships were always at sea. Losses in convoy were at the ratio of one in 750.

In 1941, one ship was lost out of every 181; in 1942 one out of every 233; in 1943 one out of every 344; and last year, only one out of every 1,000. Up to the beginning of this year, 9,000 trade convoys had safely entered or been cleared from British ports. Millions of troops and vast quantities of war material had been carried in huge convoys, which included famous peacetime liners.

Accurate statistics on the numbers of merchant ships which sailed in these Atlantic convoys remain difficult to come by, as the total number of ships which sailed does not equate to the number which participated. There are very many examples of ships returning to port as a result of poor weather, mechanical breakdown or enemy action which sailed again in later convoys or did not sail again at all. Given these qualifications, aggregation of the published figures produces the breakdown shown at Appendix A.

Finally, on 2 June 1945 Churchill sent President Truman the draft of the ultimate statement on the U-boat war. The President approved the draft two days later. The statement as published in the press on 7 June 1945 read:

FINAL JOINT STATEMENT ON U-BOAT WAR

LONDON, June 7
The final joint monthly statement by Mr Churchill and President Truman on U-boat warfare states:

'With the surrender of Germany the Battle of the Atlantic has ended, German U-boats have ceased to operate and are now proceeding under Allied orders.

Beginning in September 1939, it has been a long and relentless struggle, demanding not only the utmost courage, daring and endurance, but also the highest scientific and technical skill.

Germany's object was to cut Allied sea communications, upon which the maintenance of the Allied war effort depended. This included the movement and supply of our armies and air forces during successful campaigns in four continents.

Losses, both of lives and materials, have been heavy,

At the peak in 1941 and 1942 the issue of the struggle hung in the balance.

On the other hand, more than 700 U-boats were sunk, and many others destroyed by the Germans themselves in the final stage. Most of these successes have been achieved by the combined Allied naval and air forces. Others are due to mines laid by aircraft or ships, or to bombing in harbour, and a few U-boats were lost through marine dangers.

But success was achieved thanks to sailors, airmen, scientists, technicians, shipbuilders, and factory workers, our convoys reached their destination and enabled our soldiers and airmen to fulfil their tasks.

We, the President and the Prime Minister, in this, our last joint statement on the U-boat war, can now report that the Allies have finished the job.'

This was not quite the end of the story. On 10 July *U-530* surrendered at Mar del Plata Argentina,[2] followed by the very last U-boat (*U-977*) to surrender, on 17 August 1945 also at Mar del Plata, Argentina, after a 66-day submerged trip from Norway.

Chapter 15

Retrospection and Reflection

As the Minutes of the Führer Conferences on Naval Affairs and related BdU reports suggest, it had been very much left to Dönitz alone to orchestrate the U-boat campaign against the Atlantic convoys, Hitler having shown little understanding of the wider strategic implications or willingness to commit the necessary resources to achieve Dönitz's aims. In his post-war *Essay on the Conduct of the War at Sea* Dönitz provided a succinct and objective assessment of the causes of the failure of the U-boat fleet to sever the flow of merchant shipping to and from the British Isles:

> The war was in one sense lost before it began, because Germany was never prepared for a naval war against England. The possibility of having England as an antagonist was not envisaged until 1938, the government was ill-advised politically and Hitler had never been abroad. A realistic policy would have given Germany a thousand U-boats at the beginning of the war. As soon as war started, shipbuilding policy was completely changed; but even on 1 September 1939, Hitler had stated England would not come into the war
>
> The final outcome resulted from a number of German naval weaknesses. These included a gross lack of U-boats at the start of the war due to the faulty political concepts of the Third Reich. The naval construction programme was then relegated to a role secondary to the development of the Luftwaffe, resulting in failure of the Kriegsmarine ever to obtain any semblance of surface superiority; and this lack of naval strength was definitely one of the primary causes of 'postponing' the invasion of England.
>
> The success of wolfpack tactics was dependent upon reconnaissance to locate convoys. Aircraft were the logical instrument for the accomplishment of this mission, but the navy was dependent on the Luftwaffe for air support. Eventually, sufficient pressure was exerted so that a squadron of FW200s was placed at the disposal of the U-boat command. However, results proved to be painfully slow [from Dönitz's point of view], due to lack of cooperation and time consumed in arriving at mutual understanding, common terminology and mediums of communication, and in training

pilots in navigation over water, recognition, correct reporting of contacts, etc. In my opinion, the lack of an adequate naval air arm was a decisive disadvantage in the German conduct of the war at sea, and conversely, the outcome of the U-boat war in 1941 would have been quite different if the navy had had its own air arm.

The US Navy Division of Naval Intelligence's Introduction to Dönitz's essay concludes:

The Second World War was a war of logistics, and VE-day came only after many weary months of supplying men and materiel to Europe. What greater successes might Germany have had in the Atlantic, what further destruction might have resulted to Allied convoys, had the Kriegsmarine possessed even the minimum sea power which should have been contemplated as necessary for global war?

Churchill for his part later offered the following assessment:

The immense scale of events on land and in the air has tended to obscure the no less impressive victory at sea. The whole Anglo-American campaign in Europe depended upon the movement of convoys across the Atlantic, and we may here carry the story of the U-boats to its conclusion. In spite of appalling losses to themselves they continued to attack but with diminishing success, and the flow of shipping was unchecked. Even after the autumn of 1944 when they were forced to abandon their bases in the Bay of Biscay they did not despair. The Schnorkel-fitted boats now in service, breathing through a tube while charging their batteries submerged, were but an introduction to the new pattern of U-boat warfare which [Admiral] Dönitz had planned. He was counting on the advent of the new type of boat, of which very many were now being built. The first of these were under trial. Real success for Germany depended on their early arrival in service in large numbers. Their high submerged speed threatened us with new problems, and would indeed, as Dönitz predicted, have revolutionised U-boat warfare. His plans failed mainly because the special materials needed to construct these vessels became very scarce and their design had constantly to be changed. But ordinary U-boats were still being made piecemeal all over Germany and assembled in bomb-proof shelters at the ports, and in spite of the intense and continuing efforts of all Allied bombers the Germans built more submarines in November 1944 than in any other month of the war. By stupendous efforts and in spite of all losses, about sixty or seventy U-boats remained in action until almost the end. Their achievements were not large, but they carried the undying hope of stalemate at sea. The new revolutionary submarines never played their part in the Second World War. It had been planned to complete 350 of them during 1945, but only a few came into service before the capitulation. This weapon in Soviet hands lies amongst the hazards of the future.

When Dönitz ordered the U-boats to surrender, no fewer than forty-nine were still at sea. Over a hundred more gave themselves up in harbour, and about two hundred and twenty were scuttled or destroyed by their crews. Such was the persistence of Germany's effort and the fortitude of the U-boat service.[1]

The Official Account of the 'Fight Against the U-Boats in the Atlantic', published in 1946,[2] contained the following summary of the outcome:

Until the very end the German U-boat arm fought with discipline and efficiency. There was no relaxation of effort or hesitation to incur risks. Had the U-boat war continued for any appreciable period, there is little doubt that it would have imposed an increased and severe strain upon the Allied resources.

Despite the dislocation and interruption caused by the severe Allied bombing of German building yards, bases, communications and assembly plants, which had a very considerable effect in delaying output, the U-boat fleet would have increased substantially in numbers and power.

New and improved types of U-boats were also coming into operation. Their war potential was not exhausted when the victory of Allied arms brought about the downfall of Nazi Germany. .

But the U-boats nearly succeeded. The anti-U-boat war was one of the most vital, protracted and bitterly fought sea-air campaigns in which the British Empire and Allies have ever engaged.

It is hardly necessary to point out that the severance of our Atlantic supply lines would have brought us to our knees through the eventual starvation of our war industries and population.

Appendix

North Atlantic Convoy Codes and Convoy Routes

The distance from Halifax, Nova Scotia to Londonderry, Northern Ireland or Liverpool is approximately 2,500 nautical miles. It would take a 'slow' convoy roughly seventeen days and a 'fast' convoy about eight days to make the voyage in good weather. Fog and ice caused delay, whilst the threat of U-boat and aircraft attack forced radical alterations of course, adding miles to the voyage. Westbound convoys faced strong headwinds, which slowed them even more. Storms forced ships to heave to for days at a time, damaging or disabling them and scattering a convoy over hundreds of square miles of ocean. Each delay increased the risk of attack.

Eastbound from Canada to UK

There were initially two departure points for eastbound Atlantic convoys: Halifax, Nova Scotia for fast convoys (designated 'HX'), and Sydney, Cape Breton for slow convoys (designated 'SC'). Later, the convoy assembly point was temporarily shifted from Halifax to New York.

Halifax to UK: HX convoys, 13 September 1939 to 6 June 1945

The HX convoys assembled at Halifax, Nova Scotia, from where the merchant ships sailed nominally to Liverpool, although as the convoys entered British coastal waters individual ships would detach to various west and east coast ports. The HX convoys were joined at sea by convoys from Bermuda designated BHX (Bermuda to HX rendezvous: May 1940 to July 1941) and sections from Sydney, Cape Breton designated SHX (Sydney Cape Breton to HX rendezvous: July 1940 to August 1941). These were 'fast' convoys made up of merchant ships capable of a speed of between 9 and 13 knots. The first convoy of the Halifax series (HX.1) sailed with a local Canadian naval escort at 14.00 on Saturday, 13 September, followed three days later by the first fast Halifax convoy (HXF.1). The HXF series was a short-lived series of seventeen convoys running between

Halifax, Nova Scotia and Liverpool or Dover. These convoys included merchant ships returning from the Panama Canal or Caribbean whose speed was in excess of the 9-knot maximum set for the HX series, but less than that required to sail independently (13 knots). The series which ran from October 1939 to February 1940 contained 199 ships.

Until 25 September 1942, the HX convoys were routed from Halifax to Liverpool. The last Halifax convoy, HX.207, departed on 13 September 1942 and terminated in Liverpool on 25 September. Thereafter, from HX.208, which sailed on 17 September 1942, until 6 June 1945, the series departed from New York. This convoy series ran throughout the Second World War. In the very early days the merchant ships in these convoys dispersed once they passed out of the range of U-boats, and received only limited naval protection during the majority of their passage.

Sydney, Cape Breton to UK: SC convoys 15 August 1940 to 26 May 1945

This was a series of eastbound 'slow' convoys originating in Sydney, Nova Scotia (designated as Sydney, Cape Breton to avoid confusion with Sydney, New South Wales), from where merchant ships assembled to sail to ports in Britain, mainly Liverpool. The first convoy departed Sydney harbour on 15 August 1940. As slow convoys of ships not capable of steaming at a speed of 8 knots or more, these were more vulnerable and attracted disproportionately more attacks than the 'fast' convoys

Until August 1940 these slow merchant ships sailed independently, often with disastrous consequences. The SC convoy series provided the only means of an escorted eastward passage for merchant ships from Canada to Britain. The Royal Canadian Navy (RCN) provided a Local Anti-Submarine Escort during the first twenty-four hours after the convoys left Halifax and Sydney. After the escort departed, the only protection for each convoy from Halifax to the edge of the U-boat danger zone at approximately 12° west was provided by a single Royal Navy armed merchant cruiser (AMC) from Halifax. Once the convoys reached the Western Approaches, an eastern Atlantic anti-submarine escort was provided by naval vessels from British ports.

Sydney, Cape Breton was chosen as the western terminus for these convoys to help ease congestion at the port of Halifax. During the winters of 1941 and 1942 the SC convoy assembly point was shifted to Halifax due to ice in Sydney harbour and its approaches.

When in September 1942 the terminus for the HX series of convoys was shifted to New York, the SC convoy assembly point was moved to Halifax, with a temporary interval when they also originated from New York between

September 1942 and March 1943, after which congestion problems there resulted in a further move back to Halifax. However, the SC designation was retained throughout.

The convoys were suspended during the summer of 1944, when a number of the naval escort groups were diverted to support the Normandy landings. During this period all of the eastbound traffic sailed in the HX series, which ran as fast or slow convoys and whose sizes were as a result effectively doubled.

Westbound from UK to Canada

Outbound Alpha (OA) convoys, 7 September 1939 to 24 October 1940

These, together with the concurrent OB series (see below), were the first outward-bound transatlantic convoys from the UK. They sailed from the Thames estuary through the English Channel out into the Atlantic via the South-Western Approaches. The first, OA.1, departed the Thames estuary for Halifax on Thursday, 7 September 1939. Until mid-1940 this series contained both ships proceeding overseas and ships bound for British ports, with the two groups separating off Land's End. Ships also joined from Southampton, Plymouth and Falmouth.

During the first phase of the war these outward ocean convoys were only given close escort as far as longitude 12.5° west; westbound ships dispersed two days after the escorts had left and continued to their destinations independently. The destroyers generally waited at the rendezvous to escort back the next inward convoy.

The OA convoys were dispersed about 750 nautical miles west of Land's End, judged to be the limit of the U-boat threat at the time, and ships proceeded independently to their final destinations. Later, they also sailed from Methil on the east coast of Scotland to Liverpool, then on to disperse in the North Atlantic.

The OA series ceased on 24 October 1940.

Outbound Bravo (OB) convoys, 7 September 1939 to 21 July 1940

The OB series sailed from Liverpool and catered for vessels sailing to North and South America and through the South Atlantic to Freetown, the Cape and beyond, together with coastal traffic. En route, vessels sailing from the Bristol Channel ports (Avonmouth, Barry, Newport and Cardiff) would join the convoy at a designated position, usually a few miles south of The Smalls Lighthouse (51.43°N, 5.40°W). The convoy was initially routed south through St George's Channel.

Off Land's End the convoys were joined by OA convoys from the Thames estuary via the English Channel. The combined OA and OB convoys were escorted for about four days to get beyond the range of U-boat patrols, then dispersed after dark in position around 50°N, 26°W (about 750 nautical miles west of Land's End), when the naval escort departed and the merchant ships sailed on to their individual destinations After the fall of France in June 1940, OA and OB convoys sailed to the north to join in the Western Approaches. As German aircraft, surface warships and U-boats were able to extend their reach farther into the Atlantic from bases in occupied France, ships formerly assigned to the OA and OB convoys were then formed into 'ON' convoys departing Liverpool via the North Channel and escorted all the way to Halifax, Nova Scotia.The OB series ran from 7 September 1939 to 21 July 1941, but the last OB convoy sailed from Liverpool on that date, to be superseded by the new ON series of convoys sailing from Liverpool via the North Channel – the strait between north-east Northern Ireland and south-west Scotland – and escorted all the way to Halifax for North America, and by the OS series to Freetown, Sierra Leone, for ships bound for the South Atlantic (later sailing with the KMS series to Gibraltar).

Outbound to North America ON convoys, 26 July 1941 to 27 May 1945

These convoys were numbered from ON.1, which departed on 26 July 1941 with fifty-five merchant vessels and an eventual total of fifteen escorts, to disperse on 9 August, to ON.305, which sailed on 27 May 1945 with seventy-six merchant vessels and an eventual total of sixteen escorts, arriving on 10 June.

Westbound Atlantic convoys, both fast (designated ON) and slow (ONS), assembled close to one of the principal UK west coast ports, with merchant ships joining in coastal waters before heading out into the Atlantic.

Often there were at least two convoys headed east and two or more westbound any one time. Although it appears to cover a large sea area, the North Atlantic was in reality quite small when there were hundreds of ships to get across safely and large numbers of U-boats attempting to intercept them.

From August 1942 the Mid-Ocean Escort Force of British and Canadian warships, together with a few US Coast Guard cutters, escorted ON convoys to meet the Royal Canadian Navy's Western Local Escort Force (WLEF) off Halifax, and the WLEF escorted most convoys from ON.125 to ON.301 forward to New York City. Most of the ships in the ON convoys were in ballast, although some carried coal or other export goods; a total of 14,864 ships sailed in 307 ON convoys. One ON convoy sailed in fast and slow sections, and two others were cancelled. U-boats sank eighty-one of these ships, and another twenty-three were lost as a result of accidents at sea. (These figures do not include stragglers, although the majority of casualties to U-boats were ships that had fallen out of convoys or were sailing independently.) Some ten warships were also lost while escorting ON convoys.

Outbound to North America ON (fast) convoys, 26 July 1941 to 27 May 1945
The ON series of mercantile convoys replaced the OB series in July 1941 and continued until May 1945. Initially, they sailed from Liverpool and were dispersed about 750 nautical miles west of Land's End, as the OB convoys were. Later, as escorts became available (from March 1942), they were escorted all the way to ports in Canada or the USA. From October 1944 sailings also started from Southend, with the Liverpool section joining at sea.

Outbound to North America ONS (slow) convoys 15 March 1943 to 21 May 1945

The ONS series ran from March 1943 until June 1945 (suspended from March to September 1944 for the Normandy landings). They included slow vessels from Liverpool to Halifax, where the convoy divided, one section sailing on to Boston and New York under the convoy designation.

Until April 1943, ships capable of speeds between 9 and 13 knots were assigned to odd-numbered (fast) convoys, sometimes designated ON(F), while ships capable of speeds between 6 and 9 knots were assigned to even-numbered (slow) convoys – until a new and separate series of ONS (Outbound North Slow) convoys commenced on 15 March 1943. It continued until 29 March 1944, when it was suspended because of the withdrawal of Escort Groups to support the invasion of Normandy. The series resumed on 29 September 1944 and continued until 21 May 1945.

The convoys departed from Liverpool, with feeder convoys from Milford Haven, Belfast, the Clyde, Oban and Loch Ewe. The convoys were routed to Halifax, Nova Scotia, but split up off Halifax, with some vessels going on to Canada, while a small detachment of ships southbound from Halifax joined. The convoy would then assume the title XB (Halifax–Boston), proceeding to Cape Cod Bay, where it terminated. Some vessels entered Boston, but the main body of the convoy continued on to New York via the Cape Cod Canal and the East River.

The last ONS convoy, ONS.51, sailed from Liverpool on 21 May 1945 and terminated at Halifax on 4 June.

Curaçao to UK convoys (CU) 20 March 1943 to 8 June 1945

CU convoys were established as an emergency measure to maintain petroleum fuel reserves in the United Kingdom for the continued strategic bombing of Europe, following heavy tanker losses along the east coast of North America during the 'Second Happy Time' for the U-boats. As modern tankers travelled at a higher speed than the 9-knot HX convoys, the CU convoys operated as a very fast (14-knot) convoy series along the HX convoy route. United States destroyer escorts provided the anti-U-boat cover for CU convoys, as the Flower-class corvettes of the British and Canadian Mid-Ocean Escort Force lacked sufficient speed to protect them.

Empty ships travelling westbound on similar routes from 15 February 1943 to 3 June 1945 were designated UC convoys.

The Western Approaches to the British Isles

The Western Approaches is an approximately rectangular area of sea in the Atlantic Ocean lying immediately to the west of the British Isles. The northern and southern boundaries of the area are demarcated by the corresponding northern and southern extremities of the British Isles – see map below. The coast of mainland Britain forms the eastern boundary, and the 30-degree meridian, which passes through Iceland, the western. The area was, and remains, of strategic importance as many of the UK's principal shipping ports lie within it.

The safety and defence of merchant shipping in the Western Approaches was the responsibility of the Royal Navy operational command, designated 'Western Approaches Command' and based in Liverpool.

The Western Approaches sea area was divided into two principal sub-routes – the South-Western and North-Western Approaches – see map below.

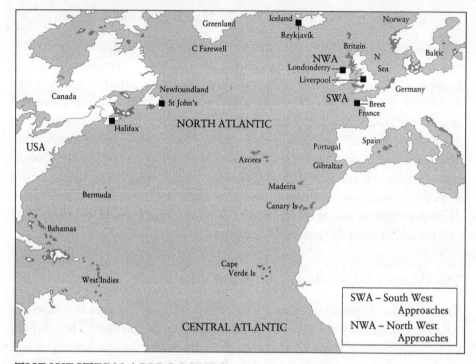

THE WESTERN APPROACHES

Convoy Code	Dates	Number of Convoys	Number of Ships	Convoys Attacked	Percentage Attacked	Ships Lost	Losses in Convoy	Convoy Stragglers	Losses out of Convoy	Percentage Lost
HX	16 September 1939 to 6 June 1945	377	19,000	71	19%	206	110	60	36	1%
SC	15 August 1940 to 26 May 1945	177	6,800	48	27%	211	145	54	12	3%
ON	26 July 1941 to 27 May 1945	305[1]	16,510	45	15%	162	81	43	28	1%
ONS	15 March 1943 to 29 March 1944 / 29 September 1944 to 21 May 1945	51	1,873	5	10%	19	16	3	-	1%
Sub Total		910	44,183	169	19%	598				1%
OA	7 September 1939 to 24 October 1940	226	4,007	14	6%	35	16	5	14	1%
OB	7 September 1939 to 21 July 1940	342[2]	9,023	70	20%	213	53	30	130	2%
TOTAL		1,478	57,213	253	17%	846	69	35	144	1.4%

Convoy Code	Dates	Number of Convoys	Number of Ships	Convoys Attacked	Percentage Attacked	Ships Lost	Losses in Convoy	Convoy Stragglers	Losses out of Convoy	Percentage Lost
CU	20 March 1943 to 30 May 1945	75	2,255	3		5			-	N/A
UC	15 February 1943 to 3 June 1945	103	2,313	1	1%	3	2	1	--	N/A
TOTAL		178	4,568	4		8	2	1		

1. 306 Convoy Codes were issued. One convoy ON.185 was cancelled.
2. 349 Convoy Codes were issued. Seven were not used.

Notes

Introduction

1. Churchill. *The Second World War*, Vol V, *Closing The Ring*, p. 6.
2. Churchill. *The Second World War*, Vol II, *Their Finest Hour*, pp. 528–9.
3. The Ministry of Shipping was formed in October 1939. On 9 May 1941 the Ministry of Transport was amalgamated with the Ministry of Shipping with the combined title of Ministry of War Transport. The first head of the combined Ministry was Mr. F. J. Leathers.
4. After 17 September 1942 the convoy assembly point was moved to New York.

Chapter 1

1. An island off the north coast of Ireland about 6 miles north-east of Malin Head, Co. Donegal.
2. Hansard: House of Commons debate Monday, 4 September 1939 Vol 351 Columns 370–4.
3. Churchill. *The Second World War*, Vol I, *The Gathering Storm*, p. 333.
4. *The Befehlshaber der Unterseeboote* or BdU (Commander of the U-boats) was the supreme commander of the German Navy's U-boat arm. The term also referred to the Command HQ.
5. An island off the south-west coast of Co. Cork.
6. War Cabinet. W.P. (39) 36 dated 17 September 1939.
7. Führer Conference on Naval Affairs.
8. Hansard: House of Commons Debate 20 September 1939 Vol 351 Column 979.
9. Only two U-boats, *U-39* and *U-27*, had been sunk by that date.
10. Hansard: House of Commons debate Tuesday, 26 September 1939 Volume 351 Columns 1240–2.
11. Hansard: House of Commons debate 17 October 1939 Vol 352 Columns 688–9.
12. The actual number was somewhat smaller.
13. Hansard: House of Commons debate 8 November 1939 Vol 353 Columns 253–67.
14. Hansard: House of Commons Debate Wednesday 6 December 1939. Vol 355 Columns 691–3
15. Once again Churchill was being economical with the truth.
16. C.B. 4501. History of U-Boat Policy 1939–1945.
17. Summary of Memorandum entitled 'One Year of U-boat Warfare' by Operations Division, Naval Staff, August 1940. CB 4501.

Chapter 2

1. RN Primary Maritime Tasks – Objective 3 – Maritime blockade of Germany and contraband control.
2. *The Second World War* Vol III, *The Grand Alliance*, p.120.
3. War Cabinet. WM (40) 113, 6 May.
4. The Northern Patrol was deployed to prevent any German warships breaking out from the North Sea to attack Atlantic convoys, prevent German merchant ships reaching their home

ports and intercept neutral merchant ships running contraband goods through the blockade to Germany.

5. On 10 June Mussolini had declared war on Britain and France.

Chapter 3

1. The official convoy terminus but not the final destination for many of the merchant ships.
2. Hansard: House of Commons debate 20 August 1940 Vol 364 Columns 1132–274.
3. War Cabinet 227 (40). Conclusions of a Meeting of the War Cabinet held at 10 Downing Street, SW 1, on Wednesday, August 14, 1940, at 6.30 pm.
4. The official convoy terminus but not the final destination for many of the merchant ships.
5. A small island group in the Outer Hebrides approximately 20 miles west of the Isle of Lewis.
6. *Knights of the Battle of Britain: Luftwaffe Aircrew Awarded the Knight's Grand Cross in the Summer of 1940* (Chris Goss). Other sources – NavalHistory.net & *Luftwaffe Aerial torpedo Aircraft and Operations in World War II* (Harold Thiele) – record the first attack was on convoy CO.203 on 23 August in the Moray Firth, when the *Llanishen* and *Makalla* were sunk.

Chapter 4

1. War Cabinet W.P. (40) 403 3 October 1940.
2. A shot fired at a convoy from a long distance in the hope of hitting something, rather than aiming at a specific target.
3. The sole survivor from *Fiscus* was rescued by the Norwegian *Snefjeld*, which was torpedoed after having stopped to pick up survivors from *Thalia*, and had four survivors from this ship in her lifeboat – this may have caused *Fiscus's* survivor to believe he had been rescued by *Thalia's* lifeboat.
4. Merchant Navy: *London Gazette* dated 13 May 1941: T 335 - Treasury: Ceremonial Branch: Second World War. Merchant Navy Awards Files. (MN Series).
5. The gazette.co.uk/London/issue/34999/supplement/6743.
6. Hansard: House of Commons debate 5 November 1940 Vol 365 Columns 1205–310.
7. Six ships were sunk – two by *U-103* and four by *U-123*.
8. Six ships were sunk and one damaged beyond repair, all by *U-100*.
9. The North Channel separates north-eastern Ireland from western Scotland and links the Irish Sea (south) to the North Atlantic Ocean. This shallow strait is only 13 miles wide at its narrowest point, between Torr Head, Northern Ireland and the Mull of Kintyre, Scotland.
10. *U-57* was salvaged, repaired and returned to service in 1941.

Chapter 5

1. An undersea feature between the north-west of Scotland and Iceland.
2. War Cabinet 27 February WM (41) 21st Conclusions.
3. OB.288 – eight merchant ships and one escort sunk.
4. OB.287, OB.288, OB.289, HX.109, OB.290.
5. 4 March 1941 WM (41) 23rd Conclusions.
6. Hansard: House of Commons debate 5 March 1941 Vol 369.
7. Merchant ships fitted with a catapult in the bow from which a Hurricane fighter could be launched.
8. The Battle of the Atlantic Committee was a specially constituted War Cabinet Committee which evolved out of two ministerial meetings of the Import Executive in February 1941 (the two unnumbered meetings in CAB 86/1), with the first meeting of the Committee being held on 19 March 1941. Initially, the Committee dealt with operational matters, but later began to deal with everything which had a bearing on imports, including protection of

convoys, measures to achieve quicker turnaround of ships, ship repairs, and progress with inland sorting depots. From May 1941 it took over many of the functions of the Import Executive and continued to meet until July 1942.

9. W.M. (41) 29th Conclusions 17 March.

10. On 14 October 1939 the Admiralty announced three U-boats were sunk the previous day. Some of the crews were rescued.

11. War Cabinet W.P. (41) 62. 18 March 1941.

Chapter 6

1. The convoy was on passage *from* Halifax.

2. This was the first and one of the serious loses of the year, but not the most serious, and the comment is curious. This appears to be another example of Churchill's economy with the truth. Ten merchant ships were sunk, and the AMC and two merchant ships damaged.

3. [Stamp] Prime Minister's Personal Telegram Serial No. T. 31 Personal and Secret *Former Naval Person to President Roosevelt 4.4.41* [handwritten].

4. WM (41) 48th Conclusions.

5. Hansard: House of Commons debate 9 April 1941 Vol 370 Columns 1587–605.

6. Royal Navy Banff Class anti-submarine warfare escort ships, commissioned at the Brooklyn Navy Yard between 30 April and 20 May 1941. Manned for passage to UK by crews from the damaged battleship *Malaya* under repair there.

7. Hansard: House of Commons debate 7 May 1941 Vol 371 Columns 867–950.

8. https://www.presidency.ucsb.edu/documents/radio-address-announcing-unlimited-national-emergency.

9. Hansard: House of Commons Debate 10 June Vol 372 Column 161.

10. U-boat.net says four: *U-147, U-138, U-556, U-651.*

11. Hansard: House of Commons Debate 9 July 1941 Vol 373 Columns 181–3.

12. Hansard: House of Commons debate 29 July 1941 Vol 373 Column 1299.

13. Hansard: House of Commons debate Wednesday, 6 August 1941 Vol 373.

14. WM (41) 84th Conclusions.

15. Ismay to Sir Charles Portal, 20 August 1941, ADM 205/8, the National Archives.

16. Hansard: House of Commons Debate 9 September 1941 Vol 374 Columns 67–156.

17. Hansard: House of Commons debate 30 September 1941 Vol 374 Columns 509–10.

18. Hansard: House of Commons debate Vol 376 Wednesday, 12 November 1941.

19. War Cabinet. W. M. (41) 112th Conclusions Confidential Annex (12 November 1941 – 5.50 pm).

20. Hansard: House of Commons debate 11 December 1941 Vol 376 Columns 1686–700.

21. German submariners named it the 'Happy Time' or the 'Golden Time' as defence measures were weak and disorganized, and the U-boats were able to inflict massive damage with little risk. The first Happy Time is described in Chapter 4.

22. BdU War Log 15 May 1942.

23. Admiral Dönitz Memoirs p.196.

24. War Cabinet W.P. (41) 308 29 December 1941.

Chapter 7

1. *The Second World War* Vol IV, *The Hinge of Fate*, p. 97.

2. Hansard: Vol 378, debated on Thursday, 26 February 1942.

3. The twenty-fourth – *Northern Princess* – was last seen late in the evening of 7 March and was sunk by *U-587* the following day with the loss of all thirty-eight crew.

4. On 10 February Churchill offered the President twenty-four anti-submarine trawlers and ten corvettes with their trained crews.

5. The number of days between each successive convoy.

6. Following an increase in U-boat attacks in the South Atlantic necessitating a recasting of arrangements for convoys in the South Atlantic and provision of escorts to deal with the U-boats operating off the coast of South Africa, the United States was asked to return the nineteen trawlers. See W.M: (42) 138th Conclusions. Minute 2a Confidential Annex 12 October 1942.

7. Führer Conference, 13 April 1942.

8. War Cabinet WM 43 (69).

9. Winston Churchill, *The Second World War* Vol IV, *The Hinge of Fate*, p.106.

10. BX.23A

11. *Ten Years and Twenty Days*, p. 237.

12. War Cabinet. W.P. (42) 311 dated 21 July 1942.

13. Convoy ON.115.

14. *Ten Years and Twenty Days*, p.241.

15. Kriegsmarine Maritime Warfare Command responsible for operational planning.

Chapter 8

1. Hansard: House of Commons debate, 8 September 1942 Vol 383 Columns 82–110.

2. The R was added to Ireland to avoid confusion with Iceland.

3. CAB/66/30 October 24, 1942.

4. Winston Churchill, *The Second World War* Vol IV, *The Hinge of Fate*, p.127.

5. The Anti U-boat Warfare Committee was set up in November 1942 as a series of weekly meetings designed to give the same impulse to anti U-boat warfare as had been applied to the Battle of the Atlantic. The Committee met between November 1942 and July 1945 and comprised various ministers and secretaries of state, including the Minister of Labour, Minister of Food, Minister of Agriculture and Fish, Minister of Supply, Minister of War Transport, the President of the Board of Trade, the Lord Privy Seal, the Secretary of State for Air and the Secretary for Petroleum.

6. Hansard: House of Commons debate 18 November 1942 Vol 385 Columns 386–468.

7. War Cabinet W.P. (42) 556. 28 November 1942.

Chapter 9

1. Hansard: House of Commons debate 11 February 1943 Vol 386 Column 1453.

2. The actual total was thirteen sunk, and one damaged. Two U-boats were sunk – one by a Liberator on 21 February.

3. These were type XIV U-boats modified to support the operational type VII and IX U-boats by transferring supplies and ammunition at sea.

4. Change of Operational Control. A CHOP line is a line at which operational control of forces transfers from one command to another.

5. Roskill, *The Battle of the Atlantic – The Triumph of the Escorts, 1 January–31 May 1943*.

6. Hansard: House of Commons debate 3 March 1943 Vol 387 Columns 566–611.

7. C added to Iceland to prevent confusion with Ireland.

8. W.M. (43) 22nd Conclusions. 18 March. 6.00 pm.

9. Churchill had written: 'However as the German concentrations at Narvik may disperse, it is not proposed to unload convoy JW 54. It may therefore start under the protection of the Home Fleet as a blind, being called back to Iceland if the enemy keeps his station.' In the event, JW.54 was cancelled.

10. In a stationary position with head to wind: at a standstill.

11. The sea area to the south and west of Norway.

12. Lorient, Brest, Saint-Nazaire, La Rochelle and Bordeaux.

13. Code name for Mk 24 Mine.

14. An acoustic torpedo designed to home in on the propeller noise from a ship.

15. Karl Dönitz, *Ten Years and Twenty Days*, Frontline Books, 2012.
16. Hansard: Vol 390 Columns 184–5 debated on Wednesday, 2 June 1943 Oral Answers to Questions.
17. Telegram No. 277 dated 3 June 1943.
18. War Cabinet WM (43) 83.
19. Hansard: House of Commons debate 8 June 1943 Vol 390 Columns 566–8.

Chapter 10
1. War Cabinet WM (43) 93rd Conclusions 5 July 1943.
2. W.M. (43) 96th Conclusions.
3. ONS.7, HX.238, SC.130 15 – 26 May 1943.
4. A radar warning device designed to detect enemy aircraft.
5. Also known as an Anti-Submarine Projector. A forward-throwing anti-submarine weapon platform capable of firing up to 24 spigot mortar bombs ahead of a warship when attacking a U-boat.
6. A balloon 3ft in diameter which floated above the surface anchored to a raft. Deployed on a line 50m long, with three strips of aluminium foil attached to act as radar reflectors.

Chapter 11
1. 'Strength through joy'. Physical training exercises.
2. Hansard: Vol 392 debated on Tuesday, 21 September 1943.
3. The Convoy Commodore's Report gives 21.55 BST on 22 September.
4. ONS.18/ON.202.
5. Seven more arrived as reinforcement – one on 25 September, two on 27 September and four on 6 October.
6. Reinforced by three more on 7 December for a total of nineteen.
7. *Rügen I* comprised eight U-boats, *Rügen II* six, *Rügen III* seven, *Rügen IV* eight, *Rügen V* seven, *Rügen VI* nine. All 23 December to 7 January 1944, but *Rügen VII*, three U-boats, was 28 December 1943 to 2 January 1944. The total number of U-boats in these groups is often quoted as the sum of the seven – up to fifty-one – but U-boats were reassigned between groups; the actual number deployed was twenty-eight.
8. HX.270, HX.271, ON.291, ONS.27, SC.150. HX.273, HX.274, SC.150, ON.220, ON.221 and SC.151.
9. CB.4501.
10. *Rügen VII* had been disbanded on 2 January.
11. *U-757, U-305, U-307, U-757.*

Chapter 12
1. Hansard: House of Commons debate 22 February 1944 Vol 397 Columns 680–1.
2. SC.153, SL.150, MKS.41, CU.16, SC.154, HX.281 and ON.227.
3. Hansard: House of Commons debate Tuesday, 29 February 1944 Vol 397 Columns 1280–1.
4. Hansard: House of Commons debate 7 March 1944 Vol 397 Columns 1880–957.

Chapter 13
1. Hansard: House of Commons debate 2 August 1944 Vol 402 Column 1460.
2. Hansard: House of Commons debate Thursday, 28 September 1944 Vol 403 Column 486.
3. Hansard: Navy Estimates debate, Vol 408 Wednesday, 7 March 1945.

Chapter 14
1. Churchill to Truman (No 66). 2 June 1945. Prime Minister to President Truman Personal and Top Secret. Prem 3/413/7.

2. For a copy of the interrogation report on the crew see http://www.uboatarchive.net/U-530A/U-530NAReport.htm.

Chapter 15

1. *History of the Second World War*, Vol VI, *Triumph and Tragedy*, p. 472.
2. 'The Official Account of the Fight Against the U-Boats 1939–1945'. Prepared for the Admiralty and the Air Ministry by the Central Office of Information, 1 January 1946..

Chapter 16

1. 306 Convoy Codes were issued. One convoy, ON.185, was cancelled.
2. 349 Convoy Codes were issued. Seven were not used.

Bibliography

Published sources

Admiralty, *The Führer Conferences on Naval Affairs*, Greenhill Books, 1990

Blair, Clay, *Hitler's U-Boat War: The Hunters 1939–1942*, Random House, 1996

Blair, Clay, *Hitler's U-Boat War: The Hunted 1942–45*, Random House, 1998

Carruthers, Bob, *Hitler's Wartime Orders: The Complete Führer Directives, 1939–1945*, Pen & Sword, 2018 (see also https://der-fuehrer.org/reden/english/wardirectives/01. html)

Central Office of Information, *The Official Account of the Fight against the U-Boats 1939–1945*, prepared for the Admiralty and the Air Ministry, 1 January 1946

Churchill, Winston, *The Second World War*, Volume I, *The Gathering Storm*

Churchill, Winston, *The Second World War*, Volume II, *Their Finest Hour*

Churchill, Winston, *The Second World War*, Volume III, *The Grand Alliance*

Churchill, Winston, *The Second World War*, Volume IV, *The Hinge of Fate*

Churchill, Winston, *The Second World War*, Volume V, *Closing the Ring*

Churchill, Winston, *The Second World War*, Volume VI, *Triumph and Tragedy*

Cressman, Robert J., *The Official Chronology of the U.S. Navy in World War II*, Naval Institute Press, 2000

Dönitz, Admiral Karl, *The Conduct of the War at Sea: An Essay* [1946], Lucknow Books, 2014

Dönitz, Admiral Karl, *Memoirs: Ten Years and Twenty Days*, Frontline Books, 2012

Edwards, Bernard, *The Twilight of the U-Boats*, Pen & Sword, 2003

Edwards, Bernard, *From Hunter to Hunted: The U-Boat in the Atlantic, 1939–1943*, Pen & Sword, 2020

Grove, Eric, *German Capital Ships and Raiders in World War Two*, Volume II, Routledge, 2016

Kimball, Warren F., *Churchill and Roosevelt. The Complete Correspondence*, Vols I–III, Princeton University Press, 1984

Kindell, D., Bertke, D., Smith, G., *World War II, Sea War*, Vol 9, *Wolfpacks Muzzled*, Lulu.com, 2016

Llewellyn-Jones, Malcolm, *The Royal Navy and Anti-submarine Warfare, 1917–49*, Routledge, 2005

Roskill, S. W., *The War at Sea, 1939–45*: Volume I, *The Defensive*. Volume II, *The Period of Balance*. Volume III, *The Offensive Part 1, 1 June 1943–31 May 1944*, *The Offensive Part 2, 1 June 1944 –15 May 1945*, HMSO, 1954

Sternhell, Charles M., Thorndike, Alan M., *Antisubmarine Warfare in World War II*, Operations Evaluation Group Report No. 51, Library of Congress, 1946

Syrett, David, *The Defeat of the German U-boats: The Battle of the Atlantic*, University of South Carolina Press, 1994

Westwood, David, *The U-boat War: The German Submarine Service and the Battle of the Atlantic*, Bloomsbury, 2005

Other sources and websites

hansard.parliament.uk (House of Commons debates)

https://www.kbismarck.com/fuhrer-conference (the Führer Conferences on Naval Affairs)

https://www.gale.com (German Naval Staff Operations Division War Diaries)

https://www.history.navy.mil/research/archives.html (US Naval History and Heritage Command Archives)

https://www.nationalarchives.gov.uk/cabinetpapers/cabinet-gov (War Cabinet Minutes, Memoranda and Conclusions. CAB.65 and CAB 66 Series)

http://www.uboatarchive (C.B. 4501 History of U-Boat Policy 1939–1945)

www.convoyweb.org.uk (details of composition of convoys)

www.ibiblio.org (US Naval Administration in WW II – History of Convoy and Routing: Chapter III – Ocean convoys)

www.naval-history.net (Royal Navy Home Fleet War Diary)

www.thegazette.co.uk (*London Gazette*)

www.warsailors.com

www.worldnavalships.com

u-boat archive.net (BdU War Diary and War Standing Orders of Commander-in-Chief, Submarines)

U-Boat.net (details of U-boat and wolfpack operations, attacks on convoys and Allied merchant ships and warships)

Index